VERGEEN

VERGEEN

A SURVIVOR OF THE ARMENIAN GENOCIDE

BY
MAE M. DERDARIAN

BASED ON A MEMOIR BY
VIRGINIA MEGHROUNI

ATMUS PRESS
PUBLICATIONS
LOS ANGELES
1996

PRINTED IN THE UNITED STATES OF AMERICA

Copyright 1996
by
Mae M. Derdarian, Vahe Meghrouni and Victor Meghrouni

All rights reserved. No part of this book may be reproduced or transmitted in any form by any means, electronic or mechanical, including photocopying, recording or by any information storage and retrieval system, without permission in writing from the Publisher.

ATMUS Press Publications
Los Angeles, CA

Derdarian, Mae M.
Vergeen.

ISBN 1-888156-02-3

First Printing 1996
Second Printing 1997
Third Printing 1998
Fourth Printing 2000
Fifth Printing 2002

Art direction: Andy Takakjian / Layout design: Kent Bancroft

Dedicated to

*Victor A. Meghrouni
and
Vahe Meghrouni, M.D.
and to the
surviving victims of the Armenian Genocide*

"Who today still speaks of the annihilation of the Armenians?"

- ADOLPH HITLER -

The German dictator made this boast to his military officers during World War II. It is now on display, etched on a granite wall, in the United States Holocaust Memorial Museum in Washington, D.C.

Acknowledgments

In many ways, this was a difficult book to write.

Vergeen was a compelling influence in my life, someone whose valor and inner strength I admired greatly. She and my mother had been survivors of the Armenian genocide, the first of the 20th century. In the cauldron of this catastrophe, their lives had converged leading them to a close, lifelong friendship that has endured with their children and even with their grandchildren. Before she died in 1975, Vergeen asked me to prepare her story for publication. Thus, I was entrusted with the mission of her storyteller.

Although I had the benefit of Vergeen's written memoir detailing her incredible experiences, it took several ensuing years to produce a final work because, at times, I found the relating of her saga much too painful. Perhaps because my own late mother also went through the agonies of the holocaust, I felt I actually lived their deprivation, their degradation, and their harrowing fear.

During the months spent in editing and rewriting Vergeen's account of her ordeal, I received the generous support of some special individuals. First and foremost, I am grateful to Vergeen's sons, Victor A. Meghrouni and Vahe Meghrouni, M.D., who helped enormously in furnishing typed drafts of their mother's memoir plus additional information and photos, and whose adoration of their mother was inspirational.

In addition, I owe special thanks to my daughter, Christine, and to my friends, Ardemis Kalousdian, Mary Georgilas Ball and Betty Pernick for their consistent encouragement and advice as well as their periodic critiques.

Of enormous value was the oral history articulated into recorders by many survivors, including my own mother's oral account taped before she died in 1982. It provided unequivocal testimony about the genocide of the Armenian people and their subjection to "death caravans".

In researching the world's reaction to Turkey's planned annihilation of Armenians, I gathered vital material from Richard D. Kloian's significant collection of news accounts by the American press from 1915 to 1922. These articles appear in his remarkable book, *The Armenian Genocide.*

Most important of all, I must acknowledge the objective of Vergeen's own powerful words: *to immerse the reader in her story and to refute historical revisionists who deny and distort the facts of the Armenian holocaust.*

Contents

Chapter: *Page:*

One: Remembering My Family 1
Two: Armenag 15
Three: Cruel Fate 19
Four: Last Tender Years 23
Five: Strife Heightens 29
Six: The Ultimatum 33
Seven: Deportation Begins 39
Eight: Katma: The Herding Place 51
Nine: Syrian City of Aleppo 55
Ten: Godforsaken Ras-al-Ayn 61
Eleven: The Abduction 71
Twelve: Yousuf and the Beduoins 81
Thirteen: Life in the Desert 95
Fourteen: An Attempt at Escape 107
Fifteen: The Final Flight 117
Sixteen: The Railroad Company 131
Seventeen: Joseph 143
Eighteen: The Family 153
Nineteen: The Hospital 163
Twenty: Serpouhi 179
Twenty-one: The War Nears End 193
Twenty-two: Peace Comes to Aleppo 201
Twenty-three: Mending Torn Lives 219
Twenty-four: Beginning Anew 233
Epilogue 255
Historical Notes 259
List of People 265
Glossary 269

Foreword

Vergeen was born in early 1902 in *Kayseri* which she depicted as a popular city in central Turkey where Armenians were among the minority. Set in a large valley covered with brown willow trees, the city's 12,000 houses were built back-to-back along unpaved, often muddy streets. Most were unpainted, dilapidated structures that gave the impression of a poor, undeveloped town. Yet, the city was flanked by nature's bounty – the snow-covered peaks of the *Erciyas* mountains towering nearly 13,000 feet above sea level and the solemn *Ahi River (Kezel Ermak)* flowing quietly down across the city of *Sivas* into the Black Sea.

In 1915, Christian Armenians and Greeks comprised a third of Kayseri's predominantly Muslim population of more than 56,000. Providing the only means of educating Armenian children, the churches – Armenian Apostolic, Evangelical, and Roman Catholic – offered French, American and Armenian schools.

Vergeen often recalled how the harsh climate of Kayseri brought severe winters and blistering summers. Affluent families spent the hot months in their comfortable vineyards and orchards while others vacationed in the cooler, nearby villages.

Use of the Armenian language was restricted in Kayseri and in some other locales throughout the country. After conquering Armenian communities, the Turks stipulated that Armenians speak Turkish exclusively. Otherwise, the severe punishment for the unfortunate violators was the amputation of their tongues. Many foolhardy Armenians were punished in this barbaric way even during the days of Vergeen's great-grandmother. For some obscure reason, Armenians living in many of the villages were spared the compulsory language compliance, often causing awkward communication problems between Armenian city dwellers and villagers.

Frequently, the dialects as well as the language differed. So did the culinary specialities vary according to the inherited traditions of various townspeople. Such scant differences in provincial speech and cherished customs became inconsequential for all Armenians – villagers and city people alike – when, starting in 1915, they were forced to bow to the brutal ultimatum to leave the land where Armenian life had prevailed for four millenniums. Nearly three-fourths of the deported Armenians did not survive. *Vergeen* was one of the fortunate half-million who miraculously prevailed.

ONE

Remembering My Family

In my later years, my husband and I had a grocery in Pasadena, California. Whenever customers who frequented our store asked about my background, I always replied: "I was born in Turkey, but I'm Armenian."

Usually the response was the same. "Oh, really! I'm sorry, Vergeen, but I don't know much about Armenians."

Sometimes, when I had an interested listener, I'd embark on a lecture about what Armenians endured during World War I.

It always amazed me how little my neighbors and customers knew about one of this century's most shameful episodes even when history books speculate that Turkey's plan to exterminate its two million Armenian subjects served as a strategy for Adolf Hitler in his scheme against the Jews during World War II. When occasional news stories appear in the press about Turkey's rigid denial that the genocide of my people ever occurred, it arouses a passionate anger within me about the Turkish government's attempt to revise history. I want to scream out: I was *THERE!* I was an *EYEWITNESS!* I was a *VICTIM!*

For me or for any Armenian who survived the massacres, extinguishing those searing memories is inconceivable. Those horrible events following the deportation from my family home still gnaw at my soul despite the passage of more than a half century. Only thoughts of my dear parents and relatives sustain whatever cherished recollections remain of my early years.

Especially, I remember the devotion of my loving parents. I treasure the memory of the cheery aura that continually illuminated our home, the pride we shared in each other's accomplishments, and the joy we derived from exploring new ventures and ideas. Yet my parents experienced a great deal of sorrow, too. Both suffered the loss of their own parents at an early age, and they lost three newborns before I came along.

Mama was just seventeen when her first child, a girl, died a week after birth. A second child, also a girl, survived only three weeks. Her third child, another girl, lived two months. During her fourth pregnancy, Mama was placed on a special diet and told to rest as much as possible. Worried Papa, fearful about losing another child, employed a Kayseri woman to come to our home every day to cook meals, clean our house, and look after Mama's needs.

For a while, desperate to try anything to safeguard her pregnancy, Mama followed the bizarre advice of a midwife who recommended a weekly meal of porcupine meat to make certain the baby would develop to full-term. Some of our relatives claimed the diet of porcupine meat was a dreadful mistake. They suspected it caused Mama's milk to be tainted as she could not breast-feed me, her newborn.

"*Aman, Allah!* (Oh, God!)" Mama always called on the Almighty whenever she wanted to stress a point. "Your Papa searched the whole village and finally found a woman whose baby no longer needed her breast milk, and he hired this woman to come to our house every day to nurse you. You caused us a lot of trouble, Vergeen, *ghiz (*my girl) – just to be born and to stay alive!" Mama would tease and smile at me. "But we just wanted to make sure you grew up healthy and strong. I guess you were worth it."

"Thank God!" I'd exclaim, grateful that I was seldom sick.

My parents had two more children: a son, *Manoog*, who died after contracting diphtheria at age three; and a daughter, beautiful *Khenarig*. She was a cheerful brunette with curly, brown hair framing a delicately-molded face with adventure-searching, dark eyes. I adored her!

The only ones missing in my family life were grandparents. Neither Mama's nor Papa's parents were alive.

Remembering My Family

⚘ ⚘ ⚘

Papa often told me stories about my paternal grandfather, *Hagop Tachdjian*, a warm and good-natured man who was a native of *Darende*, a village near Kayseri. A widower with three children, grandfather's eldest child, *Baghdasar*, was my father. Another son was my uncle, *Melkon*; and the youngest was my aunt, *Veronica*.

Grandfather Hagop found it impossible to provide for his three children in the village of Darende, so he decided to move his family to Kayseri where he hoped to find better opportunities for earning a living. Within months, he was able to set up a successful shoemaking shop in the city's business section. He truly must have been a congenial man because, according to Papa, grandfather made friends quickly and easily. Soon, prying neighborhood women were secretly scheming to alter grandfather's marital status and they spent a great deal of time searching for a suitable wife for him. (In those days, matchmaking was a prevalent activity of older women who delighted in finding husbands for the single females in their midst.)

The women had decided on *Maryam Indjejian* as the perfect mate for grandfather. Widowed two years earlier, Maryam was left alone with the weighty responsibility of raising her son, *Parsegh*, and she was known to favor the idea of marrying again.

As I learned from Papa's entertaining story-telling, grandfather had seen Maryam months earlier in the marketplace. He'd inquired about her and liked what he'd seen and heard.

As hoped, the matchmaking was successful and grandfather married Maryam two months later. Papa happily recalled how the newlyweds provided a loving home for their blended family.

"Maryam was truly an angel, a wonderful mother to all of us," Papa said. "She was as devoted to me, to my brother and sister as she was to her own son, Parsegh."

Papa spoke about his family's comfortable life, and how his father's shoemaking business flourished with the help of the older boys, Papa and Parsegh.

"Our family life was wonderful! Parsegh was such a great brother to me and a fine son for my father. We both worked hard in father's shop and helped the business grow quite a bit. But," Papa recalled sadly, "we were crushed when my stepmother died suddenly just three years after she came into our family. My poor, grieving father died six months later."

Since Aunt Veronica was not yet old enough to run the household by herself, the responsibility of finding someone to help care for the children rested on Parsegh, the oldest member of the orphaned family. He felt he should marry, and he found a suitable young wife who moved into the family home right after the wedding.

"I thought we all got along fairly well," explained Papa. "But, after a year, Parsegh's wife complained about doing the cooking and washing for everyone. So, my stepbrother had no choice. For the sake of his marriage, he decided to move out of our home, and he also left our business."

Although only sixteen at that time, Papa ran the store with some help from his little brother, Melkon.

"I want you to know something, *kezel ghiz* (my pretty girl)," Papa said with spirited pride. "Customers liked my work and I had quite a good reputation. Remember that!"

With Mama listening to Papa boast about his business acumen, I could see her from the corner of my eye nodding in agreement.

Things went so well for Papa the next few years that he thought it was a good time to look for a wife. He had envisioned the kind of girl he'd like, someone from an upper class family. A friend had told Papa about the orphaned niece of a wealthy business man, named *Haji Hagop Balian*..

"My friend told me the niece's name was *Lousaper* and he said she was pretty, very smart and a gifted homemaker."

Papa grinned broadly, glancing at Mama. "I wanted to make sure I saw her first before I asked for her hand. Luckily, I happened to see her one afternoon as she was leaving her house, and I knew instantly," Papa paused teasingly. "Your Mama was the one for me!"

"What did you do, Papa?" I giggled impatiently, clasping my hands over my mouth. Like so many children who romanticize, I was thoroughly captivated by the story of how my parents met. Sometimes, during Papa's description of their betrothal, Mama would stifle a chuckle and turn her head away to keep me from noticing her reaction to his exaggerated story.

"Well, I didn't dare go alone and ask for your Mama's hand," Papa said, shaking his head. "That's not proper. I needed an older man, maybe an uncle or cousin, to talk about marriage for me – you know, that's a very important custom for us!" Papa looked at me to make sure I understood the importance of that age-old tradition before he continued. "But I had no uncle, no cousin, no one; so I decided to go alone to the Balians' home and speak for myself."

I still remember clearly how entranced I was by Papa's dramatic tale as if I didn't know how the story would end.

"I guess Haji Hagop had already heard about me because he greeted me warmly when he answered the door. He invited me into his parlor and listened politely to the purpose of my social call." Papa paused and glanced at me again to add to the suspense of his tale.

"But in my haste to get to the point of my visit, I almost spoiled everything," he said, chuckling. "Right away I blurted out that I wanted to marry his niece, Lousaper."

"Oh, Papa! That was wrong, wasn't it? Did Mama's uncle get angry?"

"No," my father replied, grinning widely. "But he asked me if I made a good living. I told him even though I wasn't rich and I was responsible for taking care of a young brother and sister, I had high hopes of becoming very successful one day."

"Then what happened?"

"I relaxed a little bit when Mama's uncle didn't say 'no' to my proposal. Instead, he said they'd have to have a family conference and I'd get my answer in two weeks. So, when I returned two weeks later, your Mama's uncle greeted me nicely again and he asked me to sit in a big, red, velvet chair – it was a place of great honor. As I sat down, I got the idea that my luck was going to be rosy, just like the color of the chair."

Then, Papa imitated Haji Hagop, by lowering his voice and speaking slowly. "Well, *oghloom* (my son), you have my blessings. Any young man who has the guts to come alone to ask for my niece's hand deserves to be her husband."

※ ※ ※

Mama seldom spoke about her childhood until one summer afternoon. Before that time, she had always responded to my questions with bits and pieces about her early years. I must have been nine or ten years old when I learned the whole story of her childhood. The memory is still vivid. I sat eagerly at Mama's feet, listening intently. As she spoke and crocheted a dainty doily, her fingers rapidly escorted the needle without the guidance of her eyes, as though her hands belonged to someone else.

I learned that Haji Hagop, the man who consented to Mama's betrothal, was the brother of my maternal grandmother, *Arshalous*. She was married to *Boghos Kashisian*, the son of an affluent family in *Aghin*. They were together almost ten years when Grandmother Arshalous became critically ill. Since the town of Aghin had no major medical facility, she was taken to Kayseri to live with her brother's family while she underwent the imperative treatment.

Without close relatives in Aghin to care for her three children, my grandmother insisted on taking them with her – her nine-year-old daughter, *Haiganoush*; her five-year-old son, *Mardiros*; and my mother, three-year-old *Lousaper*. At first, my grandmother was welcomed warmly by her brother Haji Hagop and his wife, *Filor*. But, eventually, for Filor, the burden of having so many more young ones in the house plus the additional responsibility of caring for a sick sister-in-law became more than she could handle. Consequently,

Mama was placed in the home of her widowed great-aunt, *Soultan Kala*, whose two adult, unmarried daughters lived with her.

"They were wonderful to me!" Mama said wistfully; her voice softened as she recalled those gratifying times. "I loved them. They tried everything to ease my separation from my sick mother."

While living with Uncle Haji Hagop's family, Mama's six-year-old brother died after an accidental fall and her sister, Haiganoush, although sickly and frail, was expected to help with housework and look after her ailing mother.

"My poor mother never recovered," Mama said sadly. "After three years of suffering, she died one cold, winter night with my inconsolable sister at her bedside."

Remembering the heartaches of those bleak days, Mama stopped talking, obviously blunted by the emotion of her sad memories.

"Where was your father?" I wanted to know.

"Oh, he was still in Aghin. When he heard that mother had died, he came to Kayseri for the funeral," Mama murmured almost inaudibly. In her portrayal of what took place after the funeral, Mama stopped crocheting and bowed her head.

Mama then described how she and her sister sat stiffly next to their father in the Balian parlor as he acknowledged the condolences of the mourners. She remembered being kissed by all the weeping women as they passed by, muttering over and over again: *"Khetch chojoogh nereh! Khetch chojoogh nereh!* (Poor children! Poor children!)"

Mama's brows meshed as she remembered that day.

"When everyone left, father finally noticed how awful my sister looked. Normally, Haiganoush's face was round and rosy, but it'd gotten very thin and pale; and her arms looked like sticks hanging out of her big dress. Yet, she was terribly swollen here." Mama pointed to her abdomen.

"Uncle Haji Hagop warned father that my sister had a serious kidney problem and she needed special attention. And he also scolded father, claiming my sister and I should go back home to

Aghin because we needed our father's affectionate care."

Mama hesitated before continuing. "Even though I hardly knew my father, I could tell by the look on his face he was not going to heed uncle's request to take us home with him. He only said he'd return for us in a month or two." At this point in her story, Mama's eyes moistened. After a few seconds, I heard her say under her breath, "He never kept his promise; he never came back. I don't know what happened. I never saw him again."

For the next seven years, Mama lived with her great-aunt, Soultan Kala. "I was really happy there." Mama recalled how affectionately she was treated, especially by her great-aunt's daughters.

"But Haiganoush's health got so bad that my uncle came by one day and took me to his house so that I could help with my sister's care. Just three months later, darling Haiganoush died."

Mama was thirteen at the time of her sister's death and, crushed by her father's callous indifference, Mama said she felt lost and so alone – a pitiful orphan. All members of her immediate family were gone – her mother, her father, her brother, her sister.

Although she spoke kindly about her uncle, Haji Hagop, I got the impression that his wife treated Mama like a servant. But, without other options, Mama remained with her uncle's family until she wed at age sixteen.

Mama finally found happiness when she married Papa. He was a devoted and considerate husband, an irresistible charmer with a contagious sense of humor.

Having been denied a family life with her own parents, Mama liked having a bustling household with lots of people always scampering around. She was especially fond of Papa's sister and brother who continued to live with us until each got married. Their departure from our home truly saddened Mama; she missed their incessant chatter and clatter.

My memories of Papa are still so vivid and endearing. He was a dynamic man, vigorous and self-assured. He was truly gifted in many ways, even though he'd been denied a formal education because he had to work, far too early in life, to support his siblings. Yet, remarkably, he taught himself to read and write, to keep business books, to develop a love of music and art. He learned to paint and to play the *Baklama* (a smaller replica of the mandolin). Perhaps his most acknowledged accomplishment was his painting which graced a drape on the altar of our church: a portrait of Jesus surrounded by his apostles. The clergy valued the painting so highly that it was saved to be exhibited only twice each year, on Christmas and Easter.

I remember how much I loved to watch my handsome Papa dance! What a dashing figure he made, what a marvel he was! He'd twirl a pair of long-handled knives as he circled the floor in the popular saber dance. Frequently, at gatherings, onlookers would clap loudly for more; and Papa would oblige them again and again.

Reminiscing now about my early childhood, I wish I could have salvaged at least one of Papa's paintings or a piece of Mama's beautiful needlework. A sweater! A hand-made dress! A scarf! Just one memento of the exquisite creations of her hands!

I remember how Mama always sang softly while doing her household chores, as fate would one day allow me to do the same for my children. Sometimes, now in my dreams, I relive sitting at her feet and watching her braid her long, shiny brown hair as she sang her favorite songs, mostly melancholy chants.

※ ※ ※

I recall how I bubbled with gleeful curiosity the day three "girl searchers" came to see Papa about his sister, Veronica. The men represented the parents of *Steppahn*, a young man whose family was wife-hunting on his behalf.

In the kitchen that evening, Mama whispered instructions to my nervous aunt, "Now, do you know what to do?"

"Not exactly." Confused, my aunt first nodded, then shook her head.

"Here!" Mama handed her a large tray of small cups filled with steaming, thick coffee. "Just go slowly and make sure each person takes a cup."

Mama gave my anxious aunt a reassuring smile and gently nudged her toward the parlor where the men were seated.

Peering through the curtains screening the kitchen from the other rooms, I watched Aunt Veronica admirably perform the ceremonies of Armenian hospitality. She paused in front of each guest, smiled, bowed her head demurely and offered a cup of the aromatic coffee. In offering the beverage, *"booyourahnez,"* she said politely.

Each guest smiled back at my pretty aunt; their favorable impression was so apparent. I wanted to clap my hands because I knew my aunt's secret. She'd seen Steppahn before and hoped to win his attention one day.

A week later, there was the socially expected, official visit from Steppahn's family to propose marriage and my parents accepted, confirming the *"khosgob"* known as the "tying talk". The betrothal was sealed with a gift from Steppahn's family: a large, gold coin attached to a long, gold chain. My aunt wore it every day, exhibiting it proudly.

Our two families visited often to get better acquainted. Yet, in adhering to age-old Armenian custom, the betrothed couple could not see one another, not even at their engagement celebration which, as tradition dictated for the bride's family, was hosted by my parents. However, years later, I learned to my delight that Steppahn's loyal friends had arranged clandestine occasions where the anxious couple managed to see one other.

The engagement lasted almost a year while Steppahn's parents, designated by tradition to be responsible for the wedding feast, prepared all the special wines, liquors and foods.

The obligatory dowry – a protocol stipulating the bride enter her new husband's home with an assortment of fine jewelry and a trunk full of clothes – became a concern for my parents. They'd already given a lavish engagement party, and the timing of the wedding conflicted with the costly expansion of Papa's new shoe factory; thus he could barely handle all the extra expenses connected with his sister's marriage.

Realizing they might have an embarrassing situation with the new in-laws, Mama came up with the solution. "Vergeen is nowhere near marriageable age. Let's give Veronica the jewelry and the clothing items we're saving for Vergeen's trousseau."

Wondering about my reaction to Mama's suggestion, Papa silently questioned me with a searching look.

"Oh, sure," I blurted, fully aware of how much it would please my parents and my Aunt Veronica. "And what's more," I added quickly, wanting to be the little heroine of the moment, "I want *horakooyr* (father's sister) to have my trunk, too!"

I was so proud of myself! My dramatic, seemingly selfless gesture had pleased my parents. Nonetheless, I felt a twinge of guilt, knowing that Papa would replace my trousseau's jewelry and clothes before too long. After all, I was only seven years old, and any thought of marriage was far off in the future, at least another eight or nine years.

As the wedding day approached, my parents and relatives scurried noisily while trying to perform all the pre-wedding rituals. Two days before the big event, Aunt Veronica and her close girlfriends went to the baths for the traditional ceremonial bathing. On the eve of the wedding, the female members of Steppahn's family came to our house, accompanied by musicians, for the henna ceremony. This ancient, fertility rite – performed only by a professional female *hennaoum* – involved the marking of the bride's fingers with a copper-colored substance.

The next morning, flushed with excitement, I put on the special blue frock Mama had made for me and I watched my aunt dress in her bridal finery – a softly-draped lavender dress, a pale yellow hat and veil, and new shoes. All had been blessed by the parish priest the day before.

The sound of music and voices resounded down the street. "Mama, listen!" I yelled as I peeked out the front window and saw a long string of celebrators led by two eager musicians.

"Our new in-laws and their relatives are coming for the bride." Mama laughed as she headed to the door with Papa just before sustained knocking almost shattered the door panel.

"Let us in," a male voice insisted.

"You can't come in," my parents shouted back in unison.

Mama suppressed a giggle, tickled with amusement at this age-old Armenian game of bride-snatching by the groom's relatives.

"But we promise to give you many gifts," the voice pleaded mockingly from outside the closed door.

"Well, that's different." Papa laughed and opened the door wide to welcome the revelers.

My lovely aunt sat entranced as a virgin bride, crying softly as she listened to the sad songs lamenting her departure from her family's home.

The rituals of the wedding day were memorably picturesque, especially the long, bridal procession accompanied by musicians to the groom's house where the families and all their guests gathered for the long-awaited nuptials.

The groom's parents greeted us warmly and ushered us into the parlor. Then they took my aunt's hand and led her gently in front of the priest. Seconds later, Steppahn appeared, escorted by his godfather, and he stood beside his trembling bride. As the priest began the hour-long ceremony, a huge lump grabbed my throat as I somberly watched the handsome couple take their sacred vows.

The wedding festivities lasted two days with the merrymakers singing, dancing and indulging their unsatiated appetites with lots of wine and delicious food. I remember being completely exhausted, but I didn't want to miss a thing.

My joy at having a married aunt and a nice, new uncle, whose home I could visit often, ended a month later when the newlyweds moved to the village of *Everek*. My other favorite relatives,

Uncle Melkon and his wife, moved to the town of *Talas*.

Meantime, Papa's shoe business grew vigorously. Twice, he went to Istanbul to explore new methods in shoe manufacturing. While in this cosmopolitan city, he discovered a yearly calendar; it fascinated him so much that he made a momentous decision. On his return to Kayseri, Papa changed his surname from *Tachdjian* to *Kalendarian*. His brother, Melkon, also adopted the new name, choosing *Kalendarian* out of respect for Papa.

TWO

Armenag

I would hear my parents talk about the strange phenomenon of *Mounjousoun*, a small village about ten hours from Kayseri by horseback. For some inexplicable reason, the Armenians of Mounjousoun were considered wiser, more enlightened than those in other villages. Nearly 200 families made up the Armenian community. All these families spoke Armenian since the exclusive use of the Turkish language was not required here.

One of the community's comfortably situated Armenian families was headed by *Sarkis Balian,* unrelated to Mama's uncle who was also a Balian. Sarkis and his wife, *Yeghsahpett,* had a married daughter and three sons: *Movsess*s; *Krikor;* and the family's youngest child, *Armenag*. (Many years later, Armenag became a vitally important person in my life.)

Eager to learn a trade, Movsess had gone to live with friends in Kayseri at a very young age while the two younger boys remained with their parents.

Yeghsahpett, the daughter of a medical doctor in Istanbul, was exceptionally bright, a natural born healer who treated many of the village's sick. She was affectionately called "doctor" by the families who sought her help. Yet, when she was suddenly stricken with a grave illness, no physician was immediately available to treat her; and she did not recover.

After his wife's death, Sarkis sent his middle son, Krikor, to Kayseri; and a short time later when unable to find much work as a mason in Mounjousoun, Sarkis followed his two sons to Kayseri, leaving nine-year-old Armenag in the care of his married daughter.

Finding a well-paying job in Kayseri, Sarkis considered marrying again in order to make a new home for his sons. A friend told him about a family who had an older, unmarried daughter.

"She comes from very fine people," the friend said. "And I hear she loves children. She'd make a good mother for your sons."

The friend was referring to Aunt Soultan Kala's daughter, *Elimon*, one of the sisters Mama adored during the seven years she lived with them.

When Sarkis saw Elimon, he liked her instantly and sent someone to offer a proposal of marriage. Although considered an "old maid" by the antiquated standards of those days, Elimon was, nevertheless, appealingly attractive, gentle and good-natured.

My parents, childless at the time, attended the small wedding and shared Aunt Soultan Kala's unabashed joy as she watched her daughter promise to honor and obey her new husband, Sarkis. In fact, all the relatives and friends were pleased to see Elimon marry such a fine man; it was something most older, unwed girls hardly ever achieved.

Elimon loved her husband's boys. They were devoted to her, an observation that made Sarkis supremely content. He had an enviable family situation; but, one person was missing: his youngest son, Armenag.

"Before winter comes, I must go to Mounjousoun and bring Armenag back here," he told his new wife.

Armenag was overjoyed when he heard he'd be living in Kayseri with his father. An extraordinary student, Armenag greeted his father warmly and quickly exclaimed: "I can go to a better school!" Then, realizing his tactless omission, he added, "Of course, I want to see my brothers and meet my new stepmother."

There were other reasons why Armenag wanted to get far away from Mounjousoun. He'd been treated with contempt in the home of his sister who resented being dumped with his care. One way she'd vent her anger about her unwanted responsibility was to feed her husband and children first before giving leftovers to Armenag, sometimes only bread.

Exhilarated by the prospect of taking Armenag to Kayseri, Sarkis also conceded his daughter had been burdened by the responsibility of his youngest son. Swiftly, he made arrangements for the return trip and Armenag couldn't leave his sister's home fast enough.

Sarkis bought a donkey to transport Armenag. Carefully hoisting his son on top the animal, Sarkis made sure Armenag's poorly shod feet slipped safely into the warm saddlebags hanging on each side. Traveling alongside his father, Armenag kept dreaming about the anticipated good life ahead of him. But, now and then, his thoughts were interrupted by his freezing feet which were covered only by woolen socks and sandals.

"Now, Armenag, when we get home, you must remember to kiss the hand of everyone who comes to see us." Sarkis cautioned his son lest he forget his manners.

On the day they arrived home, friends and relatives kept going in and out of the house; and Armenag was obliged to kiss each extended hand. One of the hands he kissed that day belonged to my Papa. He and Mama had joined the visitors in helping Elimon celebrate the return of her husband. Instantly, Papa noticed Armenag's torn trousers and flimsy sandals.

"Take this boy down to the shop right now," he told another visitor who happened to be a supervisor in Papa's shoe factory. "Fit him with a pair of one of our better shoes, and buy this boy some clothes from the shop next to ours."

(Years later, Armenag laughingly told me that my father had given him his first real pair of laced, ankle-high shoes.)

While his brothers, Movsess and Krikor, were learning a trade, Armenag went to Armenian school. In addition to his regular classes, he took a class in Turkish so that he could communicate better with his new stepmother, Elimon, whom he grew to love.

Movsess was eager to go to the United States where so many of his friends had preceded him and, after a few years, he managed to get to America and easily found employment. Within a few more years, Movsess sent for his brother, Krikor, and both worked in Bain, Wisconsin, where some of their young Armenian friends had settled earlier.

※ ※ ※

School attendance was fairly costly in Kayseri. All parents had to pay tuition for their children, from kindergarten through high school. Since Sarkis' work was seasonal and he wasn't able to rely on wages all year long, sometimes his family's income was meager and the support from his sons in America was sporadic.

There was a time when the family could not manage Armenag's high school tuition. He was devastated when his teacher informed him he'd have to quit school if he was unable to come up with tuition.

Angry and humiliated, Armenag grabbed his books and started to stomp out of school that day when the principal stopped him in the hallway and ordered Armenag to come into his office.

"I understand you're an excellent student," the principal noted. "So, I'm going to let you stay, without paying tuition, as long as you keep up your good marks."

Armenag kept his promise to his principal and completed high school in 1908, graduating with the highest marks in his class. His grades, customarily inscribed on diplomas in those days, were in the high nineties for all his subjects – Armenian, Turkish, French and English languages; and also for religion, health, bookkeeping, physics, reading and photography. His only poor mark, just seventy, was for drawing. It was never one of Armenag's interests.

THREE

Cruel Fate

Papa became restless after his last trip to Istanbul. No longer satisfied with the progress of his business, he wanted to pursue new ventures even when his financial situation did not coincide with his extravagant dream. In order to expand his business, he speculated about forming a company and he discussed this possibility with his wealthy friend, *Haig Dormadjian*. "Why do you want to divide the money? Why split the earnings with so many people?" Dormadjian had been insistent. "I'll invest all the money if you do all the work. Just the two of us will share all the profits."

Thus, Papa and Dormadjian became partners and established a modern shoe factory, the first in Kayseri. Shoes were produced by machines and no longer made by hand, making the cost-saving, manufactured footwear far more affordable to the city's people. The factory eventually employed more than thirty workers.

Papa was a pioneer in other ways. He was far-sighted and well-informed, always looking for new methods to enhance and protect his family's lifestyle. In fact, Papa was the first man in Kayseri to insure his life with the New York Life Insurance Company, and he persuaded two of his close friends to do the same. "This way," Papa would reassure himself as well as Mama. "I'm certain you and the children will be all right if anything should happen to me."

By now, Papa was thirty-three years old. One day when he was talking to a customer, an employee came into the sales room to ask for Papa's help in fixing a pattern on an expensive piece of leather. Taking a knife, Papa started to cut the leather and the knife slipped, deeply gashing the thumb on his left hand. Hastily, at first, he wrapped his bleeding thumb with a cloth and then waited for the customer to leave before dashing to the pharmacy across the street.

"I cut my thumb pretty badly and I don't think the knife was clean," he told the pharmacist who was waiting on an old man. "Please, I need some disinfectant right away!"

"Would you mind getting the disinfectant yourself. I'm busy now." The pharmacist pointed to a bottle on a shelf.

Papa found the medicine and immediately spread it on his thumb, unaware that the drug first needed to be diluted with water. He applied a thick bandage on his thumb, but by mid-day his entire hand began to throb. Ignoring the pain, he continued to work until closing time and then rushed home to tend to his injury. Removal of the bandage exposed a swollen, discolored hand.

"Get the doctor!" He ordered my frightened Mama to hurry.

The pain was becoming acute even with the application of the medication prescribed by the summoned physician. Next morning, concerned about the worsening condition of Papa's hand, the doctor brought two consulting physicians.

"We believe it's blood poisoning," the perplexed consultants concluded. "The poisoning appears fairly advanced. We're really not sure about the best way to treat it. Frankly, he really should be seen by Dr. Dodd at the American Hospital in Talas."

Dr. William Dodd was an American missionary physician considered God-like by everyone. However, reaching the good doctor was out-of-the-question since the hospital in Talas was a four-hour journey by horseback, and Papa's condition would not permit such a long trip.

Papa's physicians summoned Dr. Dodd by telegram: "Please come immediately to Kayseri," the wire pleaded. "This person's life is in danger. He's a unique man who truly deserves your immediate attention."

Dr. Dodd's wired response was quick, but he indicated he was scheduled to perform surgery that day. "I can't get away now, but I'll be there tomorrow. For sure."

As he promised, the kind doctor came the following morning. After examining Papa, he shook his head, "I'm afraid nothing can be done. Maybe had I been able to amputate his arm yesterday, he might have had a chance." Dr. Dodd lowered his head and spoke softly, "It's too late now. The poison has spread through his entire blood system."

Three days later, my precious Papa died.

During the days before his death, Mama tried to shield me from the sight of my dying father, and she sent me to a cousin's home several kilometers away. The cousin's three daughters treated me well, but I missed my parents and my sister, Khenarig; I wanted desperately to go home. Each day I was told, "Tomorrow. We'll take you home tomorrow." Tomorrow never seemed to come.

Finally, after a week, my cousin took me home; but no one was there. I ran from room to room looking for Mama. "Maybe she's at the neighbor's house," the cousin tried to reassure me, and we hurried next door where I found Mama in a large room, seated on a cushioned chair in the corner. She looked exhausted; her red eyes were moist and she was dressed in black.

I had been in this room often; it was usually cheery and full of revelers. Now it was gloomy, silent and dark, like all the women dressed in black. I looked imploringly at Mama as she wiped her tears. "What's wrong?" I asked, yet afraid to hear the answer.

Bending slowly to kiss my cheek, she replied, "Vergeen, *yahvroom* (my child), I must tell you that Dr. Dodd came yesterday and took your father to the hospital in Talas. I'm sure the doctor is going to take good care of him."

She kissed me again and whispered, "Don't stay here. Go out to the courtyard and play with your girlfriends."

I suspected something awful had happened to Papa when I saw the women dabbing their eyes with black-bordered handkerchiefs. I pretended to believe Mama when she said my father was going to get well; I thought it was her way of trying to break the bad news to me gradually. In my heart I knew I had lost him. My beloved Papa was gone! GONE!

He had been so caring, so generous. I worshiped him; I could not imagine life without him. I knew he loved me dearly. He'd always spoiled me with his gifts and constant attention.

Papa had always insisted on photographs being taken on every one of my birthdays. Even at the tender age of three months, I was taken to the town's photographer for a portrait.

"If anything happens to me," he'd always instructed Mama. "Please make sure you continue to have pictures made of Vergeen on her birthdays."

She kept her promise until 1915, the year the genocide began.

Papa was also emphatic about my education, wanting me to attend the most reputable schools because he believed that such schools would help me achieve my full potential. Consequently, I attended the Jesuit School; it was rated one of the best in Kayseri.

My parents' ardent hope was to see that I was well-schooled. Especially Papa! He was waiting for the time when he could place all my diplomas side-by-side with all my photos and, on my wedding day, present them to my husband along with his blessings.

FOUR

Last Tender Years

Five months after Papa died, fate crushed us with another blow. We lost my darling sister, Khenarig. For weeks, I brooded until one day I realized Mama's grief must be much greater than mine. She'd lost five children and her beloved husband. I was the only remaining member of her family. Finally one day it occurred to me: she doesn't need to see me crying all the time. Don't be so selfish, I told myself. I really should try to cheer her.

One way Mama seemed to lighten her grief was to travel every summer to popular vacation spots. Fortunately, Papa's life insurance made it all possible, providing Mama and me with a comfortable living.

We'd escape the summer heat by going to the villages and the nearby monastery where Armenag's parents, Elimon and Sarkis, joined us one year.

That summer, Armenag could not take time off from his job to accompany his parents. He'd been hired, right after graduation, as a bookkeeper by one of the area's largest textile merchants. His brothers, meanwhile, kept sending letters from America urging Armenag to join them so that he could advance his education and make his mark in the land of many opportunities.

Convinced his brothers were right, Armenag announced to his parents that he was going to America to be with his brothers. "I believe my future lies in that new country," he told his father who feared he'd never see any of his sons again. "But, I'll be back," Armenag promised.

Before leaving for the United States, Armenag always helped my widowed Mama with her shopping and other outdoor chores since Kayseri's women were still not allowed to go outside their homes without male escorts.

In this culture of countless customs, young people always referred to the peers of their parents as "aunts" and "uncles". It was considered a polite gesture of respect toward older individuals, and this was the way Armenag addressed Mama. He always called her "Aunt Lousaper".

On the other hand, for any young woman, custom demanded that she address an older male by the respectful, Turkish title of *agha*; so I always added the word *agha* after his name every time I spoke to Armenag.

Making sure I was in plain sight whenever Armenag came to our home, I enjoyed watching him talk to Mama and hoped he'd talk to me once in a while. And he always did, asking me about school and my marks.

He's not very tall, but good-looking, I'd say to myself. His best feature – large, almond-shaped, brown eyes – fit so perfectly on his pleasant, round face.

One day, while in an adjoining room, I overheard Aunt Elimon hint to Mama, " My stepson, Armenag, would make a great husband for someone."

Mama seemed stunned by the suggestion that came next as Elimon continued, "I think he'd be perfect for Vergeen."

I heard Mama's shocked response. "*Dallyseen?* (Are you crazy?)"

They were talking about me! I listened closely to hear what Aunt Elimon was engineering. I peeked around the door and saw Mama shake her head in protest as Elimon said, "*Meghah* (my goodness), just wait a minute. Listen to me! LISTEN! Yes, I know, there's quite a difference in their ages, but they're both very bright. I honestly think they'd be a great match."

Elimon waited for Mama's softening expression and then continued, "I'm only suggesting that we seal the idea now, and marriage can take place much later when Armenag returns from America. Lousaper, listen to me! Don't let this young man get away!"

Elimon stood up, walked up to Mama and asked eagerly: "Well, my dear, *nehdeeorsun?* (What do you say?)"

I heard Mama reply, " I don't believe this!"
Several minutes later, after considerable discussion, I heard her say, "I'm really very fond of Armenag. True! He's such a fine, young man with so much potential for great success. Do you really think it would work out?"
"Yes! YES!" Elimon was insistent. "I'm positive it will work!"
There was a silent moment before Mama agreed. "Perhaps you're right, I think it may be a sound idea."
I heard Aunt Elimon screech with delight. I felt so grown-up. Just think, I said to myself, you're engaged – to that nice young man. I wondered how Armenag would feel when he found out what our parents had just negotiated. I was not quite eight years old and Armenag was a fairly sophisticated eighteen-year-old when Mama and my Aunt Elimon made the pact on our betrothal. There was no formal engagement ceremony, no announcement, no gold coin on a gold chain as the traditional *khosgob* (the tying talk) dictates. It was just a mutual understanding between Mama and Elimon that Armenag and I would marry one day.
The following year, in 1910, Armenag left for the United States.

   ⊳   ⊳   ⊳

Prior to the outbreak of World War I, many young Armenian men from Kayseri, like Armenag, decided to try life in America, and they left with the understanding that they'd be back within a few years. A few did return; most of them did not. Their families, meanwhile, spent their time waiting in their homes for loved sons and husbands to come back or, if family incomes permitted it, they travelled extensively like Mama and I did, at least every summer.
One of my favorite vacation spots was the village of *Everek*; an eight-hour journey on horseback from Kayseri. Its adjoining twin village, *Fenese*, had more modern houses and better streets, yet nothing could equal the gardens of Evereg. Its vineyards and orchards produced the region's most luscious fruits and vegetables.

Everegzhee villagers, at every opportunity, boasted about their artisans, coppersmiths and bankers. They were equally justified in bragging about the town's healthy climate; the weather was always moderate, both in summer and winter. Perhaps the village's greatest treasure was its beautiful pool, the *Elbize.* Looking from the top, one never paid much attention to the depth. It was the sea-blue, ice-cold, clear water of Elbize that was amazing. Frequently, in the summer, the villagers used the pool to refrigerate liquids and fruits. It was also used extensively to irrigate Evereg's luxuriant gardens.

Papa's sister, Aunt Veronica and her husband Steppahn, made their home in this pleasant village. One year, we spent our vacation here with my aunt and her family. I loved being with my cousins, but our stay in Evereg was not enjoyable for Mama because she could not communicate well with many people there. Since she spoke only Turkish, my frustrated Mama really had trouble understanding most of the conversations around her.

On reflection, I know now why I liked spending summers in this quaint village. Even though Armenians constituted a minority, they were the town's leaders in industry, business and cultural activities. Their church, one the largest in the region, welcomed both men and women to pray together. And, too, Evereg's women had more freedom than the women of Kayseri. They were allowed to go outdoors without covering their faces; they could carry water from the wells without escorts; and they could go shopping without male companions. Oh, how we envied their freedom!

Mama's favorite vacation spot was *Talas,* a Turkish-speaking community five hours away from Kayseri by horse-drawn carriage. Its more fortunate residents were only sporadically subjected to Turkish persecution. Such periodic reprieve from fear allowed the Armenians of Talas to pay more attention to the education of their children, and many of their sons and daughters attended Armenian boarding schools.

Talas was also noted for its large, well-equipped hospital with its diverse services, including surgery which was usually performed by the renown American missionary, Dr. William Dodd.

Years before, like so many young Armenian males from other communities, several of Talas' young Armenian men had gone to foreign lands, made a lot of money, and returned to build large mansions for their families. These homes were elegant, erected mainly on hilltops, with majestic courtyards and streaming fountains.

To get to these homes, it was a challenge to climb the steep, winding streets; but the view from the top was so picturesque that one seldom minded the fatiguing ascent. Below the hills, the buildings were generally older and housed mostly Turks, some Greeks, and middle class people like Uncle Melkon who lived in a nice, but modest house near Talas' lower section.

We spent several summers in Talas because Mama enjoyed this locale more than any other vacation spot. One summer, my stepuncle Parsegh and his family came to Talas from their home in Egypt, and we all gathered there for a pleasant, season-long reunion. Every Sunday, Mama and I would get together with the families of both Uncle Parsegh and Uncle Melkon, and we picnicked at hilltop locations on the banks of running brooks. We made hammocks and amused ourselves with all kinds of games, playing hide-and-seek with the girls and leap frog with the reluctant boys. I loved frolicking with my cousins even though we fought sometimes. Our childish battles brought the grown-ups into our midst, loudly scolding the young trouble starters; and the adults always took my side because I was fatherless. I hated this pity! It depressed me at times. Yet, that summer was the most memorable vacation I ever had.

FIVE

Strife Heightens

"How come all our last names usually end in *i-a-n*?" I asked Mama one evening as she combed my waist-long hair. "We had to distinguish ourselves from the Turks," she replied and then went on to explain how most Armenians derived their surnames.

Armenians added the letters, *i-a-n* or *y-a-n*, to the end of their compulsory Turkish names. Usually, the three letters were tagged onto names to denote an Armenian family's trade or the head of a household. The word *dasje*, for instance, means mason in Turkish; and by adding *i-a-n*, the surname became *Dasjian*. Or a household head whose name was Hagop would add *i-a-n* to make it *Hagopian*. This practice was observed by nearly all Armenians after the Turkish takeover of their country. Since the conquest of their land, Armenians had periodically been subjected to Turkish ferocity: the scorching of their homes and churches, the indiscriminate killing of adults and children, the pillaging of farms and vineyards. Yet, through the years, in nearly every city and village, Armenians had prospered. They were the major merchants, the artisans, the importers, the manufacturers, the professionals.

Generally, most Armenians got on well with their Turkish neighbors and, in many instances, close friendships developed between Armenian businessmen and local government officials. But, some historians claim Turkey's leaders resented the progress of Armenians; their own people had not advanced as far.

World War I was the opportune time for Turkey's despots – the triumvirate of Enver Pasha, Djemal Pasha and the most malevolent of them all, Taleat Pasha – to carry out their plot: the decimation of all Armenians living in cities and villages throughout the country. The timing was precipitous; most of the world's attention was centered on the events of World War I.

Unaware of the explosive political situation brewing in Europe in early 1914, Mama and I joined a group of Armenian families at *Sourp Garabed Monastery* that summer to enjoy the monastery's unique environment and await its popular August festival. Mama would often make arrangements for us to attend the annual festivals, frequently with our friends and relatives.

Just an hour away from Kayseri, the monastery was famous for its academy where only rich parents could afford the tuition and where only exceptionally gifted children were accepted.

With its glorious gardens and fruit trees, the monastery was also noted for its huge courtyard which was surrounded by large cottages, each with the name of a city or village painted above the door. These cottages were available only to those who came from the designated locales.

Usually the visitors to the monastery were devoutly religious, God-fearing people. Many crawled on their knees to the altar of the monastery to donate money, jewelry, even livestock.

Mama and I loved visiting the monastery, especially the last year we vacationed there with mother's cousin, *Nvart*, and her daughter, *Anoush*, who was a little older than I. She was enviably beautiful and intelligent, her mother's great pride.

Anoush and I would explore fields around the monastery, steal fruits from the courtyard's fragrant trees, and peer into the windows of the boys' dormitory. One time, looking through a classroom window, I saw a skeleton. "What's that?" I asked Anoush and listened raptly as she explained all she knew about the workings of the human body.

I was enthralled. "Wouldn't it be wonderful to be a doctor?"

Anoush laughed, "Oh, don't be silly. There are no female doctors in Turkey. Women are not allowed to be doctors."

Well, if I can't be a doctor, I said to myself, I'll be a midwife. There are some midwives in Kayseri.

One afternoon, we scrounged around hurriedly to find charcoal to blacken pieces of glass and, from the cottage balcony overlooking the lush gardens, we looked up at the sky, watching intently through the dark glasses as the moon slowly covered the sun. What a momentous thrill it was for me to view my first eclipse of the sun.

That summer with Anoush was wonderful, full of new adventures. However, it was to be the last time we'd be able to indulge in childhood pleasures.

While we were at the monastery, war broke out. I remember so well that it was Monday morning, August 1, 1914; and the elaborate preparations for the anxiously awaited, month-end festival were abruptly halted.

We watched in terror as invading police searched for ox carts and buggies, horses and mules. They informed us that Germany and Turkey had declared war on England and Russia, and they needed all the transportation animals and vehicles belonging to the monastery's visitors.

Worried that we might not be able to find transportation to get home, we cut short our vacation and, fortunately, found someone willing to let us hire an ox cart from him. The man also agreed to take us back to Kayseri.

He threw the belongings of three families on the cart, and we sat on top of the baggage as he drove away from the monastery. The cart's owner and driver was, of course, a Turk; no Armenian dared to attempt this hazardous journey without Turkish escort.

In my sinking heart, I realized this was to be the last vacation we'd ever have.

SIX

The Ultimatum

In September of 1914, schools started and the Armenian merchants opened their shops for business. Yet there was widespread alarm and distrust of the Turks. Even long-term friendships with Turkish neighbors deteriorated.

All able-bodied Armenian males, aged eighteen to forty, were inducted for road work, not the army. Thousands of artists, physicians, writers, professors – all educated men were rounded up to work on the roads, usually without food and in extremely unsanitary conditions. A few fortunate ones were released after bribing officials with thirty lira every six months.

On the first day of September, I went to my regular class at the French Jesuit school and, as required every first day of a new semester, I had my tuition money in hand. I was astonished when our teacher did not accept it. "Take your money home right now," she said. "You can pay later."

I was confused; so were all my classmates. Something was happening, something was wrong. Terribly wrong! But what?

Always encouraged by Armenag's stepmother, Elimon, to write to him, I was frequently in a quandary about what to say in my letters. Sometimes, I'd even ask one of my favorite teachers to help me compose my messages. During the second week of school, I learned that mail between the United States and Turkey was going to be forbidden. Somehow I had no difficulty finding the words to write a long, last letter to Armenag.

At the end of that week, we were informed school would close.

"The Turks and French are at war and we're being sent back to France," our teacher announced to the class.

The news shocked us; the entire class burst into sobs. "Please don't go back to France," we begged.

After a while, we realized the school faculty had no choice. We kissed the hands of all our teachers and left weeping.

When I got home, I was still crying and told Mama the school had closed, and all the teachers and my French friends were returning to France. I really thought it was the end of the world.

"Don't worry! You can go to the Armenian school." Mama tried her best to console me. "You'll find it has some very good teachers."

There were twenty-eight pupils in my class at the French school which had a weekly policy of seating the best students at the front. Those top, coveted seats were always occupied by my friends –*Haji Marie, Seranoush* – and me.

In the Jesuit school, Catholic sisters were regarded excellent needlework instructors and, at the end of each season, they displayed the works completed by their students. A few times, one of my needleworks had been selected.

I wanted to do another piece, hopefully to be selected for display. It was silk loom work I was making for a floral-designed frame to hold a future photograph of Armenag and me. When the French school shut its doors, my loom was still unfinished; so I brought it home to complete it with Mama's help.

All my classmates from the closed Jesuit school had already registered at the Armenian school and started to attend classes. At Mama's suggestion, I delayed registering for school in order to finish my loom work which was getting a bit messy and occupying a lot of space in our house.

Mama thought it unnecessary to accompany me to school. I went alone to register and asked for the principal, *Baron Hemyak*.

"What do you want?" The principal demanded curtly. "Where are your parents? Why didn't they come with you?"

"I would like to attend this school," I replied. "I have no father, and Mama didn't want to come because she doesn't understand or speak Armenian well."

"Well, what school did you attend before?"

"The sisters' school," I answered, now fearing something was wrong.

"Oh, I know they were deported. So, now you want to come here," the principal circled his desk impatiently as he spoke.

"All the students from the sisters' school registered here last week. Where were you? Why weren't you here?"

After I explained my situation, the principal asked about my grades and he gave me a brief oral and written examination. Then he handed me a note and told me to report to the classroom across the hall from his office.

I gave the note to the teacher who introduced me to the class, and I sat where the teacher directed me. I looked around at all the unfamiliar faces; my Catholic school classmates were not here. I wondered where they could be.

Before lunch, we assembled in a large hall where I finally spotted some of my former classmates; not one returned my smile. How come I wasn't in their class? I was bewildered.

When we went out to the courtyard to have our lunch, I walked directly to Haji Marie. "Are you angry with me? Why?"

"We're all wondering why you were placed in a higher class," she snapped, obviously miffed.

A big fuss ensued. Haji Marie and Seranoush complained to the principal that they, too, should have been promoted into a higher class since their grades were equal to mine at the Jesuit school.

"But Vergeen passed my examination with a higher score," argued Baron Heymak. He was tired of defending his decision. After a few weeks, the exasperated principal called me into his office to tell me he had decided to put me in the lower class with my former classmates.

I was crushed with disappointment. "Why? Is there something wrong with my school work?"

The principal smiled and replied, "Oh, it's very good! But, I have to treat all three of you the same."

I knew I could have been penalized for what I was about to say; nevertheless, I continued, "If I'm doing well, they must be doing well, too."

The principal shook his head, perturbed a bit by my audacity and then he sent a directive to transfer my former schoolmates to my class.

The Armenian school graded their pupils according to the seating arrangement, just like the Jesuit school. I made sure I worked hard so I could sit in the first row.

I was learning Armenian, French, science, history, art, arithmetic and economics. When the war started, however, the school was forbidden to teach Armenian history and Armenian music.

※　※　※

In early April of 1915, one of Mama's cousins visited us to bring news about a dreadful rumor that was beginning to circulate in Armenian homes throughout Kayseri. "Oh, my God," our cousin began. "People are talking about a secret plan being hatched by the Turkish government to deport us – to deport all Armenians in the country!"

Our cousin was shaking as she spoke, but Mama did not seem surprised at the news. "I've been expecting the worst," she said calmly. "There have been so many signs that we're going to have terrible days ahead."

Later that week, we heard the persecution of Armenians had started with the rampant seizures of noted men – community leaders, poets, teachers, clergy, bankers and businessmen who were shackled and led off to prisons for the alleged purpose of deporting such terrible "undesirables" to nearby Syria. That was Turkey's ruse to cover its real intent: the annihilation of the Armenian nation.

In May, the schools closed by order of the Turkish government. It was yet another disturbing cause for growing apprehension. Most parents had already been afraid to send their children to school without chaperones.

Within weeks, there were increasing governmental searches for hidden ammunition. Our fears intensified when we saw many of our Armenian neighbors carted off, always shackled to each other, without any clue of where they were headed. Usually, the destination was to the city's outskirts where, we later learned to our horror, they were slaughtered with stones, hatchets or bayonets.

Military officials in Kayseri began to accuse several Armenians in our neighborhood of illegal acts. Actually, in towns east of Kayseri, there had been some underground fighters who'd gathered forbidden weapons and explosives. We heard other rumors about the eastern city of Van where underground members had slain several Turks at a tremendous cost to their own lives. We also heard a number of Armenians were assisting the Russian army as guides and fighters.

Continually, day and night, officers searched for weapons in Armenian homes, and any one caught with weapons of any kind faced execution. Even small kitchen knives were confiscated; so were historical materials and books listing names of Armenian leaders. Such findings meant prison for the offending head of the household, no matter how old he was. In many cases, death was preferred to the prison treatment – beatings, floggings, amputations, tearing of fingernails, slashing of torsos. Every form of torture was used to force the imprisoned men to reveal the names of underground leaders and persons hiding ammunition.

We heard about one prominent Kayseri businessman we knew well. He'd begged: "I'll give you all the money you want. Please use a gun to kill me."

"Why should I?" The officer had taunted him. "I can have all your money after you're dead. So, why waste expensive bullets."

Finally, the officer had sniggered, "Why don't you ask your God to spare you?" Then he'd swung his ax, severing the head of our family friend.

Frequently, members of Kayseri's Armenian community related eyewitness accounts of the great number of our townsmen being beaten and left dead at the side of roads where they became prey for vultures and wolves. Soon, it became almost daily that we heard stories of these atrocities, committed mostly against the educated

Armenian males.

One morning, I saw the brutally beaten, elderly landlord of the house where Armenag's parents lived. The poor man had just been released from prison. His face was slashed; blood was gushing from his head; his feet were swollen twice their size.

On June 15, we were not shocked when deportation notices were posted in Kayseri; and, as we discovered later, the same notices were posted throughout Turkey, stating all Armenians would be transported to Syria.

The notices stated: "Leave all your belongings – your furniture, your beddings, your artifacts. Close your shops and businesses with everything inside. Your doors will be sealed with special stamps. On your return, you will get everything you left behind. Do not sell property or any expensive item. Buyers and sellers alike will be liable for legal action. Put your money in a bank in the name of a relative who is out of the country. Make a list of everything you own, including livestock, and give it to the specified official so that all your things can be returned to you later. You have ten days to comply with this ultimatum."

Immediately after the postings, officials rounded up the horses, mules, wagons of Armenians – anything that could be used to transport governmental supplies. The about-to-be-deported Armenians of Kayseri, who had no animals left after the Turkish seizures, hastened to buy or charter whatever means of transportation they could find for the long journey to Syria. Only families with large sums of money were successful. Others had no choice; they had to leave on foot.

Within days, the exile began. One day, it was the Armenians of one town or a village; next day it was another. Among the first to be forced into exile were the residents of Mounjousoun, suffering unprovoked atrocities. Next, it was the people of Talas, then *Devrek, Efkerah, Gemereg, Everek* and more.

Even now, I can still hear my dear, devout Mama's desperate cry, "*Allah, beezah yardumed!* (Dear God, please help us!)"

SEVEN

Deportation Begins

No Armenian males remained in Kayseri, except for a few, feeble elderly men and boys under age fifteen. The able-bodied, mostly intellectuals, had been gathered, jailed, and then slain in what came to be known as "slaughter valley" where the earth was painted by the blood of the dying.

Early one morning, to accelerate the killings, Turkish soldiers hanged twenty notable Armenians in Kayseri; and they summoned the families to bury their bodies. A week later, dozens more, mostly from nearby Evereg, lost their lives to the busy hangmen.

Also that week, the government ordered the town's Armenian priest to conduct the burials, without religious ceremony. Several Armenians, including Mama and me, watched from rooftops, looking down on officers shouldering rifles and escorting our old priest who was reading from a bible cradled in his trembling hands. Four other officers followed, pulling two carts, each carrying three mangled corpses, banging together. I looked as closely as I could, despite Mama's shielding skirt; and I was horrified to see the swollen, bloody heads of the corpses and their dark blue tongues sticking out of their grotesquely open mouths.

The curious townspeople, all Turks, marched behind the second cart. Grinning tormentingly, they looked up at us and yelled, "This is where you'll be soon! Allah is going to reward us!"

⚘ ⚘ ⚘

Since Papa's death, we'd been living comfortably on his life insurance money; and Mama had granted loans to several families. In preparation for the inevitable, Mama collected a considerable amount of the money she had loaned and, weeks before the deportation ultimatum, she carefully arranged its concealment.

Deciding on the items we could carry on our forced exile, Mama doubled two quilts as the containers. In one, she spread yards of wool and silk, and, in between, she tucked her fancy handwork, our good clothes, silver and other valuables. Then she covered the quilt with a heavy, unattractive cloth, and sewed all four sides. This made one bed for us.

One of Mama's loan recipients, a rug merchant, did not have the money to repay her. Instead, Mama accepted his offer of two small, silk rugs. They were placed in the fold of the second quilt. Thus, we had our second bed.

To create two pillows, Mama folded soft shawls and filled them with her fine handwork and some of our underwear. She wrapped yarn around all her jewelry and anxiously sewed them inside the hems of the large-sized garments she and I would wear on our long journey.

Mama sewed some precious stones as well as money in the seams of our bloomers in the hope that she might be able to barter the stones for food when our original supply was gone.

Our house was near the Turkish quarters, and many Turkish families asked if we had anything for sale. Consequently, Mama was able to sell quite a few articles, accepting whatever amount the buyers were willing to pay. Predicting the worst, she sold all she could before the government's deportation ultimatum was posted.

Five sections, housing twelve to fifteen thousand people, made up the Armenian quarters of Kayseri – *Bahjebache, Dicharechar, Icharychar, Jawikyou Malacy* and *Kechy Kapou*. In September of 1915, Armenians in each of these communities received notice of the day designated for their departure and they were ordered to leave their house keys with the police. The notice further stated: "Anyone caught selling or buying articles will be apprehended and will face the court's severe punishment."

The following week, another posted notice announced: "Families whose men folk are serving in the army will be spared deportation.

Also, Catholics and Protestants can remain in their homes as well as those who will accept Islam."

Some, who'd hastily shunned the idea of abandoning their Christian faith, later anguished a thousand times over their decision while struggling desperately to stay alive.

Mama informed me she'd decided to stay in Kayseri. "Vergeen, *yahvroom,* (my child), I'm going to accept Islam so that we won't be deported."

"But, Mama," I pleaded. "You've already sold practically everything we own, If we stay, how can we live in this empty house?"

"We'll manage," Mama said, almost convincingly. "We still have this house, our beddings and our kitchen utensils."

Insisting, I said, "No, Mama! I won't stay. If you want to turn into a Muslim, that's up to you. Aunt *Haji Marie* is leaving and I'll go with her."

Our relative, Haji Marie, was a fanatic Christian who was childless, and she'd already said, "I'll never remain here even if I have to crawl."

"How do you know if she'll take you with her?" Mama tried to reason with me.

"Well, then, I'll go alone."

I was obstinate. Mama realized there was no way she could change my adolescent mind, and she continued to prepare for the deportation.

During the following, excruciating months of exile, my insistence about leaving Kayseri tormented me. Why didn't I listen to Mama? Why didn't we stay with some of the others who pretended to accept Islam? Why? Why? Why?

My enormous, gnawing guilt has lived with me ever since.

Mama's last preparation involved the making of a tent. She bought several yards of heavy canvas and three poles; one pole was seven feet long for the center of the tent and the two five-footers were to be staked in the front and back of the tent.

I helped Mama make two saddlebags to store utensils and food –

flour, bulgur, wheat, noodles, dry beans, dry meat, biscuits, bread and shortening.

Our section made up the last caravan to leave Kayseri. Mama had paid an enormous amount of money, in advance, to rent three mules and to hire a muleteer, seemingly a pleasant, eager-to-help Turk. He placed the saddlebags full of food on two donkeys; and, on the third animal, he loaded the tent and bedding. Mama was astride one saddle-bagged donkey, and I was alongside on the second one. Occasionally, the muleteer would mount the third donkey.

Mama was always suspicious. "I'm worried. I don't trust him," she'd whisper to me. "I hope he doesn't run off with our things."

"Oh, Mama! He won't. He seems like such a nice man."

Totally oblivious to the devastation facing us, I was exhilarated at first by all the excitement as the soldiers directed us to the outskirts of Kayseri. Some of our neighbors were on horses or donkeys, others had wagons drawn by horses or oxen, still others were traveling on foot. Many suffered extreme fatigue that first day, sweating and choking from the heat and dust. Temporary relief came when the officers announced the resting place for the night. Earlier caravans had arrived before us and they were setting up their tents. They appeared pathetically exhausted; so were we after we pitched our tents and lugged jugs of water from a distant well.

That night, we saw looters; more than a dozen Turkish men and a few Turkish women entered some tents. They snatched valuables and smashed everything else in their way, including innocent little infants. Our alleged protectors, the Turkish soldiers, did nothing.

My biggest worry was managing my sanitary napkins. A modest thirteen-year-old, I didn't dare have anyone know I was menstruating. But, one night, after seeing a few trickles of blood in my bloomers, I stopped flowing completely. Frightened, I asked Mama for an explanation of the stoppage. Even Mama seemed a bit concerned at first since I'd been menstruating for a few years.

"Don't worry, *Yavroom*.," Mama tried to assure me. "Your young body is probably trying to adjust to all the stress you're going through right now."

Finally convinced I was not dying, I was secretly glad: that filthy, messy, female thing had stopped. It took two years before I was able to menstruate again.

A few days into our journey, our muleteer demanded more money. Mama knew she had little choice; she paid him. He was good at his job, he always kept the three donkeys together, and he stayed close to Mama and me.

The looting and killing of deportees went on every day at both ends of our caravan; so to gain some assurance of safety, Mama made certain we always stayed in the middle. Our caravan moved continually, forced over mountains, into valleys, frequently targets of thieves who took our shovels, bags, beddings – whatever they could carry off.

Weeks into our exile, we reached *Arable Kane* where earlier caravans had been before us. Abandoned tents were stuck in the muddy soil. Then, all over the landscape, I saw dead bodies strewn here and there. I recoiled in fright, horror-struck by the grizzly sights and overpowering smells.

"Oh, Mama! Is that what's going to happen to us?" I hid my face in her bosom desperate to erase what I'd just seen.

"No! No! That's not going to happen to us! Have faith, Vergeen."

Mama's assurance usually helped. I had a lot of confidence in her ability to protect both of us, but I couldn't get the sight of the swollen dead bodies of the small children and elderly women out of mind. I thought this was the worst I'd ever see during our exile. Oh, how wrong I was!

Water was always precious; and, one night, only one well was open to accommodate us. It was guarded by soldiers who were selling cups of contaminated water for two *gourouch*, the equivalent of twenty cents. In their clamor for water, the deportees in our caravan trampled each other until the early morning hours.

Hardly anyone slept that miserable night. Since the soldiers forbid us to pitch our tents, we flocked closely together in the open field, silently fearful of plunderers. Fortunately, the night was quiet. Yet, next morning, the soldiers collected money from each family alleging it was payment for the bullets they used to protect us.

"What cruel liars!" Mama cursed the soldiers. "It's just another excuse for plundering."

The following day we headed for *Bozanti*. The weather was brisk and the surrounding scenery was glorious. Nature had lavished this area with her best. Orange trees – the first I'd ever seen – covered the landscape for miles and wild flowers of every color lined both sides of the road. Another first for me was a peculiar, repetitive sound coming closer and closer – *choo, choo, choo*.

"My, God, what's that?" I asked our muleteer.

"A train is passing," he explained.

Several minutes later, I saw billowing black smoke emitting from a chain of wagons moving on rails. I fixed my eyes on the first trains I'd ever seen until they melted into the dusk.

At night we stopped at another open field. Our muleteer was very sympathetic and helpful. He pitched our tent, bought some food from Turks for less money, and got water from the well without paying the soldiers.

The farther we went, the soldiers added more people to our caravan; they were earlier deportees from Kayseri. We traveled for many weeks, perhaps months, passing through *Eslahia, Hassan Beyli, Tarsus, Adana*. We saw still more shockingly tragic victims of persecution.

One morning near dawn, our caravan slowly passed a field outside a refugee camp where several very young girls had obviously been brutally raped. Some of the victims lay silent, unmoving, half-naked in the sun-scorched, brown field; others cried as they struggled to cover their exposed torsos from the sight of horrified onlookers in our group. The guards hurried us on, forbidding Mama and anyone else to stop and tend to the ravaged girls.

As we approached the camp, we could see that dysentery was rampant; many of the young and elderly were stooped or lying outside their tents, moaning in painful agony. Further on, we saw unattended infants crawling in and out of a tent, their faces covered with insects; they were screaming for mothers long gone.

"*Allah, nerdehseen?*" Mama cried out over and over again, crouching in revulsion at the misery of the people. "Dear God, where are you?"

Before reaching the city of *Katma*, our muleteer had been kind and solicitous; but one morning I watched raptly as he spoke to Mama, and I didn't like her disdainful expression. It frightened me!

"DON'T go near that man unless I'm with you" she cautioned me later.

Next morning, the muleteer was nowhere. Vanished! So were the mules! He'd carried out his threat to Mama after she refused his proposal of marriage. He'd run away and taken our mules with him.

"He wanted me to be his second wife," Mama said angrily. "AND, he wanted you for his son's bride! *Pehzahvank!* Bastard!"

Left without our animals, Mama appealed to the guards; and they allowed her a little time to sell some of our belongings so that she could buy two more mules and hire another muleteer. Within four or five hours, we continued on our perilous journey, again witnessing and experiencing utter deprivation.

One day, we heard even more incredible tales from escapees of the "death march" into the Syrian desert. About nine women had somehow stumbled into our caravan and, in the quiet of the night, they would describe the horrors they'd witnessed or endured. They told us how the desert was packed with young mothers and their small children, and with old women who tried to conceal their last, few precious mementos of the homes they'd never see again.

"The Turkish guards took great pleasure in separating our families," one young woman told us.

"When some of us with heavy bundles got far behind other family members, the lead officer would pull out his saber and swing it wildly, scattering us in all directions. In our confusion, we'd be divided into groups and ordered to speed up our pace. Some of us were pushed southward, others eastward and still others westward. Mothers were wrenched away from their children."

The woman began sobbing convulsively. "Those cold-blooded officers ignored the cries of our sweet babies who were left behind."

The distraught woman began tearing her hair. "*Aman Asvatz, aad chojoogh nereh eench ehghan!* (Oh God, what happened to those children!)"

"I lost my two little girls and my mother." The young woman insisted on telling her story even though spent emotionally. "Wherever I went, from camp to camp, I searched for my babies. I'm so afraid they were killed by the soldiers, like so many of the children and older people who couldn't keep up and were left behind."

Again, she wept uncontrollably. Mama tried, but the poor woman could not be consoled. We never found out if she ever located her family.

Week after week, our caravan moved on. The sickening scenery was becoming all too familiar. Even though I was becoming numb and hardened, I could not bear looking at the ghastly sights, thinking that could be Mama and me one day. Decaying corpses were often scattered all over the terrain, some half-eaten by dogs and wolves, some with gaping stomachs slashed by scavenging soldiers looking for ingested lira. The pitiful sounds of the dying and the stench of those long dead assailed the air for miles.

One unforgettable evening, our caravan happened on some revulsive evidence of depraved savagery. Mama cried out: "Vergeen, please! Don't look!" She tried, although unsuccessfully, to turn my head quickly away from the ghastly sight of five, severed heads of young Armenian males pierced on long sticks and propped haphazardly against a high stone wall. For days afterwards, the five, young faces with closed eyes haunted me.

A week later, on a particularly hot afternoon when the soldiers allowed us to rest early, we saw running water some distance away and our instinct was to rush and quench our thirst.

"If you go for water, you can only take fifteen minutes," the guard threatened, pointing his rifle at us.

No one dared go for water because it would obviously take much longer to run there and back; and we all knew the consequence of a disobeyed order was death.

Sometimes, civilian Turks came out of nowhere and invaded our caravan. Childless women grabbed babies and ran off; the men kidnapped pretty girls to sell to harems; still others robbed many tents, leaving families few belongings.

Yet, the guards did nothing, pretending that they saw nothing. Instead of providing protection, they often engaged in the same kind of depravity. They stole money; they pilfered food; they forced attractive young women and girls into their tents at night and returned them at dawn, violently raped.

Our situation worsened each day. Lacking food and clean water, many people in our caravan lost their lives to starvation and dysentery. I thought Mama and I were luckier to have outlasted the others until one day I heard her say, "Your Papa and sister were blessed to have been spared this nightmare. At least theirs were naturally-caused deaths, and they died in their own, clean beds. But maybe dying anywhere is better than this misery."

The following day, I realized what Mama meant when I saw a pregnant woman give birth while trying to walk; and she was forced to leave her newborn baby at the side of the road. A cold tremor went through me. I shuddered, feeling her helpless agony as she screamed over and over again, "Please, let me stay with my baby! *Khentrem! Khentrem!* (Please! Please!) *Ashvatz, okhneh inzhee!* (God, help me!) Please, I want to die with my baby!"

Death was merciful at times; but, most often, ugly, stinking death vilely affronted us everywhere our caravan took us.

We marched under the scorching sun, breathing dust and burning with thirst. When we saw some streams one afternoon, we risked punishment by the guards and ran right into the water. Even though the water was muddied by our shuffling feet, we used our head scarves to filter the soil as we lay flat on our stomachs, gulping the muddy, but refreshing liquid like animals.

In a reckless attempt to join us at the streams, a large-bellied, pregnant woman fell and began to twitch in painful labor. She never made it; the merciless guards killed her and her unborn child.

I'd become almost immune to this deliberate barbarity; it was becoming a daily experience. Yet, with every atrocity I witnessed, I became even more resolute about surviving. I swore that Mama and I were not going to end up being one of the dead. Never, never would we become prey for the cruel guards or for the scavenging wolves. But, I'd not yet figured out how, as a thirteen-year-old girl, I'd be able to stop any attempted barbarity.

One evening, weeks later, we saw a small brook along the road and some of our parched deportees ran toward the water without asking permission. Before reaching the precious water, they were gunned down by the guards who shouted, "*Giaour*! Hey, you dogs! Ask first!"

The flagrant soldiers got bolder. They spotted the young girls during the daylight hours, marked their locations and, at night, slipped swiftly into the girls' tents and dragged them into the hills. Occasionally, some of the poor violated girls would be released only to be subjected, night after night, to repeated sexual assaults. Several girls who resisted or, for some reason, didn't satisfy the soldiers, were never seen again; or their dead bodies were dumped outside the tents of their families.

Beauty was nothing to be desired then. Many girls tried to make themselves ugly by blackening their faces with dirt or soot.

"Vergeen, don't forget to rub dirt on your face," Mama would caution me every day. She was so afraid a soldier would notice my youth.

As the march went on, several deportees just gave up and found ways to commit suicide. That was welcomed by the callous soldiers because it meant less people to guard.

Early one evening, after a day-long baking under the hot sun, we initially welcomed the start of cooling rain; but, the accelerating storm unleashed thunder, lightening and a driving downpour that continued until the following morning. Suddenly, the weather turned extremely cold and the weak ones among us, soaked and shivering, died from exposure. I learned quickly that constant hunger was endurable; our incessant thirst was not. Neither were the increasing taunts of the accompanying soldiers who, as time wore on, became more and more brutal. They completely lost touch with humanity one dreary afternoon when they made sport of a pregnant, young woman in our caravan.

The soldiers started with profane jeers, then a dozen of them dragged the hapless woman into their midst, formed a circle around her, and pricked her enormous belly with their sabers and long knives. Moments later, with fiendish glee, they knocked her down and two held the screaming woman on the ground while two others hastily slashed her abdomen up and down, up and down, UP AND DOWN, finally pulling out a small, bloodied fetus on the end of a saber. While the young mother bled to death, the jubilant guards paraded around noisily with the dead infant exhibited on the tip of a gleaming saber, still attached to her dangling umbilical cord.

I wanted to scream! Scream madly! I wanted to RUN, RUN, RUN far away from this monstrous butchery. My earlier self-pledges at bravado disappeared. Instead, I turned my head and vomited wildly, ejecting green bile in poor Mama's lap.

"*Allah, Nerdehseen?* (God, where are you?) Have you no mercy! I beg of you; please stop this slaughter!" Mama pleaded, straining to stifle her sobs.

EIGHT

Katma: The Herding Place

The town of *Katma* was like a huge depository for human debris. Armenians from all over Turkey had been herded into this camp – people with different customs, different dialects, even different outlooks about their plight. Thousands of deportees were crammed into a small area with unbearable conditions. Mama's resolute endurance finally failed her, and she became quite sick a few days after we reached Katma.

We still had a fair amount of bread and bulgur, but water remained a problem. Just getting a jug of water for Mama was a strenuous challenge since I had to fight others and scramble for the precious water. None of us had a large container to hold a day's supply of water; we used every form of receptacle and trekked back and forth to the distant well.

In an open field not far from our camp, Turkish villagers had set up a bazaar to sell food, clothing and other needed items to the deportees. Few, however, had enough money left to buy anything. Some, like Mama and I, had been more fortunate; we'd never been robbed and we'd succeeded in hiding pieces of jewelry, even a few lira, from the thievish soldiers.

While Mama was ill, I had to take charge of the shopping and cooking, things I'd never done before. Although I was inept at shopping and economizing, I managed to take great care that no one discovered we had hidden money.

Our small tent faced the street, exposed to the busy traffic of overflowing carts and pedestrians. At first, whenever I left to go on an errand, I kept the flaps open so that my sick Mama could look at the passerbys.

"Don't ever do that again," scolded Mama.

"Why?" I was a bit hurt by her reprimand. I'd really thought the sights would do her some good. "Maybe you wouldn't feel so lonesome if you looked at the people going by."

"Just obey me!"

I understood why the view repulsed Mama when I saw an increasing number of bodies being carried by family members, right past our tent each day, to the large holes dug by the refugees for mass burials. After every sunset, a priest in our camp prayed over the dead as volunteers shoveled dirt over the growing piles of corpses. Sometimes, bodies were not completely covered; and, at night, they'd become food for the hungry, furiously digging wolves.

Conditions in Katma got increasingly wretched; millions of swarming flies made it impossible to even move from tent to tent. Mothers, unable to nurse their famished babies, gave them rags dipped in sweetened water to suck on, hoping it would keep their infants alive; but the sugary water attracted more flies. Every tent, housing at least two or three critically sick or dying family members, was overrun by the harmful pests.

"Go and find *Deegeen Timourian* and tell her I want to see her," Mama, still ill, instructed me one day.

We'd seen Lisabett Timourian the evening Mama and I arrived in Katma. We knew her husband was among the first victims of the government's hangmen in Kayseri.

Going from tent to tent in my search for Mama's friend, I ran into dear Aunt Elimon. I was so happy to see her; so excited about finding Armenag's stepmother, I kissed her hand repeatedly. Then taking a closer look, I was stunned by her appearance. She was alarmingly thin and pale.

I drew my eyes away from her emaciated body and asked about her husband. "Where's Sarkis *agha*? Is he all right?"

"Yes. He's at the bazaar right now trying to sell my ring and the gold chain and watch my mother gave me. We need some food money. We haven't had anything to eat for days."

How I wished I had something to give her. I had nothing with me. Besides, at this moment, my main mission was seeing that Mama got well.

Katma: The Herding Place

I finally found Deegeen Timourian in one of the last row of tents, told her about Mama, and she followed me to our tent.

"I want to go to Aleppo," Mama spoke firmly. "Join me, Lisabett. Let's get out of this filthy place. We'll die if we remain in this devil's pit. No one knows what's to become of us if we stay here any longer. We can split the expense of an ox cart for the trip. At least Aleppo is a big city and its sanitary conditions must be better."

Deegeen Timourian nodded. "You're so right, Lousaper. I've heard some terrible rumors that all of us are going to be driven to the Arabian desert and those who don't die en route are going to be slaughtered in the desert."

The plan for our two families was mapped out and Lisabett left immediately to find an ox cart and some essential provisions.

Mama was distressed when I told her how I had found Aunt Elimon and how awful she looked.

"She and Sarkis *agha* don't have any food money; they've starving." I said, wanting to cry. After all, they were Armenag's parents, my future in-laws; and they were totally destitute.

"Let me look under the *yorghan* (bedding)," Mama said as she pulled out two lira. "Here, take this to them. But, please make sure no one sees you."

I rushed to Aunt Elimon's tent and gave her the lira. She thanked me profusely. "I'd like to see your mother. Please take me to her."

Although very weak, when Mama saw Elimon, she quickly lifted her head and embraced her cousin tightly. After both wiped their eyes, Mama asked, "Where's your husband?"

"Sarkis went back to the bazaar today, still trying to sell my gold watch and chain. As soon as we sell them, we're going to leave Katma, too."

Elimon thanked Mama again and again for the lira, and I hung on to her as we said our tearful goodbyes. I had an overwhelming premonition that I'd never see her again.

Finding transportation was fairly easy if one had money; and two days later, resourceful Lisabett Timourian returned with a cart, drawn by a big, sturdy ox, carrying her six-year-old son and mother-in-law. It was just past dawn, with our belongings tucked safely in the back of the cart, when Mama and I left ghastly Katma with the Timourians.

We had to go past the bazaar to get to the road. I was hoping I would see Armenag's father and, instantly, I spotted his familiar bald head shining in the sunlight. Trying to get his attention, I stood up and waved wildly.

"Look, Mama," I shouted, "there's Sarkis *agha*!"

He turned, catching a glimpse of us as we drove by, and he waved back. That was the last time I saw him.

NINE

Syrian City of Aleppo

After being in wretched Katma, traveling with the Timourian family provided us with some respite from the sight of the diseased and dying refugees. Lisabeth was very kind and attentive, truly a big help in Mama's recovery. Even though our food supply was meager and allowed for only one small meal each day, Lisabeth was a magician in the way she stretched out our food.

We also felt reasonably secure since we followed some other refugee families who, like us, were eager to get away from Katma and headed toward Aleppo. Fortunately, the railroad tracks served as our guiding route to the Syrian city; and we all travelled in our ox carts during the day and camped overnight in the fragrant, open fields.

I can't remember how long it took us to get to the city of Aleppo in Syria, but I do remember suffering dysentery during the trip and I was acutely ill by the time we reached the outskirts of Aleppo. We stopped so Mama could inquire about a doctor.

"Who's sick?" A nearby police officer asked after overhearing Mama.

"My daughter who's in the cart."

"Take her there." The officer pointed to a tall, unfinished building about a half mile away.

The French had started construction of this building for a hospital before being expelled from Turkey, and now the Syrian government was using it as a hospital for refugees. Although its floors were unclean and its open windows had no glass, the building at least had a roof. Armenian deportees, from all over Turkey, were allowed to stay in this building with sick members of their families. Each family received living space measuring about nine feet by twelve feet.

Mama and I were sufficiently content; we had decent shelter for a while. Even a kind doctor came by to examine me and he gave me medication for my diarrhea.

Lisabett came to see us the next day with the news that widows were being permitted to stay in Aleppo if they could prove the loss of their husbands.

"First, you have to go through certain channels in order to make your claim," she told Mama. "Come with me tomorrow and we'll go into Aleppo together to file our applications for affidavits."

When Mama returned from Aleppo, after applying for her widow's affidavit, she brought a few pieces of candy, some cheese and a small loaf of Syrian bread. I hadn't had such a treat for a long time. As I enjoyed each morsel of the cheese, Mama described Aleppo and its colorful people.

"You should see the buildings, the marketplaces, and how people dress."

"Mama, please, will you take me next time you go? I want to see that."

"Well, first you must get well. So, rest now and be sure to take your medicine," she chided me.

Finally I was well enough for the trip. Impatiently, I waited while the building's gracious doorman gave Mama the required pass and it pleased me greatly to hear civility once again. Crinkling into a smile, the doorman said, "Have a good day."

Aleppo was astonishing, much bigger and much more progressive than Kayseri! There were so many things to buy, to eat, to wear. The strolling, elegantly dressed women wore attractive clothes and shoes; and they were adorned with extraordinary earrings and necklaces with rows and rows of heavy, gold bracelets up to their elbows.

I dared not blink my eyes in case of missing something. What a delightful time I had!

It was the last day for securing permission to stay in Aleppo. Mama and Lisabett, along with a few other widows, went from one office to the next trying to obtain the necessary permits to stay. One of the women had her small son along, and I was asked to look after him while our mothers met with officials inside.

Sitting on the steps of the last office building, the little boy and I watched the procession of people: boys in caftans and suits; some women in European attire, wearing large hats; Muslims in long, black dresses with only their eyes exposed above opaque shawls.

Young and old vendors were selling candy, biscuits, bread, halva, walnuts and other treats strung on long, rectangular tablets hanging temptingly from their necks.

We were totally absorbed by the street's sights when a good-looking, tall officer ascended the steps. We got up to make room for him; he looked down at us and swung his arms for us to move. Realizing we were refugees, he spoke in Turkish, loudly demanding: "What are you doing here? Get away!"

"Our mothers are upstairs. We're waiting for them," I answered.

"I think your mothers are waiting for me. COME! Come with me. You can't stay here; you'll be kidnapped."

Mama and her friends were seated around a large, wooden desk in a spacious office. I walked rapidly to Mama's side and sat rigidly next to her when the officer questioned her.

"Where are you from?" The officer approached Mama first.

"Kayseri, *Effendi*.."

"How long have you been a widow?"

"My husband died seven years ago." Gratuitously, she also added, "He was never against the government."

The officer looked unimpressed and asked, "How many children do you have?"

"Just one, Effendi. I have one daughter."

"Is this girl your daughter?"

My smart Mama immediately recognized the officer's personal motive. "No, Effendi, she's not my daughter. She just came with us to take a tour of the city."

"Where is your daughter?"

"My daughter is sick in the hospital."

The officer turned to me and glared silently for several seconds.

"I KNOW you are this woman's daughter. Don't try to lie to me!" The officer rose from his chair, sat on the edge of his desk, and folded his muscular arms.

"Let me remind all you ladies of this one important fact. You'll only be able to stay in Aleppo for a very short time. All of you will be going to the Arabian desert."

Again he turned to me and said casually, "You and your mother look like you come from a refined family. I'd like to save you both."

I was joyous for a moment – but, only for a moment, until I heard his next odious words.

"I have another Armenian girl; she's my wife now. I know you two would be good company for each other. Today, you and your mother can come home with me. Next week, we'll get married, and you'll become one of my wives."

The officer looked at Mama for her reaction, but she said nothing.

"I'll buy you nice clothes and beautiful jewelry – whatever you like."

He stood up and this time spoke icily. "Remember this! After you leave Aleppo, you'll run into uncivilized, barbaric Arabs. They'll take everything from you. They'll rape you, even kill you!"

Mama interjected quickly at this point. "I'll check with this girl's mother and, if she gives her consent, I'll be back with her answer."

The officer signed all the permits, except Mama's.

"I'm going to the hospital one day this week," he told my apprehensive mother. "I'd like to see your daughter before I sign your paper."

I hadn't fully recovered from dysentery when I developed a high fever, and I had to stay in the hospital a while longer. Frenzied about the possible appearance of the officer, Mama spent most of her time near the hospital's entrance door so that she could watch for him. Within a few days, she saw him enter the building.

She raced upstairs to my room and breathlessly announced: "Vergeen, he's here! In the hospital! That officer is going to look for you. Please cover your head under the quilt and DON'T move!"

Surveying the hallway cautiously before darting out, Mama said, "I can't stay here. Please, God! I don't want him to see me."

Minutes went by and I could hear someone enter the room. I recognized the clicking sound of his boots. I didn't move, not even took a breath. I made no sound, and I was so relieved when I heard him leave.

Faintly, Mama's voice echoed from down the hall.

"Here's my affidavit for your signature, Effendi."

"No! You know I can't sign it. Not until I see your daughter."

I heard Mama calmly say, "Let's go to the other side of this floor, she's in one of the rooms there."

I froze, covering my quilt tighter over my head as I heard them pass my room. Several more minutes went by before Mama was speaking again.

"I don't know where she could be right now. Maybe she went downstairs to get something to eat."

I froze with fear when I heard the officer snap at Mama. "Don't shove your paper in my face!" His voice rose in anger as he shouted, "I told you! Why don't you understand? I will not sign it until I see your daughter."

Without a permit, we could not stay. We had to leave Aleppo.

TEN

Godforsaken Ras-al-Ayn

Mama was anxious to sell our small rugs, thinking we wouldn't have another chance to get a good price after we left Aleppo. Because of their bulk, she was unable to drag them to the city and, since the train station was closer, Mama hoped some of the railway employees would be interested in these two beautiful, silk pieces.

Mama's hunch was right. An interested young Syrian asked Mama to leave the rugs at the station so he could take them home that night for his wife's approval.

"Come back tomorrow and I'll give you the money," he promised. Anxious to get the money we'd need later, Mama agreed and told the man she'd be back the next morning.

"He appeared to be sincere. I hope I didn't make a mistake in trusting him." Mama seemed worried when she told me about the man interested in buying the rugs.

Mama had returned to our room in the half-finished hospital where so many Armenian families were staying with their sick relatives, most of them suffering, like I was, from energy-sapping dysentery.

Knowing we would have to leave Aleppo soon, Mama said, "We're very lucky to spend our last days here. I hope we'll be allowed to stay another week or so. Even though there's no running water, at least we have toilets."

That night, hospital officials informed us that the recovering patients and their families must leave for the train station by dawn. Since I was feeling better, we had to go with the other Armenians whose health had also improved. Once again, frantically, Mama prepared our bundles of belongings, sewing money and jewelry in our clothes. She took special care to hide money in both our dresses in case we got separated.

She also hid some of our money in one of the food bags, securing it with the bulgur, flour and shortening. "That's in case we're robbed of our clothes," Mama explained in her rush to get ready.

She placed some coins into two small, cloth bags for each of us to wear around our necks, like scarves.

"Vergeen, please remember! If we get thrown off the train and if soldiers take our belongings, be sure to grab the bulgur bag. DON'T FORGET!"

The sun had not yet emerged when the soldiers ordered us, with our bundles on our backs, to head for the train station. When we reached the railroad cars waiting to transport us out of the city, we were packed into one without windows. Glued together with scarcely any room for our feet, many of us, still suffering from dysentery, had only cans for the waste expelled from our bowels; and it took only minutes for the nauseating, foul odor to penetrate the entire rail car.

The train was still resting on the tracks when a few considerate soldiers swung open the door to allow some fresh air into our car; but they would not let anyone step out. We waited and waited, standing up in that motionless, cattle car until mid-morning.

"If I have a chance to get out," Mama whispered to me, "I'm going to get the money from the man who wanted to buy our rugs."

Around eight o'clock, station employees were arriving for work and Mama spotted the young Syrian who had the rugs. Quickly she squeezed through the partially open door and jumped from the car to catch up to him. I watched her, my heart pounding, as she followed the man into his office – just as the train slowly started to pull away.

Not only Mama, but a few others had also stepped off the rail car to empty their waste cans, and they yelled hysterically for the train to stop. I saw Mama rush out of the office, running furiously toward our rail car, but not fast enough to grab on to its door handle.

"Vergeen, Vergeen," she shouted, helplessly waving her arms. "Cook the bulgur tonight!"

She was trying to warn me about protecting the money she'd hidden in the bag with all the dry food. Terror paralyzed me! I couldn't even cry like the others whose family members had also been stranded.

Oh, dear God! Will I ever see Mama again? What would I do without her? My unshed tears were choking me when an officer, standing near the tracks, shouted to us. "Your people will be with you soon."

Our ignorance about trains had condemned us to pitiful panic. We were unaware that certain shifting maneuvers were required before a train took off for its destination. So, we were stunned when, a few minutes later, the train screeched to a full stop, and Mama quickly scampered abroad with the others who'd been left outside.

I flung my arms around her neck, nearly smothering her. "Oh, Mama! Mama!" I shrieked with relief.

"Shush! Shush! Don't make so much noise."

Guardedly, she revealed why she was so exuberant. "It's a good thing I got off the train. That wonderful man gave me six lira for the rugs. Do you realize how much six lira can buy?"

Mama was thrilled with the amount agreed to by the young Syrian. "I think it's a good omen," she remarked wishing to be heard by the Almighty. "God won't let us down. I know it! God will not forsake us!"

The train puffed on at moderate speed. Even though we had to stand for hours, crammed together in one car, I was enjoying myself. This was my first train ride and, peering curiously out of the half-open door, I was fascinated by the sights and sounds of the small train stations we passed, and I was invigorated by the cool, whistling wind.

Finally, at dusk, the train stopped to undergo another switching change. Our car was hitched to several other cars – some carrying animals or freight; but most were filled with refugees. Only one was a passenger car with seats for the comfort of soldiers. Thankfully, they left us alone throughout the long trip.

"Where are we going, do you know?"

People in our car, suspicious about the outcome of our journey, continually questioned each other; but no one seemed to have the answer. We only knew we were headed East.

I fell asleep as the train chugged on through the night. I'd awake briefly whenever the train halted for a switching maneuver, and I'd make sure Mama was still near me. Each time, I noticed she was sitting wide-eyed, keeping watch over me and our belongings.

"Vergeen, wake up." Mama whispered and shook me gently. "Get ready, we don't know what's going to happen now."

The door of our car was still open a little, and I saw a train coming from the opposite direction; it was full of Turkish soldiers jeering loudly and shouting profanities at us.

"*Giaour, Ermini millett!* (You dogs, you infidels, you Armenians!)" Some of them yelled, "You're on your way to slaughter valley! So, how about saving a few of your pretty ones! Throw them over here!"

"Thank God," someone said. "We're going East, in the opposite direction. We won't have to see them again."

Near sunrise, we came to a railroad station bearing the sign, *Ras-al-Ayn;* and the soldiers ordered us out of the cattle car. Jumping out, I saw no vegetation of any kind; we were in the dry desert. And although it was blazing hot, how good it felt to breathe in the air and to stretch my cramped legs. Many of us even went to a side area, filled with some rubble, to empty our complaining bowels

Mama and I were famished, but we didn't dare get out our food bags for fear that other, not-so-lucky refugees would be swarming all around us for food, and we wouldn't have anything left for ourselves.

"What's that over there?" I asked Mama, pointing to huge tents some distance away. Hundreds dotted the vista, up and down a steep hill. "Is that where we'll be staying?"

Before Mama could answer, the soldiers ushered us in the direction of the tents. Once again, lugging our meager belongings, we marched toward the tarpaulin structures. We'd left our own travel-worn tent behind in Aleppo; it was just too heavy to carry.

The closer we got, more tents appeared; in fact, it seemed thousands of tents of every color were set up on the other side of the hill.

We weren't allowed to enter any of the black tents. Fate has failed us once more, I thought, until I heard they were only for the critically ill, many with highly contagious diseases. Instead, we were crammed into an open area and spent our first night on the sandy desert floor.

Looking for material to make a tent for us, Mama went to the large marketplace in Ras-al-Ayn, outside the camp. Unable to find large-size pieces of tarp or suitable poles, Mama settled for other pieces of sturdy materials we could afford, in different shapes and colors which, after carefully sewn together, gave us privacy as well as some protection from the rain and the sun. Days later, she found some makeshift poles for our tiny, new tent.

Once we were settled, Mama said she'd take me to the market if I disguised myself as an older woman. Disguises were essential since it was still hazardous for young girls to be seen by soldiers and other Muslims.

"You'll see people in the bazaar you've never seen before. They're mostly Arabs."

"Are they black?" I was curious.

In Kayseri, any reference to Arabs meant black-skinned people. So, I was surprised at what I saw in the market. The Arabs were obviously Caucasian; their skins were merely darkened by sustained exposure to the sun. The Arab men wore dark blue or white caftans resembling straight, long nightshirts; and they belted their garments with leather or twisted cords tied at the end with short sticks. On their heads, they wrapped yards of scarves held in place by crown-like anchors.

The women looked frightening, at least to Mama and me. They wore long, blue, sleeveless caftans with several, very long strips of cloth, swinging from the shoulders, to shield their faces against the desert winds. Some covered their heads with turbans; some toted cushions on their heads carrying heavy loads; some had babies suspended in cloth bags on their backs; some displayed rings in their nostrils. And all flaunted garish, dark blue tattoo marks – on their faces, bosoms, hands, arms, ankles, even knee caps.

Unlike previous concentration camps, soldiers in Ras-al-Ayn did not interfere with our activities in the marketplace. So, undeterred, Mama went to the bazaar often to buy food or to sell some of our things. Although she paid less for food, the money she received for the items sold was also less.

Nevertheless, even as refugees, our situation in Ras-al-Ayn was fairly stable, and we felt reasonably safer here. We had privacy; we had bedding; we had enough money to buy food, despite the need to skimp at times; and, so far, we had not been robbed.

A few shrewd, enterprising Armenians boldly set up their own tiny markets; they bartered on all kinds of articles. Mama liked to patronize these little markets. Forbidden in Kayseri to shop without a male escort, she now savored the freedom to go to the bazaar alone. Sometimes she was accompanied by the new friends she'd found in our camp.

We remained in Ras-al-Ayn about four months, free from the Turkish brutality we'd been subjected to earlier. Most often, the soldiers left us alone; and they scared off the Arabs in the nearby hills from entering our concentration camp.

One morning, we went into one of the large black tents where we'd heard all sick people were staying with family members. Once again, we saw pathetic victims of the government's relentless persecution. Stretched out on the bare ground, side by side, some were already dead and the ones still alive looked like cadavers, barely breathing. A small boy and his sister sat motionless in one corner.

A kind woman who was trying to give them water told us, "Ever since these poor children saw their parents massacred, they haven't been able to speak, eat, drink or even cry."

We walked out of the tent, shaken by what we had just seen; yet there was nothing we could do. Our own situation was tenuous and, by now, we had become almost insensitive to the endless sights of the dead and dying.

One afternoon, returning from a visit to a friend's tent, Mama announced breathlessly, "Guess who I saw today?"

"Who?" I couldn't imagine why all the excitement, but it was pleasantly contagious.

"Melanie! Remember that beautiful playmate of yours back home? Remember, her father was one of Papa's best friends. Oh, the poor girl looks awful – in rags, just skin and bones; she was begging for bread. I gave her some money to buy whatever she needs, and I told her to come and see us."

I was elated to hear Melanie was alive. Her father, a druggist in Kayseri, had followed my father's advice to buy life insurance, and he'd died just before Papa.

"That poor girl." Mama was truly upset. "After her father died, her mother collected all the insurance money and she eloped with a young man in Istanbul. Can you imagine? She left her children with their grandmother. Now Melanie is begging for food."

I was so happy to see my girlfriend when she came the next day, but it was painfully upsetting to hear what she'd gone through.

Melanie told us that she was exiled from Kayseri with her grandmother, her uncle, and her little brother.

"We had no money to buy an ox cart or mules for transportation, and we had to travel on foot," Melanie began, almost impassively, to tell us her story.

"Four days into our march, *mentz myreek* (my grandmother) could not walk any more and she fell on her knees. No matter how hard I tried, I couldn't lift her. My uncle and brother were far ahead of us and didn't see what happened next. An angry soldier on horseback came along and screamed that we were detaining the caravan. When grandmother couldn't stand up, the soldier shot her in the head. Mercifully, my darling *mentz myreek* died instantly."

Melanie wiped her eyes with the hem of her dirty dress before continuing.

"Right after we got to Katma, my uncle died. We went on to Aleppo with another family who were headed for Damascus, but my little brother and I could not stay with them."

Mama stopped her. "Just a minute and let me get you something to eat before you tell us the rest. Also, I want to fix a food pack for you to take to your brother."

Melanie looked at the plate of cheese and bread in front of her for a moment before she started to eat slowly, and then went on.

"We were shunted from place to place, most of the time sleeping in the open. Finally, soldiers threw us into wagons and brought us here two days ago. We had no food, no money; and, because my brother has been very sick, we were shoved into one of those miserable, black tents for the dying. I had to go out yesterday to beg for food and that's when I saw you."

Embracing Mama, Melanie kept kissing her hand in gratitude. "I must take this food to my brother now. I think it'll help him get better."

Melanie thanked Mama again and left. She returned two days later with sad news.

"When I got to our tent the other night, my brother was dead," Melanie said without emotion. "Since then, I've been eating the food you gave me for him."

Impassively, Melanie described how the soldiers ordered her to remove her brother's body from the tent immediately.

"I tried to find help, but no one had the strength to assist me. So, I grabbed my brother's legs and dragged his body all the way to the pit for corpses and pushed him in. I stayed there all night and watched other people drop the bodies of their loved ones into the pit. Then I waited for the priest to come for the short burial ceremony."

Mama and I were bewildered. Despite her terrible ordeal, Melanie seemed wholly detached from her story, almost relieved.

"Now, I'm all alone," she said, staring at the dirt crusted under her fingernails. "I don't have to worry about anyone any more."

※ ※ ※

Melanie would visit Mama and me nearly every day, and we'd invite her often to share our food. Mama found a large can, filled it with dirt, and resourcefully used it to cook food inside our tent so that our prying neighbors couldn't see what we were eating. After our meal, we'd sit around the canned fire to keep warm. Melanie enjoyed being with us, especially on the days Mama bathed her and shampooed her long, black hair. She was so dear to Mama, and especially to me! We treated her like a member of our family. Unfortunately, our tent was too small to accommodate a third person so Melanie continued to live, off and on, in one of the black tents.

We worried when she didn't show up for almost a week. Mama went to the black tent area and asked people if they'd seen Melanie.

"Not since yesterday," a young woman told Mama. "She wasn't feeling well when I last saw her."

A few days later, Mama heard neighbors talk about a dead girl behind our tent. She immediately went around the back to investigate. It was Melanie! Apparently, she was coming to see us and didn't make it.

Another loved one gone! I cried until no tears were left.

Women in nearby tents helped Mama and me carry Melanie to the crowded pit. Gently, we pushed her body on top of the other corpses and waited for the nightly burning of the bodies.

ELEVEN

The Abduction

We spent the entire winter in the desert of Ras-al-Ayn. Earlier, in October, a disastrous epidemic of typhus spread through our camp. Mama heard fleas were transporting the disease from one person to another; so she dug a ditch, encircling our tent, and poured water into it every day to keep the fleas away. She forbid me to leave the tent, and she only went out herself when it was absolutely necessary. Thank God, neither she nor I contracted typhus.

Drained of money and faced with increasing hunger and spreading diseases, many of the Armenian refugees in Ras-al-Ayn sank into abysmal despair. The number of deaths escalated each day and, for the burials and burning in the pit, we were ordered by the soldiers to haul the bodies of those without any family members and toss them into the pit every evening.

One day, in the midst of this chaos, a young, well-dressed woman entered our tent.

"I'm an Armenian from Diyarbakir," she identified herself quickly.

Mama was happy to see an Armenian who obviously was not a refugee. "Come in and please sit with us for a while," Mama said, anxious to hear what the woman had to tell us.

After exchanging a few welcoming words with Mama, the woman said, "Six months ago, I was in the same situation you're in right now. Just like you and your family, my people were deported and several of us were massacred. Only I was spared because a Muslim from Ras-al-Ayn abducted me, and now I'm his wife. He likes me very much and he treats me very well, but I'm very lonely."

The young woman told us she needed to talk to someone in Armenian or Turkish. "I don't understand my husband's language," she lamented, her eyes glistening with tears. "So, I come here once in a while to have a conversation with anybody who understands me. Thank God, my husband doesn't mind my coming to the camp to visit the Armenian refugees, so I come here as often as I can."

"Do you have any relatives here?" Mama was curious about this woman.

"No. But, every time I come here, I remember my family."

"Why don't you stay here, in this camp with us?" Mama tried to convince her that she'd be better off living with the refugees. "Ras-al-Ayn has been quieter, more stable than anywhere else during our miserable exile. At least, the soldiers don't bother us very much and they stop the Arabs from coming into our camp."

"No, no, I can't!" The woman rose from her seat and came closer to Mama; and almost whispering, she said: "I happen to know they're letting you stay here until they finish with the previous caravans that were here before yours, and this camp will be next"

"What do you mean?" Mama's voice betrayed her sudden uneasiness.

"I'm so sorry I have to tell you, but you're all going to be taken to slaughter valley where all the refugees ultimately end. That's what happened to me and to my family, except I was kidnapped just before the killing began."

Mama held her head in her hands and cried, "Not again, God!"

"Sell whatever you can," the woman's voice quivered. "Use the money for food; don't deprive yourselves. Believe me, they'll take everything from you, then at the end they'll kill you."

Now the young woman rapidly continued to volunteer her advice. "Don't try to hide your money in your clothes, not in your hair, not in your shoes. The soldiers know all the hiding places; first they'll look in your vagina for gold pieces and jewelry. The only safe place for hiding money is in your rectum."

She looked wistfully at Mama and said, "Your only salvation is to marry a *Zhairkez* (cossack), a Kurd or a Turk; and, if you get the chance, you must do so if you want to stay alive."

After the young woman left, I began to shiver. I didn't know if I was really ill or frightened by what I'd just heard. When the fever started, I realized it wasn't just what the woman had predicted for us. I was really sick.

Mama worried that I'd contracted typhus, and she fussed over me day and night as I huddled in the corner of our tiny tent. Days later, she learned a doctor was visiting the sick in camp and she hurried to speak to him about me. Mama persuaded him to come to see me, and the kind doctor brushed aside her offer to pay him for his service.

"Vergeen is not seriously ill," he told my relieved Mama. "These pills should help her. Besides, I'll try to come by later this week to make sure she's all right."

Then he introduced himself, he was Armenian. "My name is *Vahan Hershdakian*. I'm the doctor for Ras-al-Ayn's railroad station and, believe me, the only reason I've been spared is because my wife is German."

Trying to help further, the doctor said, "If you have any money, I can get a room for you in Ras-al-Ayn and you can live there."

"No, we don't have much money left." Mama was honest, we didn't.

"Well, my wife likes handwork. Do you have any? I'll buy all you have." Discreetly, I told Mama I couldn't sell the needlework I'd made. Except for that cherished piece, we sold everything else to the doctor who paid us handsomely.

Before leaving, the good doctor asked Mama why I'd refused to part with my needlework.

"She made it for her dowry," Mama explained. "Her betrothed is in America."

The doctor turned to me and smiled. "If I were to buy that from you, how much would you charge?"

I hesitated a moment, then replied, "One lira!" That was a lot of money to me. Yet, I still did not want to part with my needlework; I treasured it.

He reached into his pocket and handed me two coins. "Here's a lira and an extra *mejidi*. You'll always need the money."

As he promised, the doctor came to check on me a few days later and assured Mama that I was recovering well. I'll never forget his kindness.

※ ※ ※

Hundreds of new refugees, exhausted and famished, arrived at our camp every day. The fortunate ones found family members from whom they'd been separated months before. But, for most, death had waited until they got to the camp.

Unsanitary conditions and the awful odors were intolerable, especially the dysentery-caused human feces scattered all over the camp's grounds. Stepping into it was unavoidable; this was a daily occurrence for Mama and me.

The winter was hard. Mama and I hugged each other tightly at night to keep warm. Experiencing the first freezing snowfall ever seen in Ras-al-Ayn, we thought it was God's way of killing the disease-causing germs.

Mama and I didn't have adequate clothes to withstand the cold or wet weather, and we were chilled most of the time. Our food supply was also depleting fast. The extreme cold and hunger were too much for Mama. She became quite ill and feverish, and all I could do to try and lower her temperature was to apply vinegar solutions to her forehead.

Occasionally, the government workers distributed soup with round bread to the starving refugees. However, one needed some kind of a receptacle to carry the soup from the distribution spot to the tent; and many of the refugees had nothing, not a single bowl. We, fortunately, had two bowls; and I dashed out one day, swinging the bowls over my head, shouting and running after the soup-dispensing worker.

"You're only allowed one bowl of soup." The worker chastised me severely.

"But I need one bowl for my sick mother who's inside the tent, the other is for me."

"Are you telling me the truth?"

"Oh, yes! Please! Mama's very sick! We're very hungry."

Luckily, the worker believed me. I walked slowly back to our tent, carrying two round breads, one under each arm, and two bowls of hot soup. I was oh so careful not to spill a single drop of the precious nourishment.

Word spread throughout the camp that the feared extermination of our camp's refugees would soon begin. The icy rain was pouring down heavily when the soldiers started to dismantle all the tents and ordered us to get ready to leave Ras-al-Ayn within the hour. Mother was still feverish, still unable to rise from her bed. I thought the soldiers might let us stay a day behind if I pleaded with them.

"Please let us stay just until tomorrow, my Mama is very sick." I hoped the officer would show some compassion.

"That does not matter! Both of you must leave Ras-al-Ayn NOW!"

Two young brothers occupied the tent next to ours, and I ran to them for help. They were in their early teens, and they were always grateful whenever Mama cooked for them.

"If each of you will carry my bundles and help me with Mama, we'll feed you all the way." I was almost euphoric when they accepted my proposition right away.

I dressed Mama lightly in the only warm jacket we had, making sure she would not be dragged down by the weight of heavy garments. And, rather than bundling them, I wore as many clothes as I could, including a hideous smock and a voluminous skirt with a torn hem.

Mama had a difficult time walking, so we slowly followed the moving line of stricken refugees. The brothers shouldered our heavy bundles in the pouring rain; and the soaked bundles, mostly bedding, got heavier. Hanging on to me, Mama found it increasingly hard to keep pace, and she stopped now and then; but, we were forced on by the angry soldiers who frequently whipped us with their batons. Our shoes fused with the mud; our feet bled and swelled badly; infections erupted around the heels. Anxious for respite from bruised, blistered feet, we took off our shoes and dragged our bare toes in the deepening mud, endangering them to even greater risk of infection.

At noon, we ate our bread, and I wondered if I could find twigs later to cook the last of our noodles.

We were still marching when the weather broke and small patches of dark blue appeared in the sky, readying for dusk.

"Stop! This is where you'll rest for the night," an officer shouted.

Mama urgently needed to rest, so I spread our wet bedding on the soggy ground and gently lowered her on it. I looked for something to light a fire to boil our noodles and went hunting for twigs. Finding none, I returned looking for the noodles. They were gone; someone had stolen them. Cold and wet and hungry, Mama and I fell asleep on the muddy ground.

In the morning, we saw Bedouin women selling some food items; and we used the few coins Mama had left in her neck bag to buy some milk and yogurt, adding a few more days' food to our dwindling supply.

The next day was bright and sunny, and our clothes and bundles had finally dried. Although still weak, Mama did feel better since her fever had broken during the night.

On the second day, the guards woke us early. After walking some distance, we saw a wide river, only five feet in depth in some sections; and we were helped across, carried on the shoulders of some volunteers. They grasped each other, forming seats with their arms for Mama and me while struggling to remain upright in the rushing water. Finally, they set us down safely on the opposite bank of the river. Profoundly grateful, Mama gave them all the change hanging in the small bag around my neck.

Ignoring the jeering guards who sat at the river's edge, Mama and I looked for the two brothers who had helped us earlier. We found our bedding they'd been carrying for us; but, not the boys. "I think they drowned along with a dozen others who just could not make it across," a tall, weary woman told Mama.

※ ※ ※

Remembering the advice of the young woman in Ras-al-Ayn, Mama had hidden three lira in her rectum. But, we dared not use them to buy food; we knew the guards would take them from us.

On and on we went for many days, perhaps even several weeks. Yet, the guards prohibited us from walking on the smooth roads and forced us to keep to the rough roadsides. Uphill. Downhill. Uphill. Downhill. We knew we were nearing our destination when we sighted amputated hands and feet. A little further, we saw swollen bodies of women and children covered with swarming worms.

It seemed we were marching in circles for endless days, deprived of food and water, seeing the same corpses, bumping into the same groups of people. The only difference was the new dead thrown on top of the old.

Early one morning, an order came from a stern-looking guard.

"All the people from Kayseri, come here!" He pointed to a mound of dirt "Sit together here!"

I noticed others were being grouped the same way, according to their villages and towns. Our group was the largest.

The soldier walked back and forth for a few minutes, then pointing to a half dozen people randomly, he shouted, "You, you, you! Come with me!"

One of the chosen was our old neighbor, *Yervant*. He looked back at his confused wife, daughter and grandchild as the soldier hurriedly led him away. Half an hour went by before the soldier returned and signaled to ten more people. And then he pointed to Mama and me.

"COME! Come with me," he yelled.

Shaking with palpitating fear, we followed the guard to a small hill where we saw *Yervant agha* descending on the other side.

"Stop here," ordered the guard. "Take off your clothes, except your underwear." Obeying quickly, Mama and I stripped to our undershirts and bloomers. Two guards from top of the hill came to Mama and me and took us individually to another spot where each one meticulously examined every fold of our apparel, looking for hidden money and jewelry.

There were three piles, the paltry harvests of their searches: one was for money, another for jewelry, and still another for clothes that still looked wearable.

Under a guard's watchful eyes, Mama and I stood rigidly in our underwear, several yards apart, awaiting the next deep humiliation. The examining soldier returned to me and began to survey my adolescent body roughly with his dirty hands, up and down. Finally he pulled my bloomers down to my ankles and inserted his long fingers inside my virginal vagina searching for money. The violent pain made me nauseous, but I didn't dare faint or vomit.

I still wore Papa's gold watch around my neck; both Mama and I had agreed weeks before that we couldn't bear to sell it. Now, in my undressed state, it became fully exposed, gleaming in the sunlight. The guard yanked it off and tossed my cherished remembrance of Papa into the jewelry pile.

Mama was still several yards away, being examined by another menacing guard. I groaned when I saw him take her jacket and throw it into the pile of clothes. When the first guard returned my garments, I dressed promptly and, passing by the clothes pile, I quickly retrieved Mama's jacket and gave it to her when no one was looking. She put it on under her large smock.

Shortly after, we heard the moans and pleas of people begging to be killed by bullets, one of them was the familiar voice of old Yervant. The poignant cries of children, calling out for the help of parents, was especially hard – excruciatingly hard to bear.

Seated on the ground again with the Kayseri group, Mama and I glanced at each other apprehensively, knowing full well that we'd be next. I wondered what it'd be like to feel the steel blade of a knife at my throat. Would the pain be intolerable? Would I die right away? Would Mama and I die together or separately? Would Armenag, living in safe and secure America, ever know what happened to us?

My desponding thoughts were interrupted by the woman sitting next to Mama. "I think that Arab is interested in your daughter," she said, nodding toward a well-dressed, stately Arab in a white caftan who kept sauntering around us.

"Quick!" Mama pulled me toward her. "Put your head down on my knee and don't look up. Stay DOWN!"

The Arab came alongside and this time yanked my head up by my hair, forcing me to look at him; and he left. Within minutes, a guard came to Mama and said, "That Arab over there wants this girl. You'd better give her to him; otherwise, you and your daughter will be killed with the others."

"Listen to me," whispered the woman next to Mama. She had a proposition while the guard waited for Mama's answer. "It looks like that man is going to take your daughter with or without your consent. Why don't you tell him you'll agree on the condition that he take us along, too." She pointed to her family of eight.

"Please, this way we'll all be saved; and your daughter will not be alone. We'll all watch over her."

Mama had no choice; either we'd end up on the pile of corpses or we'd risk a chance with this Arab who might let us live.

"Tell the Arab that I agree if he'll accept certain conditions," Mama told the guard.

The guard left to confer with the Arab and he returned minutes later. "The Arab wants to see you. Come!" The guard took all of us to where food was available and he gave us bread and yogurt. I'd forgotten how good yogurt tasted; it had been many weeks since I'd had anything this nourishing.

I was still chewing on a piece of bread when the Arab on horseback came from behind and grabbed a young girl in our group and pulled her up next to him on his horse. Suddenly, the same thing was HAPPENING TO ME!

I was hoisted onto the horse behind the girl; and, with the two of us in back of him, the Arab began to prod his horse into a gallop. I looked back to see poor Mama running tortuously! Shouting furiously!

"Vergeen! Vergeen! Don't leave me here!"

I jumped off the horse stumbling, then ran to Mama as fast as I could. The Arab had turned around and rode to where the Turkish soldiers were watching us. He motioned to a shabby, dirty Arab on a donkey to follow him. Then lifting me on to his horse again, behind the other girl, he instructed the old Arab to walk and to let Mama ride the donkey as the five of us headed toward a distant hill.

TWELVE

Yousuf and the Bedouins

We rode silently for an hour before our abductor began to speak to us in broken Turkish. "My name is *Yousuf*. Don't worry, you'll be safe with me and my people." Glancing back at me, he added, "Your mother will be safe, too."

I kept looking back to see if Mama was all right. I saw the old Arab pulling Mama off the donkey and he got on the wretched animal himself.

"Yousuf, Effendi," I begged. "Please let me walk and allow my Mama to ride on the horse."

I was surprised when he appeased me for a while and agreed Mama could ride while I walked. After a few hours, Yousuf stopped, dropped Mama off the horse and ordered me to climb up. Again and again, I kept checking on Mama and I panicked when I saw the old Arab beating Mama while trying to steal her jacket. Crying and screaming, she was scrambling to stop him.

"You'd better get off the horse and give him that jacket!" Yousuf yelled at me.

I hopped down quickly and ran to Mama. "Let him have it, please, Mama!"

The old Arab grabbed the jacket and took off, astride the donkey.

Yousuf wanted to rest his horse so we all sat down, silently for a few minutes before we began to talk.

I learned that the other captive, a very attractive dark-haired girl, was named Vartouhi. Well-educated, she spoke Armenian and Turkish fluently. She was more than a year older than I and came from a well-to-do family in Kayseri. Her story was a familiar one: her father had been executed, her mother and sister had died from typhus, and she had no relatives left.

We resumed our journey with three of us on horseback, Vartouhi in front of Yousuf with me behind him. It broke my heart to see my sick Mama lagging behind, dragging her feet with every step. I pleaded with Yousuf to let me walk, but no way would he let me exchange places with Mama.

We approached a flat part of the desert and I could see another hill some distance away.

"That's where we're going," said Yousuf pointing to some dunes. "My people live in back of that hill."

As Yousuf spoke, I could see men, dressed in white caftans, on horseback, coming toward us and they stopped, dismounted and talked to Yousuf. We couldn't understand one word; but I knew what their intent was when I saw them remove knives from their belts, check the sharpness with their fingers, and point to Mama.

Two of them came toward Mama and pushed her down on the ground. Immediately, I ran and fell on top of her yelling for Yousuf.

"Tell them to kill me first!" I screamed over and over again.

I don't know what Yousuf told them, but they went away.

At my insistence, when we proceeded on the journey, I walked while Mama rested on the horse. But when we neared the tents, Yousuf ordered Mama to get off the horse and he told me to get up in front of him.

Reaching his tent, we were greeted by a pretty, fair-complexioned woman with large blue eyes. She was wearing a light-colored dress similar to the Arab garb I'd seen before on the streets of Aleppo.

"This is my wife," Yousuf said. "Her name is *Aneche*."

※ ※ ※

Mama, Vartouhi and I were escorted by Yousuf into a large, black tent which was divided in the center by a long bamboo curtain. Two couches and beddings backed neatly against the bamboo; and sacks of flour, bulgur and some utensils hung from the top of the curtain. This was the family's living area, the other half of the tent was occupied by horses.

An ugly, middle-aged woman, named *Fatima*, with tattoos all over her face and arms, sat on one of the couches and stared at Mama, Vartouhi and me as if we were creatures from another world. Yousuf said something to her and left.

From the back of the tent, a pretty dark-haired woman, named *Zegariad*, entered the living area and gave Fatima some flour and left. Other women walked in, all wearing their customary blue dresses; and all were covered with hundreds of tattoos over their faces, necks and arms. Fatima's daughter-in-law, *Zahra*, wearing a small ring in her nose, brought dried camel dung to heat the food.

We learned later that Yousuf's wife, Aneche, and Zegariad were Kurds and sisters; and Fatima and Zahra were their helpers.

As we sat in the tent, we watched Fatima and her daughter-in-law prepare the day's meal. Fatima placed three, equal-sized stones on top of each other, covered it with a round sagger while Zahra started the fire. Then Fatima flattened small balls of dough with her fingers and tossed them back and forth from one hand to the other until the diameter of each measured about seven inches, and she baked them on the hot sagger. The smell of the fresh bread was so luscious!

The activities inside and outside the tent produced a feast: broiled lamb, bulgur pilaf, and a wonderful thin, round bread. Whoever walked into the tent received this food heaped high on a metal plate. However, since each household had only two plates, guests would have to take turns to eat, waiting for one of the plates to become available.

Famished, I salivated waiting my turn to receive a plate of food. Mama cautioned me not to eat much. "Remember," she said, "you haven't eaten in days, so you might get sick if you have more than your stomach can handle."

The big moment came at last. Zegariad handed me a plate steaming with bulgur pilaf, four pieces of lamb, and fresh baked bread; and Vartouhi received the second plate with the same amount of food. But Zegariad gave nothing to Mama.

I wanted to share my food with Mama and I passed my plate to her. While we were waiting for forks, two men entered the tent. Zegariad quickly snatched the plates from Mama and Vartouhi and handed them to the men. More men filled the tent to savor the food and to see us, the *Ermini* women. Several of the men were shepherds and they wore peculiar outfits: short, tight, brown, leather capes without sleeves; and their heads and faces were covered with dirty scarves barely revealing burning eyes that were focused menacingly on Mama, Vartouhi and me. I felt fearfully uneasy. Scared!

We watched them keenly so that we'd learn the proper Bedouin way of eating. Using their fingers and teeth, the men tore the hot meat from the bone and gulped it down; they scooped the pilaf into funneled pieces of torn bread, and shoved large chunks into their mouths. We saw no eating utensils.

When a plate became available, Zegariad took it and, without washing it, filled it and handed the plate of food to me; I gave it to Mama. With the second plate ready, Zegariad filled it and passed it to Vartouhi.

"Come, *yahvroom* (my child)," Mama said softly to me, tears glistening in her eyes. "Sit with me and let's eat this together. You poor girl, did I bring you up for these uncivil people."

My stomach rumbled in its insatiable craving for food, yet I could only eat a small piece of meat.

We were constantly on display, even neighboring tribes came to see the *Ermini* women. One of them, a Kurdish woman, was very sympathetic and, by gesturing, she let us know she'd like to help us, especially Mama. Somehow, she let Mama know that the Bedouins were planning to kill her, and she motioned to Mama to follow her.

Yousuf was in the tent and caught the exchange between Mama and the Kurdish woman. He raised his head and glowered, staring icily at Mama.

Summoning her courage and speaking boldly in Turkish, Mama told Yousuf: "I'd like to go with that Kurdish woman. And I want to take my daughter with me."

"NO! You cannot!" Yousuf spoke so harshly that it made Mama flinch.

Fearful about what was going to happen next, Mama and I looked apprehensively around the tent.. We thought it strange that the Kurdish women were not offered any food by Zegariad even though she was one of them at one time.

A tall, handsome man suddenly entered the tent accompanied by a young woman with reddish hair and a few tattoo marks on her chin and lips.

The stately man wore a white *djellabas*, resembling a nightshirt, over which he had a belted, brown-and-white, wide-sleeved coat. The adornment on his head was a typical Bedouin scarf held down by a double-anchored *kefyah*. He had beautiful carriage and, when he spoke, his deep, strong voice immediately commanded everyone's attention. The tribal sheik, he was Yousuf's older brother, *Mounla Salman*; and the woman with him was his wife, *Saliha*.

The brothers conversed for several minutes, and Yousuf walked to Vartouhi. "My brother and his wife want you to go with them."

She looked beseechingly at Mama and me, tears welling in her beautiful, large dark eyes, and she left with the tribal leader and his wife.

Stunned and wondering what was in store for us, Mama and I saw another handsome man, in his early twenties, enter the tent; he was Yousuf's younger brother, *Abdullah*, and Zegariad's husband.

The two brothers and their wives – the Kurdish sisters, Aneche and Zegariad – lived together in the tent where we were awaiting our fate. Yousuf and Aneche had no children; Abdullah and Zegaraid had two children. Constantly bickering, the sisters argued about who was the household's boss. Later, I met the third and oldest brother, *Ahmed*, who lived in another tent with his wife and four children.

Mama and I watched Aneche and Zegariad prepare the beddings before nightfall. Aneche's bed, neatly covered with a red and gray damask quilt, sat on top of three mattresses while Zegariad's bedding was made of cotton. Aneche made up a third bed, a composition of cotton and damask, for Mama and me. When it got dark, Aneche motioned that we had to get to bed.

I was so weary, so glad to put my head down on such soft fabrics and, half-dozing, I told Mama, "At last, we'll be able to have a comfortable night's rest."

Exhausted, I fell asleep immediately. Now and then I'd open my eyes to see if Mama was sleeping, too; and I'd notice she was still awake.

Once I woke up when it was nearing sunrise, but still dark; and I saw Aneche and Fatima standing on each side of two, tall bamboo sticks and swinging them back and forth to each other. Inside the two sticks, tied about a foot apart with heavy ropes, was a black object, looking like a small infant. I was shocked and shook Mama who'd finally fallen asleep. We both looked in terror, thinking they must be torturing a child dressed in black.

Ordering me to stay in bed with my head covered, Mama got up to check out what was happening. She came back smiling and said, "They're just churning butter in a black goat skin."

In the morning, after neatly folding our bedding, we were given bread and yogurt. We watched Fatima and Zahra working outside the tent, baking bread, and gathering and drying camel dung.

Mama and I were talking about Vartouhi and worried about her treatment by the sheik and his wife when we saw her coming toward us. I ran to her and threw my arms around her, "Vartouhi, are you all right?"

"I have no complaints," she said quietly. "They gave me a comfortable bed and some food this morning. But they changed my name to *Zenab*."

"At least, you're alive," said Mama who appeared unperturbed by Vartouhi's name change. "In your heart, you'll always know your own name. But, for now, you"ll just have to answer these people by your Arabic name. "

Walking nearby, Aneche, Zegariad and Fatima motioned us to follow them toward a small brook. Again motioning, the women indicated they wanted Vartouhi and me to take off our clothes, and they gave the garments to Mama to wash them. Naked, Vartouhi and I were taken deeper into the brook where Fatima scooped water with palm leaves and sprinkled it over our heads, praying in Arabic: *"La Ilah il lah Mohammed Nabina Rasoul La!* (There is no God, but God. Mohammed, our prophet, is God's Messenger.)"

Then she made both Vartouhi and me repeat the prayer in Arabic. "Thank God, I accept the true father!" Then she named me *Noura*, meaning bright; and she confirmed Vartouhi's new name, *Zenab*.

Still naked, Vartouhi and I were carefully examined by Fatima from head to toe while Mama spread our clothes on stones to dry.

Suddenly, it hit me! Why didn't Mama get baptized and why didn't she get a new Arabic name, I wondered and I worried deeply. I was alarmed when Mama kept saying she was going to be killed, and that's why she wasn't baptized. Silently, I begged God: "Oh, please! Don't let them kill Mama!"

Vartouhi and I got dressed in our freshly washed clothes and walked back to our tents with the three Bedouin women. They displayed great hostility toward Mama, especially Aneche and Fatima. Every time these two women passed by Mama, each spit at her three times and called her a pig, a great insult.

The second day, people from other tribes were still coming to see us, the *Ermini* women. They were friendly toward Vartouhi and me, but they'd look at Mama and shake their heads. Each would lament, whispering, "*Miskin! Agh Miskin!*"

We knew what that meant; the same word in Turkish meant "poor thing." The sympathetic women knew Mama was going to be killed. That day, I stayed close to Mama every minute. I went with her everywhere, even when she had to eliminate her bowels.

Replacing the three lira in her rectum, Mama wondered, "Do you think these lira will save my life if I bribe someone?"

Once again that second night, Mama and I were told to use the same bed; but, I was afraid to close my eyes. I stayed awake as long as I could and finally fell into a fretful sleep. Frequently, I awakened to touch Mama and make sure she was still next to me. Once when I awoke, Mama was up, standing with Fatima next to our bed. Fatima laughed as I tried to climb out of bed.

"Stay in bed, *yavroom* (my child); go back to sleep." Mama kissed both my cheeks and drew the covers around my shoulders.

I tried vainly to keep awake, but my fatigue won the battle; and I must have slept for several more hours. I awoke again, angry at myself for not being more vigilant; and I immediately checked on Mama. She was not in bed, not in the tent! I dressed quickly and went outside.

It was a cool, hazy morning. Aneche and Fatima were warming their hands by the fire. As soon as they saw me, they turned their heads and softly said to each other, *"Miskin! Miskin!"*.

Instantly, I knew something terrible had happened – please, God, NOT TO MAMA! Motioning wildly, I tried to ask Fatima where Mama was, and she pointed to Sheik Mounla Salman's tent. Before I could start to run, Aneche and Fatima stopped me, dragged me back, and forced me to sit by the fire. While Aneche held me down, Fatima went into the tent and brought me yogurt and bread. I sat there, shrouded inside myself, with the plate of food in my lap, unable to eat as the silent tears flooded my face.

"What have you people done to Mama?" I finally screamed and tried to run toward the Sheik's tent, but each time Fatima or Aneche grabbed me and pulled me back near the fire.

"At least let me see Vartouhi, please!" I protested loudly. "I know she's in that tent." But neither woman understood me; yet their faces could not hide their pity.

I don't know how long I sat next to the fire when Yousuf appeared. I jumped up and shouted, "Yousuf, please help! You can understand Turkish. Please, please tell me, where's my mother?"

Yousuf raised both hands to quiet me.

"Please! Let me go to your brother's tent. I was told Mama may be there. Let me talk to Vartouhi."

"You can't go there now. My brother is talking to some Turkish officers." Pointing to horses tied in front of the sheik's tent, Yousuf insisted, "You'd better listen. If those Turks saw you they'd take you away and you'd be killed. You stay here with Aneche and Fatima."

I went back and sat next to the fire again, watching the horses, and I saw Vartouhi walking toward me. "Oh, Vartouhi, I'm so glad to see you. They won't let me go into the sheik's tent to find Mama. Is she there?"

Vartouhi shook her head sadly. "No, she's not in the tent.

"Do you know where she is?"

"No, Vergeen."

Now unrestrained, I began to sob. Aneche motioned to Vartouhi to return to her tent, and Vartouhi obeyed instantly

I found my only consolation in my tears. Mama's dead! Mama's dead! I told myself over and over again.

Yousuf left and was gone for four days. I could speak to no one, except Vartouhi. She'd come to console me and spent as much time with me as she was allowed. She knew nothing of Mama's whereabouts, but Vartouhi tried to encourage me to have hope that she was still alive. Those miserable days spanned several weeks.

Yousuf came home with an Armenian boy named *Vahan*. He was a year younger than I, and also from Kayseri. In fact, I knew his family well; his older sister was my classmate in French school. I tried to be pleasant to Vahan, but my thoughts were always with Mama.

"Yousuf, will you please tell me, where's my mother," I asked him the first chance I had.

"Do you see this boy?" Yousuf shook Vahan's shoulders. "I bought him from Turkish soldiers, just like I bought you and Zenab. I didn't pay for your mother. She chose to tag along. She doesn't belong to this tribe. I can't keep her here, so I gave her to another tribe."

I stared at him, trying unsuccessfully to mask my hate, and wept. "Don't cry." Yousuf tried to comfort me. "Someday I'll take you to her or I'll bring her here."

Thank, God! At least she's alive, I told myself, a little relieved.

The next day, I spent several hours exchanging stories with Vahan about what had happened to our families since leaving Kayseri. His situation was the same as mine, except he and his family were in Ras-al-Ayn only two days before being forced to leave for slaughter valley. On the way, both he and his sister were abducted; she was taken by another Arab while Yousuf seized Vahan. We spent the day comforting each other; he was anxious to find his sister and I was still worried about Mama.

"When will you take me to see my mother?" I asked Yousuf that question every time I saw him.

He'd respond with a sneaky smile and never answer.

One day, I found the nerve to confront Yousuf.

"You're lying to me! You've killed Mama, haven't you?"

"Why are you so stubborn?" Yousuf showed his exasperation. "I'll prove to you that I was telling you the truth! I'll go to her and bring back any article of hers you want. Maybe that way you'll be convinced she's not dead."

"Bring me some of the papers Mama had with her. They were bank notes from my great-uncle in Tiflis. Maybe then I'll believe you."

I thought if Yousuf showed me these papers, perhaps Mama was not dead. The next day, Yousuf brought the papers to me.

"See! I told you she was fine. Now do you believe me?"

Satisfied for only a little while, I started to pester Yousuf again. Doubts about her safety nagged me. The uncertainty made me ill. Food, sleep, even chats with Vartouhi and Vahan held little interest.

On the day of his arrival, Vahan had been baptized and renamed *Hassan*. Aneche gave him my bed and I was moved to the horses' area. In my state of mind, sleeping with the horses was fine. Besides, these Arabian horses were admirable, better than my captors; and they were more precious to Yousuf than almost anyone else in his family. Painfully aware of her husband's great love for his horses, Yousuf's wife was very jealous of the animals.

My hatred for the Bedouins grew each day. I wanted to die, but I couldn't find a weapon to do the job. At first, I'd sit all day long, not speaking, not eating. Then, I lost myself in sleep, sleep, solacing sleep. It was my only liberation from grief. I slept day and night until one day Vartouhi tried to keep me awake.

"Vergeen, *khentrem* (please)! You must not sleep so much. These Bedouins have a strange custom. Anyone, man or woman, who's sick for three or four days is killed; and only the despised ones are buried."

I was beyond caring. Yet, both Vartouhi and Vahan tried to arouse me from my depressive lethargy.

Both knew about Sheik Mounla Salman's plan, but said nothing to me. The tribal leader had decided to move his people to another location and leave me behind. Early on the day of the move, after completing his shepherding duties, Vahan came to bid me goodbye. I ignored him and went back to sleep.

My eyes suddenly opened wide when Yousuf pulled me out of bed, dragged me outside, and threw me on top of a camel.

"Stay awake!" His warning would have frightened me another time. But I no longer felt intimidated by him or any other Arab in this dismal desert.

Vartouhi, seated on a larger camel, came alongside. "Vergeen, I'm so glad to see you. I was afraid they were not going to bring you along."

As we rode on, Vartouhi told me the Sheik's wife, Saliha, thought my sleep was due to a contagious illness. "She refused to let me see you. Please, don't sleep so much so that I can come and visit you when we reach the new camp."

I slept less after we got to our new location and Vartouhi came to tell me about the dispute between Yousuf and his brother.

"I think you should know Yousuf saved you from dying alone in the desert. We heard him argue with the sheik that he would not leave you to burn to death in the hot sun. He was taking you with him."

Two days after we settled, Yousuf came to my quarters with a blonde, young man who was a Kurd like Aneche and Zegariad. I knew they were talking about me. I'd learned a few Arabic words by now, and I gathered Yousuf was telling him to take me, Noura, to the stream and drown me.

As Yousuf talked, the young man kept looking at me with pity. I welcomed what I was able to understand. At last, my misery was going to end.

The next morning, I was told to accompany Aneche, Zegariad, Fatima and Zahra; I knew we were headed for the stream. Carrying goat skin and ropes, the women talked and laughed all the way. When we reached the stream, the women filled their goat skins while the blonde young man appeared and grabbed my hand. He walked into the deep waves, pulling me along. The water was over my knees when I heard Yousuf calling the young man and I turned to see him motioning us to turn back. Yousuf had changed his mind.

OH, God! How much longer was this agony going to continue? I wanted to sleep again. No, oh NO! I just wanted to think about Mama. I longed to know how she was being treated. I wondered if she missed me as much as I missed her. I wanted to plead with Yousuf again to let me see her.

One day, greatly annoyed by my relentless pleas about Mama, Yousuf entered my quarters with Vahan.

"Please forgive me," Vahan started in Turkish. "I'm here to speak for Yousuf since his Turkish is not good. He says he's tired of your nagging about your mother."

Vahan turned to Yousuf who nudged him on. "Go on. Go on, tell her."

Vahan tried to look at me again, his eyes shifting from side to side. He began speaking slowly, "I have to tell you that they killed your mother some time ago, and you're not to ask about her any more."

I lurched toward Yousuf; I tried to pound his chest with my fists, crying: "Liar! Liar! You killed Mama!"

Yousuf grabbed my hands roughly and pushed me down on top of the bedding. Reaching into a nearby basket, he pulled out a loom and some sheep wool, and handed them to me.

"You're not going to cry anymore. Do you hear?" His voice cracked from shouting.

"From now on, you're going to spin wool; you're going to weave; you're going to clean the tent; you're going to carry water for us; you're going to carry hay for the horses! And you're going to do whatever Aneche and Zegariad tell you to do!" He stopped for a second to catch his breath. "Remember this! You and Hassan are our servants!"

Yousuf turned to look at a man entering the tent and said: "One more thing. I did not kill your mother. That's the man! *Hilmi!* He's the one who did the killing."

It must have happened on our second night in the Bedouins' camp. God, weeks ago! I remembered Mama standing by my bed with Fatima. I remembered the touch of her soft lips as she gently kissed my cheeks and told me to go back to sleep. I remembered the many times she told me to have faith. I remembered how she protected me, how she loved me! Oh! MAMA! An explosive rage surged through my gut! REVENGE! I wanted revenge! But how? All I could do was weep!

Days later, I found out the details of Mama's death from Zegariad. Fatima and Hilmi had taken Mama to the overflowing Jurjub River where he'd knocked Mama unconscious with his pistol. Then, with Fatima's help, he'd undressed Mama and thrown her into the rushing river.

As payment for committing the murder, Yousuf had promised Hilmi he could take anything – Mama's clothes and any hidden money he'd find.

The next time I saw Hilmi, I wanted to shut my eyes forever – never, NEVER AGAIN to have my bitter grief inflamed by the sight of that monster! He was wearing my beloved Mama's smock!

THIRTEEN

Life in the Desert

In the Summer of 1916, we were three teenaged Armenians, given Arabic names, and living in the middle of the Arabian desert – Vartouhi, known as *Zenab*, was fifteen; Vahan, known as *Hassan*, was thirteen, and I, now called *Noura*, was fourteen.

Both Vartouhi and Vahan seemed to cope somewhat with their new surroundings, they even began to call each other by their Arabic names. I could NOT! I could NOT tolerate the lifestyle of the Bedouins; nor did I want to communicate with them.

My depression worsened as days went on. I resented having to go on with life without Mama. I hated everyone, even the innocent little children. I refused to learn the language of the Arabs.

"Vergeen, forget the past." Vartouhi often lectured me. "This is our life now. Maybe one day we'll be able to be with our own people, but you must try to adjust. Please try."

"How can you say that?" I was unrelenting. "How can I learn to live with these savages! How can I! They murdered my mother!"

As the painful, depressive weeks went by, my duties rescued me – even though Aneche treated me harshly, like a slave. I ignored her carping and completely lost myself in my work, especially with the animals.

Never comfortable with camels before, I learned to tolerate them with less fear. I was amused by the way they stomped, spit, bucked, squealed, and, yes, even laughed. They could run like machines for hours, but once they stopped, they'd refuse to budge. They exhibited their self-assured pride only when riders were in their saddles; and then they'd move nobly, taking long, elastic strides.

Camels were more than transportation providers for nomads. The old ones were killed for food and their sinewy meat was boiled for hours. Even then it was so tough that many a Bedouin's teeth were blunted or loosened.

The nomads in our camp often drank the camel's milk and, in stressful times, they'd drink the awful sour fluid secreted in the camel's stomach. On cold days, people warmed their hands – even washed their hair – in the camel's urine.

The poor animals gave so much more: their hair was woven for coats for herdsmen and garments for women and children; their dung was used for fuel; their hide was made into water bags.

※ ※ ※

It always astonished me to see how colorful, how flat the desert was in certain parts, and how its sandy surface undulated in the breeze, denting the sand into deep grooves. Sometimes, after a rain, water filled these grooves and the white mud glistened on the top like jewels. This quieting scenery afforded me many hours of peaceful solace.

Despite my reluctance to become familiar with their culture, I learned a lot about the Bedouins. I always sensed they considered themselves superior to anyone who was not one of them; the way I was treated confirmed this attitude which pervaded the entire camp. I discovered that Bedouins were hardy people who strictly followed old customs and traditions. Although their livelihood came mainly from breeding camels, goats and sheep, they also were wily bandits.

Their intense fidelity to the Muslim religion was unwavering. Before each prayer, five times a day, a devout ritual involved splashing water over the head, washing inside the nostrils and ears as well as the face, hands and feet.

Only the men prayed, first standing upright to face Mecca, then leaning forward with their hands on their knees, kneeling, and bowing down until their foreheads touched the ground.

They knew only the opening verse of the Koran and recited it

fervently:
> "In the name of God, the Compassionate, the Merciful.
> Praise be to God, Lord of the world.
> The Compassionate, the Merciful!
> King on the day of reckoning,
> Thee only do we worship,
> And to Thee do we cry for help.
> Guide us on the straight path,
> The path of those to whom Thou hast been,
> With whom Thou are not angry
> And who go not astray."

Bedouin women were not as restricted as Turkish women. They wore no face veils; their garments revealed the shape of their figures; and they could sit, talk and laugh with their men.

Led by their sheik, Bedouins wandered from place to place every few weeks, making their home wherever they found water and pastures for themselves as well as their animals. Nomadic life was usually monotonous, usually uncomfortable, and always turbulent on the days we changed locations.

We had five to ten tents in our tribe and, sometimes, other small tribes joined us when water and pastures were scarce elsewhere. Whenever it came time for another move, we rose early, gathered the household belongings, rolled the black goat-hair tent with ropes, mounted the camels, and started the journey before sunrise.

Bedouins ate only once during a 24-hour day. For the meat in their diet, they killed black goats, chopped off the heads, and blew air between the skin and flesh to separate them. Once the meat was removed, the skin was cured with lots of salt and dried. The legs were tied together tightly for use as a receptacle for transporting water. The air-tight skins were also used to store and preserve food such as butter and cooked meat.

There were few pots for cooking and no utensils for eating. At mealtime, separated according to gender, all simply ate with their hands and, when finished, cleaned their greasy fingers by rubbing them on their hair.

Bedouin wives worked hard, fetching water and firewood, gathering camel dung, and herding the animals. They spun goat hair for making tents and they spun sheep wool for warm clothes. Men, meanwhile, would spend lots of quiet time with the sheik, smoking a *nargileh* (water pipe) and drinking thick, Turkish coffee.

The men were lean, always barefoot, with leathery sun-browned skin, slender faces, and light or thinning hair. Their hair, hanging in two braids below the ears, was always covered by long twisted ropes. Their *achdachi* (robes), undoubtedly once white, were badly discolored by dirt. Their wide shoulders always sported curved sabers. Their indispensable belts, usually made out of yarn or rope, symbolized status; and the wider or silkier ones indicated the wearer was rich.

All women, especially the older ones, were tattooed from forehead to ankle, with similar symbols. Their lower lips were covered with dark blue dots; and they made their eyebrows longer by tattooing the space between them to make one, uninterrupted line over the eyes. Tattoos covered their hands, arms, legs as well as their cheeks, their chins, their necks, between their breasts, and, sometimes, from the chest almost to the groin.

※ ※ ※

The heat of the desert was at times very taxing, especially for my sun-hardened, leather shoes. I could no longer slip my swollen feet into them, so I was barefoot most of the time, like the rest of my captors. But my feet burned from walking on the hot sand and I was constantly ridiculed by the women. Feeling sorry for me, Yousuf made a pair of sandals for me from camel hide.

"Make sure you'll always wear these sandals at night or keep them hidden under this," Yousuf said, giving me a soft, white pillow.

I was so grateful for his concern; but, he neglected to tell me that dogs liked to eat anything made out of camel hide.

A week later, I forgot my sandals under my pillow and, when I returned, one of the sandals was missing. I looked everywhere, it was gone.

"I think one of the dogs got it," Zegariad pointed to a mangy dog howling around our tent.

Wearing the lone sandal alternately on one foot then the other, I soon learned how to walk on any soil, even on rocks. The soles of my feet were like the soles of my old shoes, and I could run far without any discomfort.

It was moving day again. In the haste to get ready, I rushed to help the women load the noisy, snarling camels. My job was to tie one of the female camel's forelegs to prevent her from rising while others loaded her with the household's bundles. I knew I was in trouble when I had a hard time tying the animal securely; she tried to get up and run off.

After the loading was done, Aneche and Zegariad began one of their never-ending arguments; and, this time, I guessed it was again about me and which camel I should ride. Zegariad always treated me kindly, often secretly giving me food, while Aneche resented me and deliberately made my life hell.

After the camels were loaded, Aneche grabbed me by the arm and motioned that I mount one of the last camels. Even though I suspected she had a hidden motive, I obeyed, as always. As soon as I sat in the bamboo saddle, the camel rose and ran swiftly, and headed to the front of the caravan.

Damn Aneche! She knew this camel only carried loads, never a rider before. I felt myself slipping, and fell sideways with my feet tangled in the rope which was secured tightly to the bamboo saddle. Instinctively, I managed to keep my head up as my body bounced, scraping on the hard ground.

Suddenly Yousuf was alongside. He grabbed the camel's head, forcing her to stop. He freed my feet and hoisted me onto another, more docile camel. My only dress was torn top to bottom, and red spots of blood stained the areas where I'd been dragged. Were it not for Zegariad who applied butter to the painful sores to prevent my soiled dress from sticking to the lacerations, I might have had severe infections.

※ ※ ※

As the leader of the tribe, Mounla Salman had the largest tent. It was divided into two areas, like the other tents. But what normally would have been the area for horses was used instead as a coffee house where all men, including those from nearby tribes, joined the sheik for advice, smoking *nargilah* (water pipe), and drinking thick coffee.

Moula Salman would sit on his silk mattress, propped regally against red and white damask pillows. During these occasions, he always looked like royalty, dressed in his white *djellabas*, belted with a wide silk scarf, and covered by a two-tone silk *meshlah* (long vest). On his head, he wore a waist-length scarf crowned by a handsome *kefyah*.

Usually, when Vartouhi finished her chores at the sheik's tent, she'd visit me and we'd reminisce and weep together about our lost families. One afternoon, she told me Mounla Salman's coffee boy, *Hamad*, was married to an Armenian, and we met her that day. A good-looking woman in her mid-twenties, she'd been renamed *Senat* by the Arabs.

"I was born in Tarsus," she told us. "But I was living in Alexandria, Egypt, with my husband and two children until last summer when I took my children to visit my mother. When we received word about the deportation of the Armenians, I wasn't permitted to return to Alexandria and I was exiled from Tarsus along with mother."

Almost passively, she continued her story: "Shortly after we left Ras-al-Ayn, my darling children were kidnapped. My daughter was stolen by one Arab and my son by another. A few days later, Hamad bought me from the soldiers; he married me; and we came here. Now I live with him and his mother."

Vartouhi and I saw Senat as often as we could. She talked about her children continually, and she was hopeful about finding them.

"After the war, I'm certain their father will look for them and me, and we'll all be reunited," she'd say repeatedly.

She was also a great comfort, always consoling. I still was having great difficulty coping. But now, at least, there were four of us – four Armenian captives of the nomads. My luck, however, was the worst; I was Aneche's slave.

※　※　※

I detested moving days, especially when there were sandstorms. Pitching the tents was particularly hazardous since stakes would come out, no matter how deeply pounded in the ground; and the tents would collapse. One of my duties was to fetch large jugs of water from the stream and pour it around the stakes so that the dust could settle and the ground could harden. The second, more arduous job was to find twigs and dried shrubs for fires, collect them in a large, heavy bundle, and carry them to the tent on my back. And always, I had to get the hay ready for Yousuf's splendid horses.

Before noon each day, Vartouhi, Senat and I helped each other carry the water in the saddle bags and, whenever the water source was far from camp, we used donkeys to haul the bags. Sometimes, the animals would run off with our water before we had a chance to grab onto them. That caused a great deal of trouble for us.

A water-toting saddle bag served as my bed, and often it would be still damp at night although I'd try to dry it out each afternoon.

In every camp location, the women seemed to know every inch of the area; they'd been there many times before.

One day, Aneche instructed me to make *amhiet* soup with wheat. "Go behind the fifth tent and you'll find a large rock," she said. "Put four cups of wheat in this cloth and stick it in the bowl-like hole in that rock, sprinkle some water over it and pound on it hard with this wooden mallet; then sprinkle some more water and pound the wheat again."

Aneche hesitated a moment to make sure I understood her instructions.

"Do what I told you over and over until the outer skin comes off and the wheat turns white. Blow off all the loose skins, then it'll be ready to cook.

Despite my diligent search, I could not find the big rock. Instead, I dug a large hole, covered the bottom with goat-hair material, poured in the wheat, sprinkled water over it, and pounded and pounded until I was exhausted; but I still had to make the *amheit* soup.

I hadn't yet mastered the art of starting a fire by rubbing two stones together. It was an arduously difficult job, even for the nomads; they'd borrow starter flames from each other. Looking around I saw no other fire going. I worked with the stones to ignite a flame and the camel dung never sparked; it only emitted smoke. I blew and blew on the uncooperative, dying embers until I could breathe no longer. I looked behind me for some help from the women; they were amused by my ineptitude. Aneche, mocking me, was having the best time of all. She had finally become pregnant and flaunted her growing belly.

Eventually, I became fairly good at making *amheit*; it was a daily part of the Bedouin diet. Besides, with no one looking, I could eat as much of it as I wanted. This was a better job than constantly carrying heavy water bags.

One afternoon, Aneche decided she would cook the meal, and I had no chance of getting some food. I was hungry; I knew where the bread was stored and I took a piece just as Zegariad walked in and saw me taking a bite.

"No, No! Noura, you should not steal bread!"

That night Zegariad told Aneche that she found me with the bread and Aneche was furious; she called me a thief. Her tongue-lashing was very upsetting and I felt truly ashamed.

"I'm not really a thief, I was just hungry," I told God that night. "Please forgive me."

It was the first time I'd prayed for forgiveness; every other night I'd ask the Lord to free me from my misery.

My chores consumed nearly all my time. Before bedtime on many evenings, I helped Hassan with the camels. He and I would stay with the stubborn animals to make them sit close to the tent and we'd tie their front legs with heavy rope, then we'd watch them defecate all night. Early in the morning, my first job was to collect the dung and spread them to dry far away from the tent, and I'd gather them as soon as they'd be ready to be used for cooking.

Arab women were accustomed to frequent beatings from their husbands. Yet, any wife believing she'd been neglected or maltreated by her husband was allowed to leave and go to the tent of her father or brother. While pregnant, that's what Aneche did several times. Rebellious and a shrew, she'd escape Yousuf's beatings by running off to her father's tent. Those were peaceful days for me; she wasn't around to harp at me.

Zegariad was handled gently, never slapped by her spouse. She was meek and yielding, always eager to please her husband, Abdullah.

Early one hot afternoon, Vahan, who only answered to *Hassan* now, came to our tent and talked quietly to Zegariad; and both approached me.

"Noura, Yousuf wants to see you," said Zegariad. "Hassan will take you to him."

I walked some distance with Hassan and was surprised to see a distant hill since the desert was generally flat with few steep areas.

"Where's Yousuf? I don't see him."

"He's on the other side of the hill," Hassan said as we started to climb in the warm sand.

When we reached the top, I saw Yousuf; he was grinning sheepishly.

"Go, Hassan, and come back later." Yousuf waved his hands

back and forth. "Come back without the camels. Someone else will take care of them."

I was confused and apprehensive. Was I going to be punished? What did I do wrong? Was he going to hit me like he beat his wife, Aneche?

As soon as Hassan got out of sight, Yousuf came close to me. He removed his rifle, belt, *djellebas*; and then he grabbed me firmly and started to pull my dress off my shoulders.

I flinched and squirmed in terror. My heart pounded as if it wanted to escape from my throat. My mind darted back to all our refugee marches when young girls were seized and raped by the snickering soldiers.

"Oh, NO!" I pushed Yousuf back; it required all my fear-crazed strength.

"If you don't do as I ask, you know I'll kill you."

I remained defiant, but I knew I was doomed. I stood straight and still as Yousuf picked up his rifle, loaded it, and pointed it at my head.

I stared back at him, waiting for the merciful bullet. Seconds went by and Yousuf put down his rifle. Slowly he walked over to me and gently pushed me on the ground and sat next to me.

"Listen to me," he said, trying a more cautious tactic. "If you don't submit, I'll take you by force."

"Please, Yousuf!" I thought I could appeal to him, maybe his burdened conscience prevented him from killing me or maybe he was just bluffing. "I can't do what you want. My mother taught me that only my husband can touch me. No one else."

"Ha! Ha! I marry you?" Yousuf laughed and leaned on his elbow. "You're *naserany* (a Christian); I'm Muslim. I wouldn't marry you!"

Yousuf turned me around by the shoulders and with a roguish look, he said: "You'll be my mistress until Hassan grows older. When he's old enough to support you, you'll be married to him. Then both of you will work for me."

Yousuf continued, with his legs outstretched. "That's why I bought both you and Hassan from the Turks. I saved you two! Otherwise, you'd have been killed."

I said nothing. My mind raced again, back to the days in Kayseri when marriages were carefully arranged by loving parents and relatives, always with the consent of the young couples. I'd been pleased when Mama and Aunt Elimon made the pact about my betrothal to Armenag. Now my life was over, totally invaded by this savage.

Quickly, Yousuf took advantage of my momentary silence and pinned my head down and rolled over, mounting his long, sinewy body on top of mine.

I kicked him, pulled his braids, drew blood as I dug my nails into his face; I was sickened by his foul smell and hot sweat. My defenseless body froze, overtaken by convulsive pain.

FOURTEEN

An Attempt at Escape

When Hassan returned, he stared at my dirty, bloodstained face and uttered not a sound. He asked Yousuf if he wanted anything done with the camels.

"First, take Noura home and then come back," Yousuf ordered, gesturing with one hand while he shouldered his rifle with the other hand.

Hassan lifted me to my feet. Staggering, I walked slowly alongside him as we headed back to the tent. Feeling brutally violated and disgraced, I could not lift my head nor stop whimpering. Neither one of us spoke.

It was almost nightfall when we got back; Zegariad was waiting for me outside the tent. She took my hand and motioned me to follow her inside.

"Did Yousuf do something to you?"

I nodded slowly, my head still bowed.

"*Allah!*" Zegariad's gestures and curses revealed unusual anger.

"Noura, don't mention this to Aneche."

That night, I carefully lowered my swollen, burning face on the saddle bag and cried for Mama. I could hear her prophetic words: "Did I bring you up to be used by these uncivilized people."

Since the death march from Kayseri, I'd been forced to endure so much: beatings from soldiers, unbearable hunger and thirst, devastating disease, the loss of my precious Mama. Now RAPE! Oh, GOD! What heinous devastation! I was ruined! Physically ravaged! Spiritually pulverized!

Why, Yousuf? Why did he subject me to such savagery? I did not understand why he'd shown me kindness at times; yet why did he damn me with such an indelible stain in the dawn of my life? Why, dear God; how long must I endure this nightmare? You've left me nothing, not even my barren soul!

During the days and weeks that followed, my self-torturing thoughts banished me into a deep, irreparable depression. Almost every hour, my shattered mind vaulted rashly from fiendish schemes of revenge against Yousuf to lofty contemplations of suicide and then back to gnawing emptiness. Pretending I was doing my chores, I'd escape to the nearby dunes to pray, to make decisions, and to talk out loud to Mama; I even blamed her for my torment.

"I know you tried to save me, Mama, on that night they killed you. You made me believe you were just talking to Fatima and you ordered me to go back to sleep. But, you were so wrong! You should have taken me with you; you had no right to leave me behind. You're free now and I'm still a slave."

Concerned about my depressed state of mind, Vartouhi and Senat came to see me a week after the rape. Tearfully, I told them what had happened, how I couldn't live with this disgrace heaped upon me by that animal, Yousuf!

"Oh, GOD, I'm RUINED! I'm like those poor girls in Kayseri who were raped and returned by Turks. No one looked at them again, not even their families." I cried out to my friends, remembering how those girls were stripped of their humanity! Everybody shunned them like they were dirt, like garbage!

I was shouting, blazing into hysteria. "MY GOD! What's to become of me? I wish I'd died with Mama. GOD! If you're merciful, you'd let me die!"

"It's not the same now, Vergeen; circumstances are different." Senat tried hard to be sympathetically encouraging. "What you've been through during this miserable *oxor* (exile) has happened to so many young Armenian girls – and, maybe even worse. If we get out of here, people are not going to condemn you for being raped. You've got to get it out of your mind."

For the next two weeks, Senat tried to console me, always citing the innocence of any young refugee who was sexually molested. "God is watching," she'd say repeatedly. "He is not going to let you suffer any condemnation by people."

Senat never lost her confidence, especially about locating her children after the war and being united with her husband in Egypt.

"I know we'll all be saved as soon as the war ends. My husband will find me and our young ones, and our lives will be normal again."

"That's right," Vartouhi agreed. "I truly believe we'll be rescued."

I was the only one who doubted there was any hope left for any of us.

"Vergeen, you'll see," Senat was so positive. "I am certain someone is going to save you, too. Perhaps it'll be Armenag, your fiance in America. Despite what Yousuf did to you, always remember you're a fine person. Someday, some special, young man – if not Armenag – is going to marry you for YOU, for your fine qualities."

Although comforting for a while, Senat's words also raised doubts in my mind about my worthiness for marriage. Here I was, not yet fully blossomed into womanhood; yet, I was tarnished for life. I tried, sometimes vainly, to sweep away these haunting thoughts by concentrating on my work.

One day, running an errand far from the tent, I was startled by a strange hissing sound. The mysterious noise came from several feet away. Shading my eyes from the sun, I saw a disturbance in a large section of the sand; and a zigzagging snake started toward me. It arched its head; its long, thin tongue kept darting in and out of its mouth. I turned and sped away from the venomous reptile as fast as I could.

Halfway home, the realization hit me! Why did I run when I could have had my wish to die.* It would have been easy, just a small bite from that snake could have taken care of it. But, the near encounter with death had forced me to face my long-repressed desire to live, to go on, in the hope that someday I'd be able to escape from this hell hole.

Each day, whenever alone, I'd sit in the desert and remember Kayseri, my parents, my relatives. I'd recall how joyously we spent the Christmas holidays. My stomach ached for the special foods we always enjoyed: fine dried raisins, figs, apricots, prunes, nuts, special breads and pastries. Oh, what I'd have given for just a teaspoon of that delicious rose petal preserves on a piece of Mama's *katah*, that wonderful *khohlez*–filled bread!

I remembered how the village boys traditionally sang songs and hung baskets from the rooftops for relatives and neighbors to fill them with fruit and pastries. Mama was always generous and gave the boys lots of baked goods she'd made for the holidays.

The thought of my dear, sweet Mama was unbearably painful at times. Her devotion to me after Papa died was so protective, so profound. How proud she was when I brought home good marks from school, or when I pranced around in one of her beautiful, handmade dresses! She was cheerfully confident, too, that I'd marry Armenag when he returned from America! She'd dream about a good, abundant life. "We'll all be wealthy when Armenag achieves his expected success, and we'll hire a maid to do all the menial work," she'd say, laughing in a wonderfully melodious way that was so endearing.

Oh, Mama! Instead of having a servant someday, now I'm the one who's the servant – a tormented, ravaged slave of these illiterate nomads!

Prayer was my only consolation. I'd make the sign of the cross furtively, sometimes on my stomach just like the nuns at the Jesuit school taught me, so that no one would suspect I was still worshiping Christ.

At noon one hot day, Aneche told me to go to the stream with the donkey and bring back bags of water. Risking punishment, I refused. "It's too hot to go to the stream this time of day. And I can't lift those heavy goat-skin bags of water on top of the donkey by myself."

Then trying to avoid Aneche's wrath, I said, "I'll just go with one smaller bag and carry the water on my back."

My refusal to lift several water bags on such a blistering day sparked an argument between Zegariard and Aneche. Genuinely upset, Zegariard scolded her sister. "The sun is too hot. You can't let this poor girl try to load the donkey and bring back that much water by herself."

Yousuf was not home to settle the argument between the two sisters as he usually did, and Zegariad gave in again. As ordered by Aneche, I dragged the donkey and the goat skins some distance to the stream. No way could I load the bags of water on top of the animal without help. I stopped for a moment surmising the impossible task when I heard a man's voice calling me. "Noura! Noura!" I turned around to see a young man approaching me.

Good! I thought he could help me! Before loading the water for me, he said his name was *Abu* and he lived with another tribe located close to ours.

"Everyone knows who you are and that you're *nacerany* (a Christian). We know you live in Mounla Yousuf's tent and his wife is very jealous of you, and she makes you work very hard."

How did he know so much about me? I was puzzled.

"Come with me to my tribe, or better, let me take you somewhere else."

Why was he trying to help me, I wondered.

"No, I like the tribe I'm with and I'd like to stay with them." I was suspiciously cautious. What was this man's motive?

After pausing several minutes, he said, "Do you know why I want to help you? I'm Armenian, too." But he was speaking in Arabic, and when I spoke to him in Armenian, he didn't understand me.

I asked: "What's your Armenian name?"

"*Onni.*," he answered hesitatingly.

That was a strange name, I'd never heard of it. But then I remembered the Armenian male name of *Onnig*. I was still skeptical, however; he couldn't remember his home town either.

I continued to question him. "Why can't you speak Armenian or Turkish?"

"An Arab kidnapped me when I was a very small boy and I've forgotten everything," he replied, finally somewhat convincingly.

As I started to leave sitting on top of the loaded donkey, he stopped the animal and said: "You didn't tell me where you want to go."

"Anywhere out of this desert. Maybe back to Ras-al-Ayn."

Perhaps I can take the train from there to Aleppo, I said to myself. Was it possible that this man was sincere and he'd get me out of here.

"Yes, I'll take you to Ras-al-Ayn."

"But, I'm not alone. There are three other Armenians living with our tribe, a boy and two girls."

"I'll take them, too," he promised. "I'll come back tomorrow. Look for me at the tent next to yours."

He walked away and I returned to the tent, uncertain of this man's intent.

Without delay, I wanted to tell Vartouhi about my encounter and I dashed to her tent; Senat was there, too. "I'm not confident that this man is telling me the truth," I told them. "But when I mentioned you two and Vahan, he said he'd take all of us to Ras-al-Ayn. I don't know if we can trust him."

"If he comes tomorrow," Senat took command of the baffling situation, "I'll go and meet him. After all, I'm older and I think I can judge better."

Onnig came, as promised, the next day and met Senat at the tent adjoining ours. They talked for a long time before Senat returned to give us the good news.

"Don't worry, he's really Armenian." Senat rarely got excited, but this time she was energized by the likelihood of our freedom.

"We will meet him tomorrow night by the big rocks away from the tents."

Senat outlined the plan of our escape. "Hamad is always the last one to leave the coffee house and, right after that, the sheik usually retires for the night. I'll wait until Hamad is asleep. Meantime, Vartouhi, you let Vahan know about our plan and both of you come to my stable and wait for me. Vergeen, you watch to see when we leave and follow us."

I started to shake in eager anticipation. *Asvatz, ahss onkom ohkneh mezhee.* (God, help us this time.) I prayed for our plan of escape to succeed.

Next night, Vartouhi quietly entered my quarters and whispered. "Vahan has changed his mind. He won't go with us."

We waited until we saw Senat leave her tent and hastily followed her to the big rocks, our rendezvous spot. Our rescuer was nowhere. We called his name. "Onnig! Onnig!" There was no response.

Now fearful that we'd be missed, we scurried back to the tents. Senat was especially afraid that Hamad would wake up and find her gone. The barking dogs almost gave us away, but Vartouhi and I managed to dash into the stable where I slept. Within minutes, we saw Sheik Mounla Salman outside his tent, a rifle slung on his shoulder, searching for Vartouhi.

"Look for Noura! She's with Noura!" It was Aneche, her screeching voice was unmistakable.

The sheik entered the stable and found Vartouhi next to me. He struck her in the face with his rifle. "What are you doing here?" His voice reverberated like a loud horn in the night air.

Vartouhi wiped her bleeding cheek with the sleeve of her dress. "Noura was afraid to sleep alone here; that's why I came here to stay with her."

The sheik pulled her up by her long hair and dragged her to his tent.

Still awake near dawn and afraid of my own fate, I overheard Vahan telling my captors that we were going to escape. He was one of them now, and he liked being called by his new Arabic name, Hassan.

The entire camp could hear the loud crying. Vartouhi's cries from the next tent had continued most of the night as the sheik roared in strident anger. Hamad was yelling at Senat; and I stayed in bed pretending to sleep until I heard Yousuf's command.

"Get up! GET UP!" He pushed open the flaps of the tent and threw a stone at my bed. Aneche was behind him, watching wide-eyed, as Yousuf muttered: "I should kill you for trying to escape."

Yousuf left and returned an hour later with a rifle strapped to his back and ordered me to follow him toward Senat's tent. I saw her walking in front of Hamad who was also carrying a rifle, and all four of us headed to the sheik's tent. A strange man emerged from the men's quarters and Vartouhi appeared seconds later. Now six people, we walked in silence beyond the big rocks.

Hamad, Senat's husband, was the first to speak. "We're taking you away from the sight of our tribe to kill you! You won't try to escape anymore!"

Usually composed, Senat began to cry, begging for leniency. "I just wanted to see my son and daughter for one last time."

Quiet until she heard Senat, Vartouhi began to cry. I'd been confronted by death so many times, I was indifferent to what might be our punishment.

We were walking faster and faster. Yousuf said something to the stranger and we all stopped. The strange man raised his hands above his head and announced in an admonishing voice: "If you all beg for mercy and kiss Yousuf's feet, he'll forgive you."

Standing on my right, Senat was the first to bow down and kiss Yousuf's dirty, bare feet; then Vartouhi, on my left, did the same. I stood erect, stubbornly refusing to grovel no matter what happened. Senat pulled me down on my knees and with bowed head, speaking in Armenian, she pleaded: "*Khentrem* (please), Vergeen! We'll all die if you don't do as they say. KISS his feet!"

Although I could not see his face when I bent over, I knew Yousuf was delighted by my loathing submission.

It was Aneche's plot, we learned the next day. The man we called Onnig was her decoy and she'd schemed to lure us into thinking we could escape, and it was her hope we'd be killed in the attempt.

After a few weeks, Senat and Hamad left our tribe and took his mother with them. Word reached us some time later that Hamad had killed Senat. No reason was given; perhaps she tried to escape again. Poor Senat! She was so certain she'd be reunited with her loved ones – her real husband and children – once the war was over.

She'd always been so encouraging, so optimistic! She helped me immeasurably to have faith in my ability to survive. How wrong she was about her own!

FIFTEEN

The Final Flight

Vartouhi and I spent more time with each other, practically every day. She was always hopeful about being reunited with our own people. She provided the only joy I had with her tales of fantasy and with her eternal predictions about how good life ahead would be for both of us.

"Just wait, Vergeen," she'd say, continually predicting a blessed future with the help of the Almighty. "God will be good to us. He's just testing us now. After all, we're Christians and, in time, He will save us."

Unlike Vartouhi, my faith in God had wavered. I doubted His interest in our welfare. But I never let her know how little trust I had left in the Almighty's will to help us because she still clung to her faith, and there was little else for her to count on. More often than not, I felt we were doomed; I thought we'd spend our entire lives in this sandy, hot wilderness with these nomads. I'd almost given up on fleeing from desert life and I tried to make friends with some of the younger Bedouin women in our camp. One was Yousuf's niece, *Aisha*, the daughter of his eldest brother, *Ahmed*. She was older than I, about seventeen, and very likable. We always chatted at the stream; she'd help me fill the large goat-skins with water and lift them on top of the donkey. She was one of the few women who treated me well.

Her mother had been ill for some time and Aisha had total responsibility for her care. No one entered their tent for fear of contractng a disease; even though the mother may not have had anything infectious, it was a Bedouin belief that anyone who was sick more then a week must be contagious and, therefore, must be put to death.

A few days after our first talk at the stream, I heard Aisha's voice, loudly begging for her mother's life: "Please, please," she cried. "Don't kill her! I'll take care of her. I know she'll get better!"

A few days later, I went to see Aisha when I learned her mother had been carried some distance away from the camp by two of the tribesmen who killed her.

"You mean your people don't kill the sick even if they have contagious diseases." Aisha tried to rationalize the slaying of her mother, but she had difficulty concealing her resentment about the imposed, tribal custom.

"No, we take care of our sick people and, if they're very ill or close to dying, they're taken to hospitals for care by doctors and nurses."

"Do they get better?" Aisha was incredulous.

"Yes, most of them get well. Of course, some die; but they die because of long-time sicknesses or old age." Then I told her about Papa and how the doctors had tried to save his life.

Whenever I developed a little fever from sunstroke, I'd overhear Aneche telling Yousuf, "I think she has some terrible disease." And Yousuf would chastise her for making things up so that she could have me killed.

※ ※ ※

Since our capture months before, the women had been looking for someone to tattoo Vartouhi and me; and an artist came to the camp one day to do the job. Vartouhi was secretly indignant; she wanted no marks on her face or body. "When we're free, people will know we were with the Arabs and shun us."

Because I didn't share Vartouhi's confidence about ever being freed from this tribe, I viewed the tattooing indifferently, dispassionately. I watched as the tattoo designer held four fine needles tightly together and penetrated them deeply and rapidly through the skin, etching Arabic symbols with blue dye. Made carefully from the dried, pulverized gall bladder of goats and sheep, the dye resulted from a mixture of the powder with the breast milk of a mother whose child was a girl.

The artist completed a *disini* (an Arabic symbol) on my forehead and, working fast with the needles, she drew one dot in the middle of my lower lip and several symbols on my chin. Now, I was marked as one of them, a tattooed Bedouin.

✻ ✻ ✻

I recognized Aneche's wicked attempt to get rid of me when she'd perpetually pester Yousuf. "Noura is ready for marriage. We'd get a lot for her from a rich tribesman. I just need a little time to get a dowry ready."

Weeks went by before Yousuf was finally persuaded. An Arab from another tribe wanted me for his second wife, and he was willing to pay three sheep, one camel and five *mejidia*. The deal was a profitable one since Yousuf had bought me for just five *mejidia* without including animals.

I had mixed emotions. I was glad I'd be leaving Aneche, but I regretted not being able to see Vartouhi any more. While waiting for the next occurrence, I was busy with my chores one morning and heard someone calling me. I turned to see a tall, lean Arab in a seedy caftan exposing a bare, hairy chest. Both his caftan and head covering were so dirty it was hard to distinguish the colors. His deeply sun-scorched face was thin and craggy.

"I'm glad to see you." His widening smile flashed broken, yellow teeth. "Yousuf promised our nuptial when I gave him five *mejidia*, some sheep and a camel. But someone stole my camel and I can't locate her. As soon as I do, I'll come back for you."

I just bowed and said nothing.

"My name is *Yalal*. I promise I'll treat you well, much better than you're being treated here. You won't have to work so hard."

"I'll be glad to be your wife," said a voice resembling mine. My God, it was mine!

Yes, he was so disgustingly dirty in appearance, but he sounded sincere. Anything was better than Aneche's abominable treatment.

Yousuf learned about my encounter with Yalal, and he erupted into a tirade. Pacing inside the tent, he mumbled and waved his long arms furiously back and forth. "You are NOT going to be his wife," he shouted. "NO! NO! Not until he delivers that missing camel!"

Yousuf looked fiercely at me and yelled even louder: "He'll never find that dumb animal because I sent someone to steal it and kill it!

My situation was becoming even more hopeless. Yousuf was increasingly more oppressive while Aneche's sneaky invectives were more fierce.

I wanted to see Vartouhi, she'd not been around for a few days. Saliha, the sheik's wife, met me outside her tent and forbid me to enter.

"You can't come in, your friend is very ill. Talk to her from here."

I moved around to the other side of the tent and Vartouhi, prostrate on her bedding, saw me and begged me to enter the tent.

"Vergeen, I feel awful. Please. Please come in and give me some water."

"I'm sorry, my dear friend; I can't. I'm not permitted to come in." Vartouhi looked so feverish and I couldn't even give her a drink of water. Unable to do anything for her, I returned to my quarters, extremely upset by what I had just witnessed.

Early next morning, I went back to Sheik Mounla Salman's tent hoping I'd be allowed inside to help Vartouhi. The sheik's new coffee boy was adding tarpaulin to the tent. I guessed he might have been a Turkish army deserter because he spoke Turkish so well.

When I asked him what he was doing, he said: "I'm building a new shelter for Zenab. She's very sick; the sheik thinks she'll contaminate his household and he doesn't want any member of his family to be near her."

After completing my chores the following day, I went to see Vartouhi whom everyone now called by her Arabic name, Zenab. Her face was flushed and sweaty; it was obvious her fever was very high.

She smiled faintly when she recognized me, but her only barely audible words were: "Water, please Vergeen, I need some water."

Only the coffee boy and I were around that day to help her drink water. Once again, Aneche was cruelly vindictive. She was determined to stop me from helping Vartouhi. "You stay here and do your work! You must not go to the sheik's camp any more!"

Four days later, I was horrified to see the Turkish coffee boy pitch Vartouhi face forward on a donkey like a rag doll, with her legs dangling on one side and her head on the other side. He had a small bundle in his right hand while he held on to Vartouhi's flopping body with his left hand.

Zegariad came from behind and took me inside our tent. "Don't watch," she said with genuine tenderness.

"Where is the coffee boy taking her?" I pressed her for the answer, but she didn't respond.

I looked for the coffee boy that evening and asked: "Where did you take Vartouhi – I mean Zenab? What did you do with her?"

"The sheik's wife told me to take her away." He looked grim. "I took her to the large, dry well on the other side of the dunes, and I threw her in along with a bundle of bread. But I don't think she was alive when she got to the bottom."

I waited until nightfall to cry, I wanted no one to see me. Snuggled in my wet, goat-hide bedding, I wept for myself as well as for my last dear friend, now gone. I wanted to cry out: "Oh, Vartouhi! Why did you die! You had so much faith in God's protection. But now just like Senat, your strong faith failed you, too."

※ ※ ※

It was early autumn, and Yousuf was busy buying and storing large sacks of flour, bulgur and wheat in preparation for the winter months. Since there was a rumored shortage of these items, Yousuf bought large amounts of each, especially the wheat.

All this activity tripled my overburdened workload. I'd replaced

Fatima and her daughter-in-law as the main servant in the household. Before I came, they were paid well for their work with ample bags of flour, meat and bulgur. Now, Fatima's lone responsibility was baking bread and, consequently, her food payment was decreased. She blamed me for the cutback on food, and she exhibited her bitter antagonism with her greatest insult: calling me *naserany* (a Christian).

Perhaps she also resented the friendship that developed between her daughter-in-law, Zahra, and me. After Vartouhi died, Zahra always helped me load the water bags and helped tote them back to the tent. Sometimes, she'd stop to chat when I cooked supper, and we'd discuss my life back in Kayseri. She was very curious about our houses, food, family relationships, marriage customs – everything I longed to experience again.

"I hate getting ready for winter," Zahra told me repeatedly. "There's so much heavy work to be done."

She was so right. The preparation for the colder months was unending. It started one morning when Zegariad instructed me to spend the entire day gathering and drying camel dung along with cow and sheep manure for use as fuel. It took me from dawn to nightfall to complete the job. My exhaustion was indescribable.

"Tomorrow, we're going to par-boil all this wheat," Zegariad informed me. It was like a warning to my body to rejuvenate itself for the arduous task. I fell into a deep sleep hoping the next morning would never come.

When I awoke, Fatima already had three fires started. I helped her place a big kettle on each fire, filled them with water, and poured in large quantities of wheat. When the boiling was completed, the wheat was removed from the kettles, strained, and spread on the large, woolen blanket I'd made. It had taken me all summer to spin the sheep wool and weave it into this coverlet.

Once the wheat was dry, Fatima and I poured it back into the original sacks, getting ready for the next day's work. That night, I lowered my aching body gently on my saddle bag, but I was so tired that sleep eluded me for hours.

Early next morning, four of us – Zegariad, Fatima, Zahra and I – began the most difficult part of the work. Zahra dug a large pit right in the middle of the tent and Zegariad hardened the ground by sprinkling water in the hole and over the work area. When the pit became hard, she sprayed the area with a thick substance made of goat hair and filled it with the par-boiled wheat. More water was sprinkled into the pit and surrounding work area. Then Zegariad and Zahra sat across one another with wooden mallets in hand, alternately pounding the wheat like the rhythmic beats of a metronome. They'd stop only to sprinkle more water in the pit. When the thin coat of the partially boiled wheat was pounded off, the resulting kernels were spread to dry on my handwoven blanket, and then poured back into the sacks for storage.

This process, so punitive on the arms and hands, was repeated well into the night, this time mostly with Zahra and me wielding the heavy mallets over and over again. That night was the worst; no matter where or how I placed my aching arms, I could not find relief.

Yousuf brought a small hand mill the next morning and I thought this would ease our work, but it only caused more dissension. Fatima and Zahra were the first to work with the mill. They faced each other while seated and took turns pouring the par-boiled wheat into the mill, continually turning the wheel as the grain poured out of the side and spilled on to the blanket.

My job, at first, was to prepare the wheat in smaller sacks to make it easier for Fatima and Zahra to pour it into the millstone, and then scoop up the finished grain and place it into large, storage sacks.

"I'm very tired," announced Fatima and stopped turning the wheel on the millstone. "Let Noura do it."

I was beside myself; my arms were throbbing. I was sick of hearing Fatima and Aneche say, "Let Noura do it." I wanted to object, but I knew I'd be vulnerable to more punishment. Before the words left my lips, Zegariad interceded right away and berated her sister.

"Have you no heart, Aneche. This poor girl has been working from dawn to dusk for several days now. Let her rest for the remainder of the day."

I was always so grateful to Zegariad for her kindness. More and more, she protected me from Aneche's unsparing cruelty.

Preparations for winter continued with the slaughter of the older goats and sheep. The women cut the meat into small pieces, cooked it in salt water, cooled it, and packed it in a goat skin for the cold months ahead.

※ ※ ※

The day after our tribe moved to a new camp, I was alone spinning wool when a young girl, about fifteen years old, came into the tent, smiled and greeted me in the polite Arabic manner. *"Salami-el-Allakum."*

Her friendliness surprised me and I responded in kind. *"Allakum Salami."* She was dressed in the customary long, blue Bedouin garment and she had tattoos on her face, arms and legs.

She asked: "Are you Armenian?"

My suspicious mind told me I should exhibit allegiance to my captors, and I answered, "I was an Armenian; but *Alhamdullah* (thank God), I'm a *mousoudaman* (a Muslim), now."

"Don't be afraid, I'm Armenian, too." She spoke in Armenian and took my hand, squeezed it.

How wonderful it was to speak in my language again; I hadn't spoken an Armenian word since Vartouhi died.

"Where do you live?" I hoped she was in our camp.

She pointed to a large tent about fifty feet away from our tent.

We were anxious to exchange stories about how we'd ended here with the Bedouins. Her experiences, since being deported from her home in Diyarbakir, were worse than my own. I wanted to hear the details; besides, it was nice to be able to converse with another Armenian in our language.

"My name is *Ani*;" I come from a very wealthy family," she began. "First, Turkish officials arrested my father and we never saw him again. The next day, our whole family – my mother, grandmother, two sisters and baby brother – were forced to leave our home; we weren't allowed to take a single belonging with us.

"With the little money we had, my mother bought bread and cheese whenever she could; but, within a couple of months, our money was gone and we had nothing to sell so we could buy food. Even begging didn't help because everyone in our caravan was in the same situation. The first to die was my little brother; he was just six months old. Would you believe we were all glad that his misery had ended?"

I nodded in understanding; I remembered Mama's words about the merciful early death granted by God for some in our caravan.

"Whenever we came across barking dogs," Ani continued, "some of the old men in our group killed the poor creatures for food. We even heard rumors that many hunger-crazed persons were eating the flesh of corpses found along the roadsides."

Ani hesitated to collect herself. "My darling sister was only eight years old when she was dying, and she begged mother not to allow anyone to eat her flesh. But, God help us!"

Ani's sobs were contagious. I got up and put my arms around her and cried with her. I knew her guilt prevented her from telling me that the surviving members of her family had devoured the little girl's flesh; everyone, I learned later, except her aggrieved mother.

Wanting to talk about her ordeal, Ani went on. "Four days later, my feeble and helpless mother could not continue to walk, even when the guard warned her. He got very angry when my mother wasn't able to obey his command. He hit her head with his pistol and she fell hard, on the back of her head. I tried desperately to lift her before the guard forced me to move on. I think she was dead. God, I'm not sure; she may have still been alive. We left my dear mother on the side of the road as the soldiers beat us to go on.

"One afternoon, some Arab women came into the caravan looking for a young girl. Immediately, my grandmother grabbed my hand, took me to the women and offered me in exchange for food. That was the last time I saw my grandmother and little sister."

Ani looked up at me and smiled cynically; her anguished, wet eyes revealed immense pain.

I shook my head, unable to respond. How could a grandparent do that, I asked myself. Mama would have starved to death first before giving me up.

"But, I must tell you, Vergeen, the family I'm with now is wonderful. Both husband and wife really treat me like their own daughter. In fact, at times when food is scarce, they make sure I'm fed first. They make certain I dress better than they do. And what's more, they knew I would resent having my name changed and they call me by my Armenian name."

Ani asked me about my situation and was surprised to hear about my mistreatment and my desperation to get away. "Maybe you should agree to marry someone."

"I'll do anything to escape from these people," I said impatiently.

I learned that Ani's new Bedouin parents defied Arabic custom and declined every bid – no matter how large the offer of money and animals – to marry off their adopted daughter. Hence, a week after my conversation with Ani, her parents turned down another marriage proposal and told the man: "There's an Armenian girl in that tent over there. Go ask her people."

The man was well-dressed and decorous, obviously from the city. He approached Yousuf to inquire about me; and they'd talked at some length when Yousuf came outside the tent and told me to bring the guest a bowl of water. I realized the talk was about me; quickly I took the water to the man. He drank it slowly to allow himself time for a thorough inspection of my appearance, from head to toe. He smiled, returned the bowl to me and, as I was leaving, I heard him say to Yousuf, "I'll give you four lira."

"Come back here, Noura," Yousuf barked.

As soon as I returned to the tent, the man spoke to me in

Turkish: "I work for a very rich man who wants an Armenian girl for his third wife. He lives in the city, not in a tent in the miserable desert like this. He has a large home with beautiful gardens."

The man examined my reaction before continuing. "Would you consider marrying him?"

I did not hesitate a second. "Yes, I would."

Abruptly, Yousuf said, "We can't bargain anything right now. You'll have our answer tomorrow. Come back then."

When the man left, Yousuf was stony and stared at me. Then, in a controlled voice, he asked: "Why did you agree? I thought you'd refuse."

Before I found the nerve to answer, Aneche said: "It's a good offer, and she wants to go to the city. Let her go."

"She can't go anywhere!" Yousuf was angry and unyielding.

Three days later, Ani and her family left our camp without a word, not even a goodbye from my new Armenian ally. I knew Yousuf had something to do with their hasty departure. He'd made sure I lost another friend.

※ ※ ※

Nothing else absorbed my thoughts except devising ways to escape. Perhaps if I could get close to a city like Ras-al-Ayn, I might be able to succeed, I told myself.

"Why doesn't this tribe go into the city to sell milk and Yogurt?" I asked Zahra one day.

"Oh, we do whenever we're near Ras-al-Ayn. Right now, we're too far away. But I'm told we'll be close to Ras-al-Ayn when we move in a few weeks"

Naive Zahra had no clue as to why I asked the question. She was my one true friend in this hell hole; I hated to deceive her. Yet, she was the only one I could rely on for information I needed in order to pull off any plan to flee.

A few weeks later, in a new camp location, I realized we were near a city when I heard a large group of our camp's women returning from somewhere. They were laughing and chatting about what they'd seen. I ran to Zahra's tent and asked, "What happened, where is everyone coming from?" I was anxious for information. "Did you all go to Ras-al-Ayn?"

"Yes!" Zahra answered excitedly. "We saw women wearing pretty dresses and fine earrings. We even saw a huge thing that looked like an animal and made a lot of noise; it had two big, burning eyes." Zahra stretched her arms as wide as she could to illustrate the size of what she'd seen. "Do you know what that could be?"

"I think that's a truck," I replied, even though I'd never seen one.

"Well, we'll see it again tomorrow morning," Zahra exclaimed. "There's a lot of hay outside the city and many of the girls are going with me to pick up as many piles as we can to bring back here."

She was always eager to take me along whenever she had a pleasant task. "Come with us! We'll have so much fun."

I joined the girls and older women in the morning. En route, I tried to memorize every inch of my surroundings; and I formulated a mental map of every bend of the road, every tree, every rock.

Gathering the hay with the other girls, I watched the women carefully to see which way they were going to enter the city. Headed the same way directly in front of them, I saw black-skinned, partially naked men walking in a straight line with their hands clasped behind their necks. Driving them on with lashes were the feared Turkish guards.

Tomorrow morning! I must try the escape tomorrow morning, I promised myself. All night I prayed, trying to harness my terror; but, by morning, my courage failed me.

Pregnant Aneche was nearing delivery, and everyone was anxiously awaiting the event, especially her husband Yousuf, since this was to be their first child. Two days before the birth, he'd left camp in adherence to Bedouin custom; no expectant father was allowed to be around the tent during his wife's labor.

Perhaps this is the time for my escape, I thought; everyone was busy with Aneche and they wouldn't notice my absence for hours. I had tried several times before; but each time I froze, fearing I'd be caught. Even the day before when I went to gather twigs, I took a great deal of time pondering my decision to run, run, run as far as my tired legs would take me. Again my courage faltered and I returned with a small bundle of branches to face Zegariad.

"Where have you been all this time? And you got so little!" She was genuinely perturbed.

"Twigs are getting scarce," I answered, hoping she'd believe me. "I went to many different places to collect them." I lied, thinking my delay in returning from this chore the next day would allay any suspicion about my whereabouts.

Early morning the following day, I took my rope and sickle and announced to Zegariad: "I'm going to look for more twigs. It may take me longer, but I'll try to come back with more than I brought yesterday."

"Just make sure you do. We need more fires because of Aneche's condition. I think she's ready to have the baby today. Take all the time you need." Zegariad said, busily preparing for her sister's delivery.

I ran to Zahra's tent clutching the cherished sweater Mama had knit for me long ago; it was badly torn, but it was my only memento. I made sure no one was around, and carefully I buried the rope and sickle under a large flap in the back of the tent. My heart was pounding, nearly deafening my ears. I paused again to survey the area and heard Aneche scream in labor. And I listened as the women tried to comfort her, shouting instructions on how to expedite her delivery. This big event had preoccupied everyone. The timing was perfect!

Swiftly, I dashed away from the camp! SPRINTING! LEAPING! GALLOPING!

An hour later, I stopped to recover my evaporating breath, and my heart jumped when I saw our camp's shepherd. Quickly, I flattened myself under a small bush and waited until he and his flock of sheep were out of sight. Then I started to run again, remembering the direction taken by Zegariad and the other women when they went to the city a few days before.

Although I lost track of time, I knew I was far from the Bedouins when I was startled by two chirping birds chasing each other. I hadn't seen a bird during the ten months I was forced to live with Yousuf's family.

"What a good omen!" I laughed aloud, and I followed the fluttering birds for some distance until they disappeared in the sky.

Vergeen's parents:
Lousaper and Baghdasar Kalendarian.
Kayseri, Turkey 1903

Earliest known surviving photograph of Vergeen. Probably sent to a relative in Cairo prior to deportation. Previous photos were most likely lost to the Turks during property seizure. Kayseri, Turkey ca. 1913

*Armen (back row, right) and his classmates pose for their high school graduation picture.
Kayseri, Turkey ca. 1908*

*Vergeen shown in a hospital photo.
This is a rare instance where her Bedouin
tattoos are clearly visible. In most subsequent
photos, she had the tattoos eradicated.
Aleppo, Syria 1918*

Serpouhi Kalayjian, Vergeen's close life-long friend whom she met at the military hospital. Aleppo, Syria 1918

The two friends and their mentor.
Serpouhi (left), Nartouhy (seated), and Vergeen.
Aleppo, Syria ca. 1918

Parsegh, (center) Vergeen's stepuncle and his family.
Cairo, Egypt ca. 1930

*Melkon, Vergeen's uncle (upper right) and his family.
Cairo, Egypt ca. 1920's*

*Vergeen and Armen Meghrouni pictured on their wedding day,
January 9, 1921
Milwaukee, Wisconsin.*

Victor and the author, both three-year-olds, try to intimidate the photographer. Milwaukee, Wisconsin 1924

Vergeen and her four-year-old son, Victor.
Milwaukee, Wisconsin 1925

*Vergeen's son Vahe at age 3.
Detroit, Michigan 1929*

Vergeen and her immediate family. Her two sons Victor (left) Vahe (right) and her husband Armen (seated). Vergeen wears the locket from Joseph Pasadena, California 1945

Front page photo by The Detroit News shows Vergeen (right) on her high school graduation day.
Detroit, Michigan 1943

Vergeen and Myranie Mardirosian. Vergeen's tattoo can be seen on her lower lip.
1950's

Vergeen and friend visit the pyramids
Cairo, Egypt 1964

Vergeen is surrounded by her family as she celebrates her seventy-first birthday.
August 29, 1973

*The gold locket given to Vergeen by Joseph
during World War I*

SIXTEEN

The Railroad Company

I'd escaped! I'd succeeded! Nearly a year of misery was over, but I didn't know where I was or where I was headed! I had no food, no money! Nothing, except my precious sweater.

I just kept going for hours, slowing my pace whenever exhaustion drained me. The desert sands blurred and more vegetation emerged on the horizon. Suddenly, I heard the whish of a train; but the sound was coming from behind. I stopped for a while, trying to figure out if the train sound was coming from the opposite direction or was I being misled by a resonating echo.

The sun had not yet started its evening descent, and I thought I could see a rail track if I climbed to the top of the hill a half mile or so away. I clawed up to the top of the hill and saw nothing, and I came down crushed by disappointment. After resting several minutes, I started to walk again in the direction taken earlier by the two guiding birds.

The deepening dusk was swallowing the landscape when I saw puffs of black smoke curling in the air and I hurried toward them. It seemed to take forever to get to the source of the smoke. The closer I got, tall white tents appeared in the distance. As I headed toward the tents, I saw many other canvas structures, brown and green ones surrounding a large, wooden building. This must be an army post, I said to myself.

I thought the persons living in the wooden house must be rich and they might hire me as a servant. As I mulled over my situation, I saw a woman in civilian dress strolling with a little girl; and I approached her cautiously: "What is this place." I asked in Arabic.

"This is a railroad station. My husband works here, and we live over there." She pointed to one of the green tents.

"Do you know if anyone needs a servant? I need some place to live." I hoped she'd show some compassion.

"No! I don't think anybody wants you here." She sneered and continued to walk with the little girl who kept asking who was that dirty woman.

I knew how dreadful I must have looked, but I wasn't disheartened by the woman's contemptuous behavior. I'd come this far and nothing was going to deter me now. I started to walk toward the wooden building, but changed my mind and entered one of the white tents.

An older woman was stuffing raw wool into a clean white pillow case; it reminded me sadly of Mama filling our pillows with her precious handwork before we were deported. Silently, I sat next to the woman on a soft cushion and grinned at her.

Startled by my boldness, the woman asked in Arabic: "Who are you?"

How should I answer her? How should I identify myself?

"I'm an Arab-Armenian." I replied in Arabic, uncertain of the effect of my response.

"There is no such thing as an Arab-Armenian." The woman looked annoyed.

I tried to recover my sagging strength and sputtered pathetically: "I was Armenian, but *Alhamdullah* (thank God), I'm now an Arab *Musulman* (a Muslim)."

Hungry, exhausted and frightened, I started to shake unaware that tears were flooding my eyes.

"My child," I heard the woman speak softly, "don't be afraid. I'm a Christian. I'll see what I can do to help you."

Regaining my courage, I asked: "Can I stay with you?"

"No, that's not possible."

She led me out of the tent and stopped another woman passing by the tent. "*Hanem* (madam), this girl is Armenian and she's looking for a place to live."

The young woman looked at me for a second, then spoke in Armenian: "*Aghcheekes, me vaghnare.* (My girl, don't be afraid.)"

I wanted to shout! I wanted to throw my arms around this pretty, Armenian woman! Instead, I wept in delicious relief. She patted me on the head, waited until I stopped crying. "The doctor here has been looking for a washwoman. Do you know how to do laundry?"

"No, but I can learn." I was eager to do anything.

We went outside and stopped at a brown army tent where another young woman was standing over a steaming kettle. She, too, was Armenian; her name was *Nazig*. She asked where my home was while she checked the food cooking in a large kettle.

The first Armenian woman left, saying: "You're in good hands."

"Wait here a moment," Nazig said and disappeared inside the tent.

Several minutes went by and she came out followed by four, young men; and she pointed to me. "This is the girl I've been talking about."

The men gasped at my appearance. I was embarrassed by their shocked stare. My face was parched from living under the blazing sun; my dirty hair hung in long strings under my torn scarf; my Arab garb was filthy; my leathery feet were bare; my stomach protruded; and my blue tattoos were hideously visible even under all the dirt.

Sensing my shame, Nazig stayed close to me while all the men, except one, bombarded me with questions in Arabic.

"What's your name? From what city are you? How old are you? Where are your parents? How long were you with the nomads?"

Somehow, I tried to answer every one; but my eyes focused on the silent young man who watched from a distance. Noting my discomfort and my increasing inability to satisfy everyone's curiosity, the onlooker moved forward and dispersed the group, saying: "That's enough! Save your questions for tomorrow. Can't you see this poor girl is exhausted?"

After asking a few questions about my name and age, he instructed Nazig to take me into the tent, clean me up, and change my clothes.

"I need volunteers to offer items of clothing to this girl," Nazig smiled at the young man and ushered me into the tent.

Tenderly she bathed me; shampooed and combed my long, tangled hair. Then she collected the gifts of clothing. One young man gave underwear; another gave me his nightshirt which I wore like a dress; still another contributed stockings; a short, small man gave me a pair of shoes; a generous man offered his wool jacket; and Nazig gave me one of her scarves. Even though I must have looked strange in male garments, I felt clean, a new girl.

After I got dressed in my donated clothes, I went outside the tent to breathe in the exquisite aroma of the chicken cooking in Nazig's kettle. The smell nearly drove me crazy. I was famished and could barely restrain myself from diving into the big pot for the half-cooked chicken. While waiting for supper, Nazig told me about the place and the persons who lived in the tent.

I learned the area was the property of the Railroad Company, a joint German-Turkish railway project to expedite the transport of soldiers and war supplies between Ras-al-Ayn and Baghdad. The Company's young male employees were exempt from the army; and they considered themselves very lucky to be working here. All spoke both Arabic and Turkish.

A few of the female employees, like Nazig, were Armenian refugees. Along with her three-year-old son and mother, Nazig had miraculously eluded massacre. Given a job as a cook for five of the Company's men, she and her family lived in one of the large white tents with two other employees and their families. Their responsibilities involved serving the Company workers who were sharing the tent temporarily until the dormitory was completed in the Company's new place, *Gondjouk Jourjoub*, an hour away. Many of the men were being transferred to the new location.

Of the five young men to whom Nazig was responsible, *Ghon* was the youngest, only eighteen; and he'd bribed officials to secure his job as a secretary. *Georg Kazan* was half-Armenian, an army dodger, also a secretary. *Salim* was Jewish and he headed the

Company's secretarial division. *Souren Gondjian*, an Armenian refugee from Erzeroum, was an assistant engineer. The group's oldest member was a Syrian, twenty-four-year-old *Joseph Nacouz*, the Company's accountant and the man who stood by silently until he rescued me from the questioning workers.

"Only four of these men live in the tent with us; they sleep here." Nazig pointed to four cots, four chairs and four wooden boxes which contained the men's belongings.

"Joseph does not live here. He has a tent all by himself."

It was still dusk when Joseph entered the tent. He studied my handed-down attire and grinned: "I'm glad to see the men were generous in their donations."

He walked slowly to Nazig and said, "You know that the rules of the Company require us to report any new refugee on this property. But, I'm not going to mention Vergeen's arrival. Since I've been authorized by the supervisor to employ a helper for you, I'll just tell him that I hired Vergeen for that job."

Looking at me, he spoke to Nazig again. "Both of you have your supper now. Just prepare the table for the men and we'll help ourselves later."

He started to leave and stopped. "Nazig, come with Vergeen to my tent tomorrow morning when it's still dark. Don't let anyone see Vergeen or talk to her; and when you take her to your tent tonight, don't introduce her to anyone."

How lucky I am to end up here and to find these kind people, I thought. I hadn't eaten all day, but I was so full of joy that I was only able to take a few bites of the deliciously prepared chicken and bulgur pilaf.

Darkness engulfed the tent as I helped Nazig prepare the supper table for the five men. "It's getting very dark. How will they know what's on this table?" I asked.

"Oh, everything will be fine. You'll see."

In the center of the table, Nazig placed a large glass of liquid with a half-immersed heavy string in the middle. Using matches, she lit the string and a dancing, bright flame suddenly lit up the tent.

I was strangely mesmerized by the first candlelight I'd ever seen. Somehow it blotted out all the pain of the catastrophic times I'd had since leaving Kayseri. Until I die, I'll never forget that glorious glow, nor will I ever forget the rekindling effect it had on my will to live on.

Nazig led me to the far side of the tent, and pointed to a clean mattress on the floor. "Sleep here," she said. "Remember, you are not to talk to anyone. I'll wake you in the morning, before it gets light."

She waited until I unfolded my sore body on the cushion-soft mattress and she covered me with a blanket. She patted my cheek, and smiled. "You must be very tired. Get a good night's sleep."

I fell into a deep sleep reliving, in my dreams, my perilous escape from the wretched life in the desert. I was awakened by the sound of a loud voice. Standing nearby, a woman pointed a long, shaking finger at me. "Who's this girl?"

Nazig, who'd gone to bed next to me, replied: "She's just a young girl sleeping here for the night. She doesn't know what's going on. You just go ahead and help that poor woman deliver her baby."

The woman left and Nazig whispered: "She's a midwife who was summoned by that young woman's husband."

Nazig drifted off to sleep; and I stayed awake, again reliving the day's events. I heard a newborn's gurgling cry and the laughter of the happy father who discovered he had a new son.

Suddenly, I sat up! Where was my sweater! It was the only memento I had of Mama! I turned over, shook Nazig and murmured: "Do you know where my sweater is?"

"I threw it away with your other dirty clothes."

"Oh, NO! That's all I have left from Mama!"

"Don't worry, Vergeen. I promise to look for it first thing tomorrow morning."

The lost sweater bothered me the rest of the night, I couldn't sleep. At dawn, we looked for my sweater before going to Joseph's tent. It was GONE! Nothing was there! Not a single item of clothing was left on the hill where Nazig had thrown my dirty rags the night before. I struggled to blink back my tears, but losing the only keepsake I had of Mama was heartbreaking.

As we walked to Joseph's tent, Nazig kept saying, "If I'd only known what that sweater meant to you."

Joseph was still asleep and quickly awakened when he heard us enter his tent. "What's the matter? Why is she crying?"

Nazig explained my loss to Joseph and both tried to comfort me. She started packing Joseph's things while I sat in a chair; I got up only when Nazig needed my help.

"I'm finished here," she said. "Now, I'll go to the other tents and pack the boys' things there." Looking at Joseph, she asked, "Is there anything you'd like me to do?"

Joseph shook his head, and Nazig pulled me near the entrance and told me to face the doorway and not to turn around until Joseph said it was all right; and she left.

Why did I have to face the wall? I was curious and turned my head slightly and caught a glimpse of Joseph's back. He was putting on a shirt.

"You can turn around," Joseph said, looking solemn as he buttoned his jacket. "I'm leaving now. Someone will come to carry out all these packings. Stay here! If, by chance, anybody comes in, don't talk to him. You'll have to stay alone here until I get back. When I do, I'm taking you with me to *Gondjouk Jourjoub*."

Waiting alone after Joseph left, I wondered what was going to happen to me. Was I still in danger of being caught by the Turkish guards?

Within a few hours, I heard roaring sounds, people talking in Arabic, but mostly Turkish.

Curious to know who they were, I untied the flap rope and peeked out the tiny opening. Several persons were passing in front of the tent and most were dressed in civilian clothes; some wore army uniforms.

I kept circling inside the tent, waiting for Joseph to appear. I wanted to know what was happening, so I went to the back side of the tent, stooped down to lift the bottom flap. My heart leaped! Women I knew from Yousuf's tribe were walking toward the tents, carrying large containers of milk and yogurt on their heads.

I panicked! I rushed to the front of the tent, peered through the small opening again to see if I could see Nazig or one of Joseph's men to warn them about the Arabic women. I saw no one.

I ran to the back and raised the bottom flap once more, the Arabs were coming closer to my tent. They stopped just a hundred feet away and set up their products for sale.

What if they entered this tent? What if they tried to steal something from here and saw me? Even though I was dressed differently, I told myself, they would surely recognize me from my tattoos. My panic deepened.

I got down on my knees and held my face in my hands close to the ground, hoping they wouldn't see my face in case any one of the women entered.

I was so jittery, my body shook out of control. Where was Joseph?

Another hour must have gone by and Georg Kazan came in to look for Joseph. Seeing the tent was empty, except for me, he started to leave.

"Please! Please, come back," I whispered. "See those women in the front. They belong to the tribe that captured me. If they see me, I'll be killed." I grabbed his sleeve. "Please get me out of here."

"Don't be afraid! I'll take care of you. I'll get you out of here."

He went out. Peering through the small opening, I saw him reach for a lash hanging outside his tent; he swung around and struck the Bedouin women, spilling their milk and yogurt. "Get out of here!" he yelled in Arabic. The terrified women ran rapidly toward the desert, leaving their containers behind.

Concentrating intently on the fleeing women, I didn't hear Joseph enter from the back.

"Here, I want you to put these on," he said, handing me a man's full, face mask and a tasseled fez. "You're already dressed in men's clothes, so your attire will not be a problem. But, stick your hair under the fez – right away!

"Where are we going?"

"I've decided it's best that you not come with me now. Very soon, a man named *Abdul* will be here to take you by carriage to Gondjouk Jourjoub. It's about an hour from here and that's where we'll all be living."

Not long after Joseph left, Abdul arrived. He was kind and sympathetic. He knew all about me and he was performing this covert mission to help Joseph avoid trouble with his superiors.

We rode for an hour. When we reached Gondjouk Jourjoub, the Railroad Company's new headquarters, Abdul took me to Joseph's quarters and instructed me not to leave until Joseph's men arrived along with Nazig and her family. I nodded, affirming my understanding of the danger if I were found out, and Abdul left. I looked around the large, sun-filled room; it had been a long time since I'd seen one like this. Even though the room was void of furniture, it was so cheery and pleasant.

Everyone arrived by late afternoon and settled in their quarters. Salim, George and Ghon occupied a room near the kitchen while Joseph had the private room. Again, I shared quarters with Nazig's family. She was so delighted to be able to cook in a real kitchen instead of outdoors.

The next day, Joseph received a telegram from Souren who'd remained back at the original location. The wire read: "A wild-looking Bedouin with a rifle is here looking for a refugee girl. He says he's going to kill her. He could be looking for Vergeen. Please take care."

It was Yousuf, searching for me. For the next two days, Souren sent warning telegrams to Joseph that Yousuf was still snooping around, always in a rage. Each time the telegraph office called with Souren's messages, Joseph hid me in the office of *Hans Kislenge*, the chief engineer from Germany. A week later, Souren sent word that Yousuf was no longer around.

Everyone relaxed. I felt safe – finally!

      ❈ ❈ ❈

For the next month, in my comfortable surroundings with good food, I gained back some weight. Nazig made certain I was fed well and she watched over me like an indulgent mother.

Suspicious about my protruding stomach, she asked me one day: "*Aghcheekes, hegheeyes?* (My girl, are you pregnant?)"

"NO!" I was shocked by the question, but I knew Nazig didn't believe my denial. My stomach was big and getting bigger.

Exactly twenty-four days after my escape from the desert – I remember it so well – I had excruciating, abdominal cramps.

Always watchful, Nazig was sure I was in early labor; and she was relieved when she realized I'd started to menstruate again, the first time in nearly two years. The flow of blood was very heavy, causing considerable pain for several days. For the next three months, I suffered the same painful, lengthy menstruation; and, eventually, my stomach returned to its normal size. So did my swollen, callused feet and hands after I soaked them for months in warm soapy water.

My job, officially registered with the Company, was mainly being Nazig's helpmate in the kitchen. She did most of the cooking while I served our five young men. Each mealtime, I'd clear off the writing table used by the men for their work and I'd prepare it for setting the meals. I was also responsible for fixing the beds and cleaning the men's rooms.

The Company increased the men's workload, mostly the computation of cost figures which required a multitude of copies.

"Can you copy numbers correctly?" Georg was anxious to enlist my help.

"I'll try," I answered, hoping I could do more than just clean rooms.

"GOOD! Let's see if you can copy these quickly," Georg handed me a pencil and a sheet of paper listing rows of numbers.

I liked the challenge and copied the numbers so neatly that George howled with approval. "We've found our helper, boys!"

I loved doing the copying work for the young men. The chief engineer, Hans Kislenge, saw me working a few times and said; "Maybe you should assist me, too."

Two days later, a boy came into the kitchen and told me the chief engineer wanted to see me; and I rushed to Kislenge's office. "Do you know French? Could you copy these for me?" He motioned me to come around and look at the report on his desk.

I examined the French sentences carefully. "I don't recognize some of these words; I'm not sure I can do the job."

"Oh, that's all right. I'll help you," Kislenge said, patting my hand. "From now on, I want you to work for me once in a while, not for the boys."

※ ※ ※

Georg Kazan's mother came to the Company headquarters to visit her son for two weeks. She was a lovely, elegant lady from Aleppo who worshipped her son. "My husband died in the army two years ago, and Georg is all I have left," she told me, glancing adoringly at her son each time he came into view. "I'm so happy he works for the Company and, as long as he stays here, the army will leave him alone."

I enjoyed chatting with her during her vacation. She was charming.

"I owe you and Nazig my gratitude for taking such good care of my son," she told me on the last day of her visit. "I want you to know, my dear, I like you very much."

I was so pleased to hear Georg's mother express her affection for me. It was comforting to hear such words of endearment after the long months of being subjected to Aneche's loathsome treatment.

"I've noticed that Joseph likes you, too," she said casually.

Her comment made me blush and I must have murmured, "Thank you."

How stupid of me! What an inappropriate response! But, it must be true if she spotted his interest in me! How I hoped it was so!

"If he asks you to marry him, don't turn him down. Say yes! He comes from a very good family."

I was stunned! I could barely concentrate on what else she was saying.

"When I get back to Aleppo, I'm going to talk to Joseph's mother about you and I'm going to tell her what a fine girl you are."

In recent weeks, I'd noticed Joseph staring at me quite frequently. Whenever our eyes met, he'd smile and turn away. He can't be interested in me, I often thought. I'm a refugee, a tattooed escapee from the Bedouins! A nobody! How could he love me? It must be pity!

Then just the thought of marrying Joseph would make me swoon into a sweet, hopeful dream.

SEVENTEEN

Joseph

Our irresistible, mutual attraction drew Joseph and me closer and closer; and we snatched every opportunity to be together. I lived for those times when we were able to sit together during the early evening hours and talk about the past and our hopes for the future. Armenag, my betrothed from so long ago, began to fade from my memory.

Joseph's mother, *Lizbeth,* and his little brother, *Habib,* came to visit him. I suspected her purpose for the trip was two-fold: to see Joseph, of course, and to investigate me, the Armenian refugee who'd enticed her son.

A woman nearing fifty, Lizbeth had lost her husband five years before when she was pregnant with her youngest child, Habib, who was a very spoiled little boy. She also had four daughters with whom she lived in Aleppo.

On her arrival, we all greeted Joseph's mother cordially. Yet, at first, Nazig and I sensed her coolness toward us. After a few days, Lizbeth gradually warmed up to both of us, especially to Nazig who went all out in preparing special meals for the guests.

Nazig became ill and developed a high fever. Noticing Nazig's hot, sweaty face, Lizbeth checked her forehead and warned: "You must go to bed right now!" Nazig nodded her head and dragged her body out of the kitchen.

"Vergeen, do you sleep in the same room with Nazig?"

"Yes, I do."

"I don't think you should right now," Lizbeth said with authority. "Nazig might have a contagious illness. Come, stay with me in my room until she gets well."

I was reluctant, but I felt it impolite to decline her offer.

With Nazig still ill, Lizbeth and I prepared all the meals for the remainder of the week. Thus, working together and sleeping in the same room, we got better acquainted. By the time she left, I knew she had accepted me.

I was ecstatic; Joseph's mother liked me. A little more hopeful about winning his sisters' approval, too, I immersed myself in idyllic fantasies of a possible future with Joseph.

※ ※ ※

Occasionally, Hans Keslenge sent for me to copy reports; and the last time I went to his office he gave me a short paragraph to duplicate. Sitting across the desk from him, I noticed his stare fixed on me; and my eerie discomfort prompted me to finish the job as rapidly as I could. I wanted to get out of there! I got up and placed the sheet in front of him and turned quickly to leave.

"Just a minute. Let me read what you've done here."
I stopped timidly. "Is there something wrong?"
"I can't make out this letter you wrote. Come close and see."
The situation disturbed me; I did not like this man. I walked slowly around his desk to examine the sheet before him, and he gripped my hand.

"Don't be afraid of me," he said, looking straight in my eyes. "You really did fine work. I just want you to know I'd like to be your friend."

I pulled my hand away and started to leave again.
"Wait a minute! What's your answer? Yes or no? Will you be my friend?"

"I'm sorry, sir. I'm too young to be your friend."
I was trembling when I left his office and headed directly to the kitchen to seek Nazig's advice. As a supervisor of the Railroad Company, Keslenge could cause me a lot of difficulty, perhaps even force me to return to the Bedouins.

I dropped into a chair, still shaking. "What should I do?"
Nazig listened to my dilemma and she gave me a glass of cognac

just as Joseph entered the kitchen and asked, "What's wrong?"

Getting no answer from me, he asked Nazig to explain. Immediately, after hearing what had happened, Joseph left the room, declaring: "Stay here, Vergeen! I'll be right back!"

Joseph returned a half hour later. "Everything is straightened out. You will not be working for Hans any more. Nor will you be serving the meals to our boys." Observing my bewilderment, he added, "I'll explain it all to you tomorrow."

I had trouble sleeping that night; I was restless, impatient to hear what Joseph had told Keslenge. Early next morning, Joseph came into the kitchen and asked me to come to his room within the hour. He seemed unusually solemn when he answered my knock on his door. "Come in and sit down, Vergeen. I have something very important to tell you." His face brightened into one of his infectious half smiles before he started to speak.

"For weeks, I've been wanting to talk to you about this, but I never found the right time. The situation with Hans has made it necessary to discuss it now." Joseph sat down beside me and gently grasped my hand.

"I told Hans that you and I were engaged and I did not want you to work for him any more, nor for anybody else in the Company." Joseph hesitated to check my reaction. "I'm not wrong about how you feel about me, am I?"

Overcome by unutterable joy, I could only shake my head repeatedly.

"I knew you shared my feelings," Joseph murmured as he stood up, lifted me in his arms, and kissed me again and again. Our emotions had been curbed for months; we took advantage of the fortuitous chance to embrace for several minutes, overflowing with our newly committed love for each other.

Still enfolded in his arms, I listened to Joseph describe his meeting with Keslenge.

"Last night when Nazig told me about Hans' behavior toward you, I was very upset. When I went to his office and told him you were my fiance and that I did not want you to work for the Railroad Company anymore, I couldn't believe Hans' reaction." Joseph relaxed his arms and held out his hands to clasp both of my mine to his chest.

"Vergeen, can you imagine? He was actually gracious, even congratulated me and wished me good luck." Joseph kept shaking his head in pleasant disbelief.

"Listen to me, Vergeen! I mean it! I don't want you to work in the kitchen or serve our meals! Visit with Nazig and eat with her in the kitchen, but that's all. Besides, we'll be leaving soon for another location."

"Where are we going?"

"I've gotten another promotion, this time it's in *Nesabin*."

"Is everyone going?" I was curious to know if Georg was also being transferred. Both he and his mother had been so kind to me.

"No, not everyone. Souren will go; you know, he's Armenian." Joseph grinned at me. "So will Paul Huston. You haven't met him yet. He's English and a former war prisoner who's an engineer."

Pointing to me, he said: "With you, there'll be four of us at supper every night. Just imagine how great that will be!" Joseph grabbed me again and held me tightly in his arms.

I was replaced in my kitchen job by a hard-working Indian prisoner who was hired by the office to assist Nazig. He was more helpful to her than I'd been. Young and strong, he carried large bundles of kindling wood to the kitchen every morning – something I never could do.

The Indian, Nazig and her family moved with us to Nesabin. Although she was happy to remain with Joseph and his men, she had the tough job of cooking outdoors again until the building's kitchen was constructed. Neither were all rooms ready for occupancy. Hans Keslenge had the only available room while Joseph, Souren and Paul had to manage for a while in small tents. Nazig's family and I, along with Keslenge's female servant, lived in a tall, white tent.

The engineers – Souren, Paul and Keslenge – were particularly busy, conducting surveys until sundown. To accommodate them, Nazig prepared food for a seven o'clock supper every evening. While I ate with Nazig, the Indian served the men with heaping plates of her deliciously prepared meals.

During our stay in Nesabin, Joseph began to teach me advanced French as his time permitted, from three to four times a week. We'd meet in the dining area and spread all the lesson materials on the large table. Sometimes, after the lessons, when no one was around, Joseph would tiptoe behind my chair and startle me with a fast kiss on my neck and dash out laughing.

At suppertime, he'd avoid my stare, making sure we'd keep our romance private. But, I always yearned for his response to my playful, affectionate smiles. I could not wait for the French lessons. They also provided secluded times for us to bask in our deepening love; a time for tender embraces and ardent kisses; a time to pledge, again and again, our irrevocable commitment to each other. My love for Joseph absorbed me completely! I could think of nothing else!

Joseph always worried that Yousuf would turn up or a Turkish soldier would discover I was a refugee. "Vergeen, please be careful! When I'm not here, don't leave the tent without Nazig or one of the boys."

Our stay in Nesabin was brief; the Company announced a transfer to Baghdad for our men. The frequent moves were required after every stretch of railroad ties was completed; then the employees were transferred every few months to start construction on other planned, tracking areas of the long railroad route.

On the day of our move, Joseph came down with a serious case of dysentery. Yet, he climbed aboard with me on one of the two trucks supplied by the Company to transport personnel and provisions. "I feel awful," he whispered. "I hope this is not going to be a hard trip."

Unfortunately, the ride on the way to Baghdad was rough; we bounced continually over hard clay roads and over rocks, bushes, and boulders. Joseph gripped his abdomen all the way to *Diemir Kapaou*, where we camped for the first night. Workers pitched two tents, one for Company executives and the other for all the women and children. The remaining employees slept in the trucks.

Trying to fall asleep in the women's tent, I heard Joseph calling me and I hurried out to see what he wanted.

"Don't be alarmed," he said, bent over in obvious pain. "I'm afraid my dysentery has gotten worse. I just checked with Hans Keslenge and he recommended that I remain here until I get well. I'll probably be able to proceed on to Baghdad next week."

Joseph grabbed the tent's outside pole, waiting for a sudden pain to subside. "Vergeen, I want you to stay here with me even though Hans wants you to go with the group. I don't trust him; so I told him you also were ill and that we should stay together until we both got well."

The group left early the next morning, and Joseph and I remained behind. We stayed a week with a family who'd been working for the Company for several months. But, it still didn't afford Joseph enough time to recover; his condition worsened. The Company executives in Diemir Kapaou told him he must go to Aleppo for treatment.

"I won't go to Aleppo unless I can take you with me." Joseph was adamant. "I have no idea how we can conceal the fact that you're an Armenian refugee. But we'll find a way."

We both knew any effort to hide my identity could be dangerous. The Turkish government had issued a warning that all Armenian refugees caught in any escape attempt to Aleppo would be executed along with the helping accomplices. We'd heard tragic stories of Turkish soldiers capturing Armenian women trying to flee to Aleppo. Even though these women were disguised in Arabic dresses, the suspicious soldiers had recognized them as Armenian refugees and the poor women had paid for their attempt with their lives.

It was too risky for me to try an Arabic guise. A male disguise was equally hazardous. Besides, since leaving Kayseri, I was no longer an awkward adolescent. Now almost sixteen and well-fed by doting Nazig, I had matured physically, both in face and figure.

We remained several weeks in Diemir Kapaou. As soon as Joseph got well, he rented a horse-drawn cart and we travelled to *Telhalif* where he had a few close friends. Joseph wanted to seek their advice about devising an escape plan to Aleppo. When we reached Telhalif, his friends were eager to help us, even at the risk of reprisal by Syrian officials.

"We have to make sure our lives, including yours, are not put in jeopardy." Joseph stated his concerns. "What's our best chance of getting Vergeen into Aleppo without being caught?"

"I know what can be done to safeguard Vergeen." Joseph's friend, Jacob, was the town's railroad station manager, and he was certain he'd concocted the best, hazard-free plan.

Excitedly, Jacob explained: "Every two or three months, the Turkish government rounds up hundreds of Kurds and deports them by train to the interior of Turkey. At various stops along the way, the government drops off several of the Kurds so they can occupy the unwanted, vacant houses which once belonged to the poorer Armenian refugees."

Jacob was sure his plan would work. "We're waiting to transfer another group of Kurds in a month. You can stay here until then."

"But what can we do to make sure Vergeen will be safe?" Joseph was unsure of how much protection he and I would have.

"We'll just disguise her as one of the Kurds. Like Vergeen, they're usually fair-skinned with light hair, and they have tattoos, too. Buy a Kurdish dress for her, and she will not be detected."

Aside from the need to buy the proper clothes, the escape plan was complicated. I was nervous, but Joseph kept reassuring me that we'd be fine.

Jacob's wife and family were graciously kind. They made sure I felt secure in their warm, loving home. I shared a bedroom with their daughters while Joseph slept in their son's room.

Joseph and I rarely spoke or touched each other during the month we stayed with Jacob's family. We felt that any display of our love for each other was impolite, and we busied ourselves by helping members of the family with their daily chores.

One afternoon, Jacob brought the news about the date and time of the planned deportation of another group of Kurds; and he carefully mapped out the rest of the plan.

"Vergeen will ride in the freight car with the Kurds; and Joseph, you will be in the regular passenger car with your baggage. I will instruct the engineer to decrease the train's speed and blow the whistle fifteen minutes before the train reaches the Aleppo station. While the train is moving slowly, you must get off the passenger car, Joseph. Then, run to the freight car and see that Vergeen gets off."

Jacob stopped to fish for a piece of paper in his pocket. "Here is my brother's address; his home is not far from where you'll be jumping off the train. Take Vergeen to my brother; she'll be safe there and she can stay out of sight. Then go to the Aleppo station for your baggage – it's walking distance from my brother's house. Before you return to pick up Vergeen, you can hire a carriage at the station to take you home."

It was an elaborate plan, but the only logical one in view of our situation. We were all set to leave, except for the important Kurdish dress. Unable to locate anything suitable at a reasonable price, Joseph finally found an exquisitely hand-embroidered dress for which he paid an enormous amount.

The train carrying the Kurds was always detained overnight at the Telhalif railroad station. The usual stopover gave Jacob enough time to bribe the Kurd leader into letting me ride in the same car with his people. He'd instructed the Kurd to tell his group I was the wife of a Syrian army officer and that I was going to meet him in *Adana* near the Syrian-Turkish border.

Joseph and I boarded the train the following morning; he sat in the passenger car and I stood with the Kurds in the freight car. For the most part, the Kurds were kind and seemed to be impressed by my fine clothes. I accepted their offer of food, mostly garlic and bread. But, my Kurdish was limited, I knew a few words that I'd learned from Aneche; so I spoke very little, afraid of inadvertently revealing my identity.

Feeling vulnerable without Joseph at my side to protect me, I was racked with anxiety. What if Joseph didn't have enough time to reach me? What if something went wrong and I couldn't jump off the freight car at the planned time? What if I drifted back to Turkey with these Kurds? What would I do? My mind succumbed to all the horrors which could be brought on by an escape plan gone awry, and my terrifying thoughts chilled me. Occasionally. the women interrupted my silence to ask about my dress. In order to explain my vague knowledge of the Kurdish language, I told the women I was really Turkish and my husband was a Kurd who was an officer in the Syrian army. Thank God! The leader came to my rescue and confirmed my story.

Later that afternoon, the train stopped to replenish its water supply; and Joseph appeared at the door of our car and asked for the Kurd leader. Watching Joseph calmly confer with the Kurd allayed my fears.

Joseph motioned me to the front of the car. "Vergeen, listen! The next time the train whistles and slows down, this man is going to help you get off the train. I'll be alongside as soon as I can leave the other car. So, be ready!"

We rode for another hour. When the train slowed down and whistled, the Kurd leader helped me jump off and, within seconds, Joseph was beside me, breathlessly whispering: "Hurry! Hurry, Vergeen! Please HURRY!"

Joseph walked so fast ahead of me, I had a hard time catching up to him. Fortunately, the home of Jacob's brother was not far and we found it easily. Joseph knocked on the door; no one answered. We walked through the unlocked door into an empty room. Joseph looked around and saw no one.

"Stay here, don't go out," he warned me. "I'm going to the train station to get my trunks and hire a buggy." Noting my apprehension, he smiled and added: "It should not take long. I'll be back soon."

True to his word, Joseph returned in less than an hour, sitting in a fine-looking, horse-drawn buggy with a roof and a driver. As we were leaving, Jacob's brother and his family arrived; Joseph introduced himself and briefly explained why we were there. Jacob's brother seemed to understand our situation well and invited us to have tea with his family.

"I'm sorry we must move on," Joseph said as he thanked them for the use of their home. "May I leave my trunks with you for a few days?" Joseph again expressed his gratitude for the family's willingness to hold on to his trunks until he could pick them up.

Climbing aboard the handsome buggy with Joseph, I told myself that I'd almost forgotten such pleasant civility still existed. The clattering sound of the horse's hoofs on the cobblestoned streets registered like cadent music. The line of houses, displaying pretty lace curtains in arched windows, arose in the skyline like noble mansions. The subtle fragrance of the surrounding trees and bushes floated in the cool, evening air.

Lost in the wondrous sights and pleasant smells, I was unable to speak. I felt Joseph's loving touch as he clasped my hand, and sweet tears of joy spilled down my face.

EIGHTEEN

The Family

We were near Joseph's house when the driver stopped. Joseph paid him as I climbed down from the buggy, and we started to walk silently. Once again, Joseph's pace was so rapid that I had to run to stay alongside him. Whenever I caught up to him, he'd walk even faster. Suddenly it occurred to me that my Kurdish clothes embarrassed Joseph and I slowed down, keeping some distance between us.

It was dark when we reached Joseph's home. His mother, Lizbeth, welcomed us and instantly wrapped her arms around her son, kissing him on both cheeks. She looked rested since I'd first met her in Gondjouk Jourjoub.

"It's nice to see you," she said to me.

Four young women emerged from a doorway and each one rushed to Joseph's side, taking turns to hug him. "Oh, brother! It's good to have you home with us!"

I noted that all shared Joseph's handsome looks: his wavy, black hair and his beautiful, thick-lashed, dark eyes. The four sisters turned around and stared at me as Joseph said: "I want you to meet Vergeen."

His mother began the introductions. "This is my eldest daughter; her name is *Miriam*." I knew instantly Miriam was not going to be a friend; her animosity was clearly apparent. She muttered something and slipped into a nearby chair.

"This is *Antoinette*, she's next to Miriam in age." Lizbeth continued.

Antoinette's warm smile was reassuring. In her early twenties, she was gracious and well-mannered. "Welcome to our home," she said.

Next I met *Suzanne*, the nineteen-year-old beauty of the family.

She was quiet, said very little; but her restrained smile troubled me. Contrary to Syrian custom requiring older sisters to marry first, Suzanne was engaged to a young man from Aleppo.

The youngest girl, *Louise*, was just thirteen. She was bubbly, full of energy and obviously the household's jester.

Habib, Joseph's five-year-old brother came bouncing into the room looking for his mother and, recognizing me, he grinned and stood still.

This lukewarm welcome was not what I expected as Joseph's fiance. I felt uneasy, visibly insecure. Why did Joseph's sisters dislike me? Was it my life with the Bedouins? My tattoos? Because I was a refugee? My religion? Perhaps I wasn't a Roman Catholic like they were; but after all I, too, was a Christian, an Armenian Orthodox. What could I do to win the approval of the doubting members of Joseph's family?

Sensing my discomfort, Lizbeth said: "Come with me. Let me take you to your room. You'll be sharing a downstairs bedroom with Louise. I hope you'll be comfortable here."

In the five years since the loss of her husband, Lizbeth was totally dependent on her children financially. Until the war, Joseph had worked at the local bank as an accountant; and he'd earned adequate wages, enough to support his mother and siblings. But seeking exemption from army duty like so many other young men during the war, Joseph had gone to work for the Railroad Company at much lower wages; and now his sisters were the primary breadwinners for the family.

The three older girls were masters in embroidery, and they worked long hours in a large room on the second floor of the house trying to keep up with increasing orders. Their painstaking handwork was the most delicate I'd ever seen. Many of Aleppo's wealthiest families sought their services frequently and paid them well to embroider beautiful motifs on undergarments and dresses for their daughters' trousseaus.

"Do you know how to embroider?" Antoinette's question

pleased me. Maybe if I worked with them, it could help me gain their approval.

"Yes, I do." My confidence edged upward a little. "I was taught by the nuns at the St. Joseph School in Kayseri, and I was considered one of the better embroiderers."

"Let's see what you can do." Frowning, Miriam handed me a simple piece to work on. "Use satin threads on this."

I was so careful to make sure every stitch was even, every stitch shimmered exactly right on the sheer fabric – both on the front and on the backside of the work. I wanted to prove to Joseph's sisters that I was one of them.

"I think I'm finished," I said, truly proud of my accomplishment, and I handed it to Miriam.

Her expression told me I hadn't passed her test. "Well, this is adequate for a beginner. I think you'll be able to do the fillers, but nothing else." Again, she'd shot down my already shaky ego.

After breakfast every day, Joseph went out to explore ways to stay in Aleppo. His only hope was to buy his way out of the army; otherwise he'd have to return to the exempted Railroad Company or he'd be forced to fulfill his army requirements.

Each morning after Joseph left, the routine was the same: Louise and Habib went to school; Lizbeth worked in the kitchen; and I joined the sisters upstairs helping with their embroidery work. Everyone worked meticulously, in disciplined silence, with unblinking eyes fixed on the work. Mine was the easier job of filling the areas around the intricate designs.

Whenever Lizbeth came upstairs, she'd nod, smile, and sometimes utter a word or two. Generally, that was the extent of the verbal contact I had with her and her hard-working daughters. Conversations were scattered; they seldom included me.

Joseph found temporary employment as an accountant and, since the work location was so far from the house, he was gone from dawn to late evening. I saw little of him during my month's stay, except to exchange greetings each morning. I lay awake most nights waiting for the sound of his footsteps when he came home. During those sleepless hours, I heard far-off train whistles which reminded me of the Railroad Company and all the glorious times I had with my beloved Joseph. How I wished I was back there with him again!

A few mornings, when no one was around, Joseph would brush by me in the kitchen to kiss my cheek or squeeze my hand.

Usually on Sundays, the entire family went to church and returned for a special dinner. After the meal, Suzanne always went upstairs to beautify herself before her fiance arrived to spend the evening. On the third Sunday of my stay with the family, Suzanne's primping took longer than ever. Her fiance brought along another young man and both were ushered into the parlor by Suzanne and Lizbeth. Their visit was a long one behind closed doors, and I suspected their discussion centered on me.

The following Sunday, Joseph stayed home after breakfast.

Lizbeth appeared strangely energized. "Everyone is going to church today, even Louise. She hasn't been to church for a while."

Glancing at me, she said, "Vergeen, Joseph will take you to the Armenian Church today."

I was glad to hear that I'd have a chance to talk to Joseph alone. I had to find out what was going to happen to us. The month with his family had been extremely difficult. His sisters barely acknowledged my presence.

Joseph and I left for church before the others. I wore the prettier of the two new dresses he'd bought for me soon after our arrival at his home. We walked silently before Joseph pointed out the Armenian church on a small hill.

"I was here last Sunday and I saw your priest," Joseph said. "He was going to talk to an Armenian fellow who's going to meet us here."

I was confused! What was Joseph talking about? What was he hiding?

Instead of entering the church, Joseph led me to the side courtyard into a small room where the priest was admonishing two teenage boys. We heard him tell the boys to return later, and the priest turned to receive us.

"Please sit down here," he said pointing to chairs opposite his desk.

The priest turned to Joseph and said, "The man I told you about was here this morning; but he had to leave. He said he'd be back shortly." Then the elderly clergyman spoke to me in Armenian. *"Aghcheekes, toon vor kahghaken es?* (My girl, what city are you from?)"

"Kayseri."

"Meenaghes? Endahneek choonees? (Are you alone? Have you no family?)"

"Voch, der Hayr. Ayyoh, meenaghem. (No, father. Yes, I'm alone.)"

I tried to catch Joseph's eye several times to ask what was going on here; he looked away each time. Something was terribly wrong! Before I could question Joseph or the priest, a tall man with graying hair entered the room.

"This is *Bedros Bardizbanian*, the man I told you about," the priest stood up to make the introduction. "He and his family miraculously escaped the Turkish massacres and they live here in Aleppo now."

"Yes, we were very fortunate. All of us managed to stay alive; my wife, my mother and my two sons are ..."

The priest interrupted. "They live in one room in that house just off the courtyard. The room has a built-in bed." Hesitating a minute, he looked at me and said: "They'll give you the bed, and they'll sleep on the floor."

What was this priest talking about? A stinging pain pierced my chest and I gasped for breath. I hardly heard Joseph tell the priest that he'd bring me back the next day. Walking behind Joseph, I stepped slowly out of the office and sank down on a bench in the courtyard. Joseph sat down next to me.

"I must explain why I had to do this," he said softly. "Vergeen, please listen. I'm very sorry, but I have no choice. My sisters are against our marriage – not my mother. But my mother has no voice in the matter since my sisters are supporting her, and they're also supporting Louise and my little brother."

Joseph tried to take my hand, but I pulled it back. My deep hurt was simmering into implacable anger.

"You know I haven't enough money to support everyone right now. But, I'm going to do my best to support you. I'm going to pay for your board and room; and I'll give you spending money for anything you want to buy – clothes, extra food, whatever you'd like."

Joseph tried again to reach for my hand; but I sat stiffly with my hands down my sides, not uttering a word.

"Vergeen, please understand! It's going to take some time before we can marry. Remember, there's the matter of my exemption from the army; it will cost a lot."

I knew Joseph was grappling with a multitude of problems right now, I said to myself; but why did I have to be sacrificed?

I softened when Joseph said: "Never forget, Vergeen, how much I love you. Remember! We've come a long way from Diemir Kapaou to get you here."

Joseph touched my hand again; this time I let him hold it. "I'm going to do everything I can to work things out. As soon as I get a six-month exemption from the army, we'll get married."

I nodded to convey my understanding, albeit reluctantly; and we headed to his house. I spent the rest of the day in my room, wondering what was to become of me.

The next day, after seeing the Armenian priest, Joseph took me to the Bardizbanians. All the family was not at home, just the grandmother. She sensed we needed privacy and she left us alone.

"I'll come every Wednesday to see you until I get my job back from the bank," Joseph avowed fervently. Clutching my hands tightly to his chest, he kissed me in a lingering goodbye. I escorted him to the door and watched tearfully as he walked away. Before disappearing, he turned around several times and waved his hand. I couldn't even lift my arm to wave back.

The area occupied by the Bardizbanians was one of four spacious rooms, each housing a refugee family, in a residential building near the Armenian church. The families shared a large kitchen adjacent to the courtyard. Most of the time, Grandmother Bardizbanian stayed in the kitchen, working or chatting with the neighbors.

On my first day, I was glad no one was around to ask questions. I didn't want to see or talk to anyone. I just wanted to be alone; my depressed state of mind consumed me. I resented the family's intrusion when members appeared one by one. First, it was *Bedros*, the father. Then his little boy came in followed by the seventeen-year-old son, and they invited me to join them at the table. The grandmother first spread a white cloth and then placed forks, bread and a jug of water on the table; and we waited for *Anoush*, the mother.

Finally, she bounced in, smiling warmly and swept me into her arms. "Welcome, my dear!" Her effusiveness startled me.

Sitting down at the table next to me, she said: "I want you to consider me as your new mother. Feel free to confide in me. You can always count on me to help you!"

The family ate their supper without much conversation that evening. I think they recognized my depressed state, especially when I could not eat. Everyone went to bed early in order to save lighting costs. The five family members slept on the floor, tossing and turning most of that long night. Frequently, the little boy disturbed everyone when he'd ask for water.

My depression intensified. I lay awake all night. I was numb; I had no tears left. Was I saved for this? To live in one room with a strange family? It would have been better to die in the desert! Why did Joseph bring me to Aleppo? Why was his family against me?

Everyone left the next morning, except the grandmother. She rambled on incessantly, asking innumerable questions. Where are you from? When did your deportation start? What happened to your family? On and on.

I wanted to be left alone, but I dared not be disrsptful since she was an elderly lady. I answered her prying queries, but somewhat curtly.

The family routine was the same the second night, and I still could not eat supper. While all the Bardizbanians left the next morning, I felt very weak and stayed in bed. It was Wednesday and Joseph came to see me that afternoon.

"Why are you doing this to me, Joseph?" I was heartbroken. The more he tried to comfort me, the more I cried.

"Tell me, please! What does your family have against me?"

Joseph sat down next to me. "I've always been honest with you, Vergeen; and I'm going to be truthful again. My sisters just don't want me to marry you because you're a refugee."

I covered my ears; I didn't want to hear any more. I knew what was coming next. Joseph gently held on to my hands and continued.

"They claim you're not one of us. You're not Syrian and you belong to a different church denomination. Most of all, they feel our friends and relatives would shun you because of the tattoos on your face."

There it was! The answer to why they hated me – my TATTOOS!

"Listen to me, Vergeen." Joseph was eager to tell me about his mother's feelings. "Mother is very fond of you. She has no objection to our marriage, and her feelings about you are all I care about."

Joseph dug into his pocket for a handkerchief and gave it to me. "These people seem nice," he said. "Stay here with them until I can pay for my army exemption and I can get my bank job back; then I promise we'll be married."

I was finally comforted by his assurances and we spent a couple of hours together, talking and embracing.

"I'll be back next Wednesday," Joseph promised as he kissed me goodbye.

I consoled myself with the expectation of seeing him every week. I saw him more now and spent more time with him than when I was staying with his family. I lived for Wednesdays. Most of the time, we were alone. We'd take long walks arm in arm, sneak precious kisses, and plan for our future.

Joseph paid the Bardizbanians for my second month's rent; and I learned that the whole family was living on this rent money. They were anxious to do everything they could for me. Each time Joseph visited me, he'd ask if I was being treated well.

"I'm satisfied;" I'd answer. "But I just want to see you every day!"

Rent for the third month was due in a few days when a boy came into the courtyard on a Friday afternoon. "Are you Vergeen?" When I nodded, he handed me a small piece of folded paper.

"Who gave you this?"

"A man on the street corner asked me to give this to you." The boy answered and ran off.

Hurriedly I opened the note, and three words bolted out *PLEASE FORGET ME!* It was signed Joseph.

I stood dazed! I was numb! How could it be? Just two days ago he told me he was certain his sisters were going to give him the money he needed to stay out of the army. "We'll be together forever," he had said over and over again. That was only two days ago! There must be some explanation, I told myself. I'll find out when he comes Wednesday.

I said nothing to the Bardizbanians, but they suspected something was wrong because I could not stop trembling and refused supper that night. Confused, I lay awake for hours, trying to unravel the puzzle of Joseph's message. At midnight, there was a knock at the door; it was Joseph asking for me. Quickly I wrapped myself in a blanket and went outside into the courtyard. It was a clear moonlit night; I saw Joseph huddled on a bench. I sat down close to him and waited for an explanation of his baffling behavior.

"Vergeen, I hope you'll forgive me for the note," his voice quavered. I'm going back to the Railroad Company in the morning and I just couldn't leave without seeing you to say goodbye."

"Joseph, oh, NO! What happened? You were so sure last Wednesday that everything was going to work out."

"I know. My sisters went back on their promise to help me. They're so afraid I'll marry you if I stay in Aleppo. And, Vergeen dear, if I remain here one more day without an authorized exemption, I'll have to report to the army office. I DON'T want to do that! My only hope is to go to Baghdad and work again for the Railroad Company until the war ends."

Joseph reached into his pocket and pulled out an envelop and a small box. He handed me the box first. "I had a friend make this for you."

It was a beautiful gold heart attached to a gold chain of tiny hearts. My choking tears made it impossible to speak. I could only clutch his hand to my wet cheek, and I heard him say, "It's a token of my love and commitment."

Joseph handed me the envelope. "Here are four lira to take care of your rent and other needs you might have for the next month. I'll try to send you more, and I promise to write as soon as I can."

I buried my face in his hunched shoulder. We said little; we just clung to each other in impassioned, bitter-sweet embraces until dawn.

Joseph stood up, looked at me wistfully, squeezed my hand one last time; and he walked briskly toward the train station.

NINETEEN

The Hospital

Once again God had ignored my pleas for help. A very young and bewildered refugee, I was alone in a strange country without Joseph. I had no friends, no relatives. With the money Joseph gave me, I paid the Bardizbanians only part of the third month's rent for the room; and I hoped for a miracle to sustain me through my desolate existence until the war ended. My only solace came from a new sense of freedom. I could walk down the streets, go into shops, and occasionally look for other Armenians from Kayseri with only minimal fear of being recognized as a refugee.

Initially, Syria had denied refugees safe haven in any of its cities or villages; but, by the fall of 1917, the Syrian government had acquiesced to pleas from western nations to provide sanctuary for the stricken Armenians. Hence, the more fortunate Armenian escapees from the Turkish-driven death marches into Syria finally found temporary refuge in Aleppo, and no longer did they need to hide their identity.

As the war entered its fourth year, rumors spread throughout Aleppo that the military operations were going badly for Turkey. The British army was active along the Syrian and Baghdad railroads; and news dispatches reported that the Russians, appalled by the sight of tens of thousands of massacred Armenians in northeastern Turkish villages, had destroyed Turkey's Third Army in a revengeful assault.

Conditions in both Syria and Turkey became deplorably stringent; everything, from bread to soap, was scarce. Civilians as well as army personnel suffered equally from the deprivation of the essentials of life. Typhus epidemics swept the city of Aleppo, straining the capacity of both army and civilian hospitals to serve the rapidly increasing number of typhus victims. Hospitals posted notices of the critical need for nurses to replenish a dangerous shortage. Since many Syrians considered nursing an inferior occupation, they seldom applied; so most of the nursing posts were now being filled by Armenian refugee women who gratefully seized any opportunity to earn wages, no matter how small.

Anoush Bardizbanian, my landlady, was employed at the large *Ramanazania* Hospital, one of the army hospitals located just outside Aleppo's city limits. A month earlier, I knew she'd succeeded in finding hospital employment for her young niece.

"I must find a job," I told her a week after Joseph left. "Could you please help me get one at the hospital?"

"I'll talk to the head nurse today. Don't worry, Vergeen, I'm sure something can be worked out." Anoush was eager to help; she surmised what had happened with Joseph's family and apparently was dismayed by their behavior.

That evening, Anoush got home from work with the good news that I could apply for a hospital job right away; they needed workers to fill the acute shortage. Perhaps things would improve for me if I could find work at the hospital and I could live on the remaining lira of Joseph's money until I got paid. I was almost hopeful that my luck was changing.

Scared and shaky about whether I'd be hired, I went to the hospital with Anoush; and she took me straight to the office of the head nurse. My heart pounded as I tried to stand perfectly erect during the all-important introduction. I relaxed when the nurse's pleasant face broke into an approving smile, and she spoke to me in Armenian.

"Yes, I'm Armenian, too," she said taking note of my surprised expression. "What's your name?"

"Vergeen."

"I'm sorry to see you were a captive of the Arabs." My tattoos did not escape her attention. "But I'm glad you were able to get away."

She turned to Anoush, "Take Vergeen with you and let her help you in your ward until I find another, more suitable spot for her."

As I followed Anoush down the hallway, I saw nurses dashing in and out of patients' rooms, carrying stacks of sheets, and even scrubbing floors.

"It's bed-changing day. Vergeen, you'll have to help me move the seriously wounded soldiers from side to side in their beds."

Anoush reached into a tall bin and pulled out several white sheets and blankets and placed most of them in my outstretched arms before we walked into the ward. It was a large room with several windows, and at least a dozen soldiers – Syrian, Turkish and German – occupied narrow, wooden beds.

"First help me with this man," said Anoush standing alongside a patient's bed.

Rushing to the opposite side of the bed, I noticed one droopy blue eye peering out of a heavily bandaged face held firmly on the pillow with a bag on each side of his head.

"Grab on to the sheet underneath him, yank as hard as you can and pull it out while I raise his middle," explained Anoush, struggling to lift the young man's body without moving his head. I pulled and pulled until I could feel my neck veins ready to burst, but the sheet got lodged under the soldier and it refused to move an inch. Poor Anoush had to complete the entire job by herself while I watched, feeling totally useless.

"That's all right, Vergeen." Anoush was very patient with me. "There are special ways to move patients in bed. You'll learn how to do it very soon."

"But I don't think I have the necessary strength in my arms to make the beds." It was my first hour of work and I'd failed dismally. I began to worry; maybe the director of nurses wouldn't let me keep the job.

"I know this is very heavy work; I won't say anything about today. Let's see what will happen in a couple of days."

No wonder Anoush was so tired when she came home from work

each evening. On my very first day, it didn't take long to discover the work of the hospital nurses was physically very hard; most of the patients were immobile and unable to leave their beds. I found the bedpan duty particularly difficult since other workers were seldom free from their chores to help me, and poor Anoush frequently rushed to my side to assist me.

The bedpans were round, unlike the low, flat ones currently used in American hospitals; they were about ten inches in diameter and at least eight inches high. Lifting men nearly double my weight to sit on top of these tall bedpans required gargantuan strength; the severely wounded ones with broken bones or head injuries were especially hard to move. Sometimes, the overflow of urine and feces resulted from my inability to lift the patients properly. Not only did that make the poor soldiers more uncomfortable, but it created more work for Anoush and me; we had to keep changing messy, smelly sheets.

How can I do this day after day? I asked myself this question over and over again throughout what seemed an unending morning. But I needed employment to sustain myself; the money Joseph gave me could not last much longer. Realization of my situation made me all the more determined to do whatever was necessary to keep my new job.

Late that morning, two young women, walking ramrod straight, came into the ward where Anoush and I were trying to clean spilled urine in a soldier's bed, another one of my inexperience-caused messes. Both women wore crisp, white linen aprons covering the entire front parts of their slender bodies; and both wore their obviously long hair in neatly-pinned chignons. One appeared to be about eighteen, and she was carrying a round tray covered with a clean white cloth. The other – a tall, attractive young woman – was perhaps a few years older, and she held her hands and arms crosswise against her chest to avoid contact with anything.

"Who are those girls?" I asked Anoush, thoroughly intrigued by their immaculate appearance and composed air of self-confidence.

"They go from ward to ward to dress the wounds of infirm patients. They're known as the hospital's 'permanent girls'."

Fascinated by the competence of the young women, I moved close to the bed where both were working and watched them intently. Waiting until the younger woman unwrapped the heavy bandage on the leg of a soldier, the older nurse used a tweezer-like instrument to pick up pieces of gauze from the tray and used them to clean and medicate the large, open wound; she never once used her fingers. Finally, the younger nurse rewrapped the wound with cotton and long strips of fresh gauze. I followed them from bed to bed as they repeated this important sanitary routine on soldiers, patiently attending to their ghastly, torn body parts.

"Nurse! Please, nurse!" A soldier suddenly yelled from the far end of the ward while trying to pull himself to a half-sitting position in his bed. "There's a swelling on my leg. I can't stand the pain. Will you please look at it as soon as you can?"

The older nurse walked quickly to the complaining soldier and, with her forefinger, examined the ballooned red-and-purple, walnut-size spot on the man's leg. She turned to her young partner and said, "Go upstairs and get me a sanitized knife; this thing is filled with pus and all of it has to be cut out right away."

The younger nurse hurried out and returned in a few minutes with a surgical knife wrapped in a white cloth. Once again, standing close on the opposite side of the patient's bed, I watched the older nurse use her forefinger to determine the best place to make the incision; and she quickly slit the swelling with the knife and a large amount of white pus splattered out, some of it splashed my face.

Smiling at the soldier for withstanding the obvious pain, the nurse carefully cleaned the wound and filled the hollow area with clean gauze and then she taped several layers of more gauze over the entire wound.

I was awed by the nurse's competence and what she had just accomplished. How I wished I could do that with the same kind of deftness displayed by the exemplary nurse.

That night, I went home from work totally exhausted, still questioning my ability to do the demanding hospital work. Bless Anoush! She cheered me with her genial encouragement that it would get easier day by day.

Early next morning, I went back to the hospital with Anoush and continued to help her in the wards, mostly lifting patients on top of bedpans.

"Vergeen? Are you Vergeen?" The question came from a girl who had entered the ward.

"Yes," I replied with some trepidation.

"The director would like to see you."

I followed the girl upstairs and I felt a sinking sensation as we walked through a wide, clean corridor leading to large rooms on the left and glass-enclosed offices on the right. Through the glass, I could see two, conversing nurses in white uniforms covered by white aprons. The director was seated at a desk in front of them in her official uniform; and she was the only one wearing a strange-looking, white starched high cap on her head.

The messenger told me to sit in the outer office and she left. I waited and waited, anxiously observing that the nurses were glancing at me as they talked behind the glass window. Eventually they came into the outer office and I stood up nervously to acknowledge their greetings.

"This is the girl I've been talking about," the director said. She then introduced me to one of the nurses. "I'd like you to meet Annah."

Annah looked me up and down, and the expression on her face clearly told me she was dubious about my ability to do the work they wanted to have done.

"She looks very young; I'm not sure she can do the job."

Vartanoush disagreed immediately."I know she's young, but I believe she's capable of doing the work."

Annah spoke with Vartanoush a few more minutes before gently

The Hospital

taking my arm. "Come with me down this corridor."

We entered a large room with several water basins resting on long counters against one wall and four couches on which patients were either prone or sitting. A line of several other patients stood against the opposite wall waiting to be treated. I noticed a smaller, empty adjoining room which had one couch in the corner.

As soon as I entered the large patients' room, I recognized the two efficient nurses I'd seen the day before and we exchanged smiles. They were in the midst of preparing their medication-and-bandage trays to dress the wounds of the bedridden patients in the various wards.

Oh, my God! Am I going to be assigned to the same kind of duty? My feelings were mixed; I was both delighted and scared. The director had faith in my ability to do the job, but was I really capable of handling such an immense responsibility?

"Come in here." Annah beckoned me from the empty room. "Go wash your hands and come back."

When I returned, she asked, "Why are your hands dry?"

"I wiped them with the towel next to the basin."

"NO! You must not dry your hands."

Realizing her firm tone was unwarranted, Annah softened her voice. "Go and wash your hands again. This time, use lots of soap and water, and be sure to brush your fingernails inside and out with one of the clean brushes in the dish on the counter. When you're through washing, look for the bowl filled with red-colored liquid; it's a disinfectant called *fusmanganet*. Dip both hands in that solution and let your hands dry naturally."

Annah interrupted herself to introduce me to another nurse who had entered the small room. Her name was *Orghen* and she was a pretty, cameo-skinned girl with auburn hair.

"You'll be working together in this room," Annah informed us, and she ushered in the first patient whose entire forearm was bandaged.

"Take off the bandage," Annah continued her instructions.

"Check to see if it's free of pus or blood. If it's clean, roll the bandage you removed and get it ready to replace on the patient's arm. We're short of bandages." Annah pointed to a basket filled with soiled bandages. "Throw the dirty bandages in here so they can be washed."

Fully aware of Annah' scrutiny, I removed the yards of bandage carefully from the patient's arm and, noting the absence of pus and blood, I rolled the bandage and waited for further instructions. Meantime, Annah used an instrument to pull of several sheets of bloodied gauze from the wound; she cleaned the injured area, applied medication, and covered it with fresh gauze.

"Before we can bandage this man's arm, you'll have to clean around the entire area of the wound, Vergeen. There's the bottle of disinfectant and get a clean wash cloth off the shelf."

I dripped a few drops of the disinfectant on the cloth and carefully wiped the man's arm, looking up now and then to see if Annah showed any satisfaction of my work thus far. I saw nothing in her face that would give me even a hint of approval.

"Now, Vergeen, watch Orghen. She'll do what I just completed. You'll continue what you've done here so far. Go from patent to patient and remove the bandages, see if the bandages can be reused, throw the soiled ones into the basket and roll the others for reuse, and clean the areas around the wounds with disinfectant."

Annah stopped, looked at me cursorily and asked, "Do you get sick at the sight of blood or pus?"

I shook my head. I thought about my experience the day before when I watched the nurse slit open an infected leg and the pus had splashed on my face. I'd done well, I thought; I never got nauseous.

Annah left and the line of patients started to enter the small room one by one. The wounds of the soldiers, on every part of their bodies, were results of bullets or shell shrapnel. Helping Orghen, I followed Annah's instructions and, after an hour or two, I became a little more confident in performing my job until I tried to wrap a wound on a man's heel. It required a clean, fresh bandage which came loose several times no matter how hard I tried to secure it. Luck was not with me, I got far behind in my end of the work. I just could not get the bandage to stay on the patient's foot.

I looked up to see if I could catch Orghen's eye for help when I noticed Annah was watching me. Her stare made me so nervous that my hands started to tremble.

When I saw Annah walk toward me, I feared I was going to be dismissed. "Please, God! For once, help me!" I muttered, "I need this work."

I relaxed a bit when Annah came alongside me and smiled sympathetically.

"Don't be frightened. You're doing fine, Vergeen. I sent that patient to your room to see how you could handle it. A wound on the heel of the foot is very difficult to wrap. Now, let's take off this bandage and start over."

Patiently, Annah showed me how to start and secure the bandage properly on the man's foot. "Take off the bandage and rewrap it as I've shown you."

Finally, I completed the wrapping correctly. I was so grateful to Annah for her kind forbearance and I kept thanking her the rest of the morning. She'd pat me on the head and assure me that I was doing well.

Later that morning, Annah brought an older nurse to my work area. "This is *Nartouhy*, your supervisor. If you need anything or if you have any complaints, just go to her."

Nartouhy wore a large, white apron and a stiffly starched, white cap perched squarely on her head. She was short, quite lame, and so obvious about her displeasure in supervising a young neophyte like me. Even though I smiled in the hope that she'd return it, Nartouhy stood motionless, unsmiling while checking me head to foot. To me, her whole demeanor conveyed an imperious attitude. I disliked her immediately.

Both Annah and Nartouhy were Armenian, and they were graduates of an American nursing school. Annah served as the chief nurse in the surgical unit and Nartouhy headed the general department called the *Pansement*, a French term describing the various first-aid and follow-up treatments required in healing the injuries of patients.

Nartouhy often spent long hours in the hospital's main room, working closely with the doctors and their more seriously wounded patients. Her firmness and scrupulous attention to her nursing duties scared me a bit, yet I admired her reverently for her professional proficiency. Wanting to learn all I could from this extraordinary woman, I stayed late with Nartouhy several evenings to help her and to do her bidding – clean the instruments, scour the basins, scrub the floors.

I soon realized my initial impression of Nartouhy was totally wrong. Her seemingly tough exterior masked a compassionate nature which she exhibited infrequently. I was stunned when I learned she was truly fond of me and that she had a great deal of faith in my ability to fulfill my assignments. And I was even more surprised later when she asked me to take charge of one of the bandaging rooms. Our eventual friendship meant a great deal to me.

All nurses were paid exactly the same: two loaves of small, round breads everyday; and, each month, we received two bars of soap, one pound of granulated sugar, half of a freshly slaughtered lamb, and one *midijia* which was almost equivalent to a dollar. One loaf of bread was enough for me and, since bread was not available in shops, I sold my second half to a nurse who had children at home.

After a few weeks, I left the Bardizbanian home to live at the hospital and each evening I ate with the hospital employees, mostly soldiers. The meals consisted of different soups from leftovers of the food prepared for the doctors and upper echelon staff.

"I'd like something different once in a while," I complained to my supervisor, Nartouhy. "I can't go out and buy food; there's no place in the hospital where I can do my own cooking."

"Ask Dr. Sertabid; he's the hospital administrator. Ask him if you can work out another arrangement for your meals."

Nartouhy's suggestion paid off. Dr. Sertabid offered me a way to get the same hospital meals served to the medical staff if I'd relinquish half of my hospital earnings as payment for the better meals. I accepted happily and, when informed the meals would start the next day and they'd be served on trays brought to me in the nurses' room, I was even more delighted. The aroma of the well-prepared meals evoked the envy of the other nurses who had homes where family members waited for them for their evening meals. Unfortunately, they were unable to buy the ingredients to duplicate the hospital's food because so many things were scarce or much too expensive to purchase. Yet, many kinds of meat, fruits, vegetables and breads were made available to the hard-working medical staff.

Even though I'd adapted well and was gratified by my life in the hospital, I became absorbed again with self-torturing thoughts of Joseph. I hadn't heard from him for months. Where was he? Why hadn't he written to me? Why had he abandoned me? I brooded night and day over these vexing questions without answers. I tried to hide my anguish in fear of revealing my painful emotions to the other nurses, and I'd seldom take part in their off-duty activities in the nurses' room. Instead, I kept to myself and always made excuses for not being able to spend time with my colleagues. Often I'd take the last shift of night duty so that I wouldn't have to engage in conversations with the women or answer questions about my past.

Nearly fifty of the hospital's nurses went home after work each day unless they were scheduled for one of the two night shifts: from five in the afternoon to midnight, and from midnight to seven in the morning. Sometimes a nurse would pay me take her place on night duty if, for some reason, she had to be home that night. I welcomed these opportunities for extra work. Not only did they provide me with more money; but, more importantly, they afforded me sublime protection from my co-workers who were inquisitive about my wish for privacy.

I spent my leisure hours seated on the balcony outside the large window of the nurses' room, and I'd often get lost in my gloomy reverie, staring silently at the enormous fig orchard below. I'd search and search for some sign, some explanation of Joseph in the tall, fig trees; and I'd empathize with their curving branches, heavily laden with clumps of the sweet figs. Those poor trees are also burdened, I'd tell myself; but theirs is a fruitful experience, mine is worthless without Joseph.

There was only one bed, a double-bunker, in the nurses' room; and, since I lived in the hospital, I always slept in the lower bunk. Sometimes, different night-duty nurses would occupy the upper bunk. Late one night, a tall young woman entered the half-lit room. Still awake and pondering about Joseph, I sat up when I recognized the nurse I'd admired so much on my first day when I watched her drain and dress a nasty, pus-filled wound on a soldier's leg.

She inquired genially, "Is anyone sleeping in the upper bunk? I just got off duty and I need some sleep before I head home. Is this upper bed vacant tonight?"

"Yes." I didn't want to answer any more questions and turned my back.

As I started to lie down on my pillow, she spoke in Armenian. "I'd like to introduce myself. My name is *Serpouhi – Serpouhi Kalayjian*."

Embarrassed by my rude behavior, I turned around, sat on the edge of the bed and managed a smile. "I'm Vergeen Kalendarian."

"Like you, I'm an Armenian refugee who's fortunate to still be alive," she said. Getting no response from me, she tried a more exuberant approach. "We're lucky to have jobs here, don't you think?"

I nodded in agreement. Then feigning fatigue, I excused myself politely and laid my head back down on my pillow.

"I'm scheduled for several more nights of late duty this month, but I don't like to walk home so late each night after I finish my duty. So I plan to stay in the hospital until daylight, and I'll probably be using the upper bunk quite often."

"That will be nice," I mumbled as I heard Serpouhi quickly

undress and climb to the upper bunk.

Serpouhi was back the following night and, when she discovered I was still awake, she indicated she'd like to chat a bit.

"Where are you from?" Serpouhi started our conversation.

"Kayseri."

"The city?"

"Yes."

"That's very interesting. I come from the nearby village of Everek. Have you ever been there?"

"Oh, yes!" I felt a slight surge of energy when hearing she came from the town I loved to visit with Mama. "I have an uncle, my father's brother lived there with this family." Sadly remembering my dear Uncle Melkon, I said: "I don't even know if they're still alive."

"Are your parents alive?"

"No."

"Have you any brothers or sisters?"

"No. I have no one left. I'm all alone."

"*Aman! Ahdee shad tzhvareh!* (Oh! That's so hard!) What terrible losses we've all suffered! My mother and I are the only ones left since our deportation from Evereg. We started out with ten family members."

Serpouhi hesitated; her eyes misted.

I thought of Mama and I wanted to change the painful subject.

"How long have you been working at this hospital?"

"Almost six months. How long have you been here?"

"A little more than three months."

"When were you forced to leave Kayseri?"

"In September of 1915. That's more than two years ago, but it seems like a hundred years ago. So much has happened. So much misery." I found myself sadly remembering Kayseri and I wanted to erase my thoughts quickly. "Serpouhi, when were you deported out of Everek?"

"A month before you – in August. I'll never forget it. It was August 19."

Both of us became silent for several minutes, deep in our sweet recollections of our homes and the good life we once had.

Serpouhi spoke again. "I can tell you were a captive of the Arabs. I'm so sorry you had to go through that horror. How long were you with them?"

"I have no idea of the exact number of days or months I lived with those people in the desert, but I think it was about a year."

"Oh, my dear. How awful! Did you escape or were you rescued?"

"I managed to escape on my second try." Shaking my head in agitation, I remembered the cruelty heaped upon me by Yousuf and his wife, Aneche.

"Why did you have to go through such agony? Why were all of us – all Armenians – made to suffer so much?" Serpouhi also began to show her anger. "I've lost my faith in God, Vergeen. How could He have allowed the massacre of our people?"

I didn't want to talk anymore. Suddenly, I remembered my darling Mama again and Aunt Elimon and Sarkis *agha* and Melanie and Vartouhi and Senat; and I remembered the pregnant woman whose belly was slashed by the fiendish guards who spitted her bloody fetus on a bayonet. I remembered Armenag, my betrothed of so long ago, and how Mama always talked about my life with him when he returned from America. Would I ever see him again? Then I thought of Joseph and his mother and his arrogant, unyielding sisters. An icy chill overtook my body.

"Are you feeling ill?" Serpouhi seemed genuinely concerned when she saw I was shivering. "Can I get you some water?"

"No. I guess I'm just tired. Maybe I should try to sleep now."

"Yes. I'm tired, too. *Keshare paree* (Goodnight)."

Our conversation had aggravated my memories, especially of Joseph; and I lay awake most of the night imagining we were together again, walking blissfully hand-in-hand under the glorious fig trees and pausing frequently for tender embraces, for ardent kisses as we lavished each other with our love.

Oh, Joseph! We were so committed to each other! We made so many plans to spend our lives together! What made you change? How could you forget me?

I turned my face to the wall and tried to muffle my sobs in my pillow.

"Vergeen, what's the matter?" Serpouhi jumped down from the upper bunk and sat on the side of my bed. "Are you sick? Is there anything I can get for you?"

"No. I'll be all right. I'm just a little upset."

"It's my fault, I'm sorry. I know, talking about our past is so very painful. And it must be terribly hard on you. You've gone through so much."

Serpouhi thought I was thinking about my massacred loved ones; yet, I couldn't tell her I was weeping because of Joseph. Despite all his professed love, he'd deserted me.

She stroked my hand in a comforting gesture, and I drew my hand away. I wanted to be left alone so I could wallow in my misery.

Bewildered by my odd behavior, Serpouhi returned to her bed. I did not see her for a while.

The following week I had great difficulty controlling my growing depression and, to conceal my troubled mind, I busied myself with my duties. Once or twice, during our leisure hours, I joined the other nurses in conversations in the hopes of seeing Serpouhi. But I didn't see her that week. I missed her.

Several nights later, I heard a gentle knock on the wall. "Vergeen, are you awake?" It was Serpouhi. She had just completed her work on the first night shift and she wanted to sleep for a few hours before going home.

I was so glad to see her and, for some inexplicable reason, I hoped we could talk a little before she went to sleep.

"Are you feeling better?" Serpouhi asked as she sat in the room's lone chair to remove her shoes and stockings. "You weren't feeling so well when I was here last week."

"I guess I'm better." My halfhearted answer brought Serpouhi to the side of my bed and she sat down on the edge.

"What's wrong, Vergeen? The girls think you don't like them because you always shy away from us. But I think it's because you're so depressed. What's the matter?"

I shook my head as a huge lump gagged my throat. "Nothing. It's really nothing." I could not reveal my feelings about Joseph, not to anyone.

"Vergeen, I'd like to be your friend. Maybe talking about what's bothering you will help greatly. I believe there's more to your hurt than the dreadful things you've been through during this terrible exile. Won't you please tell me what's troubling you?"

I turned my face away from the wall and looked for understanding on Serpouhi's face; I could see she was genuine in her compassion, in her desire to help me. Her wistful smile and misty eyes imparted the encouragement I needed to shed my armor of silence.

I told her about Papa, about Armenag, about Mama and how she died so brutally at the hands of the Bedouins. I told her about Yousuf and Aneche, about Melanie and Vartouhi. And finally I told her about Joseph and how he had deserted me because of his family.

It felt so good to talk, to unburden myself. Still, I could not stop weeping, saying over and over again. "I have no one left."

Serpouhi reached out and clasped my hands. "Vergeen, *khentrem* (please) consider me your close friend." Tears filled her large, dark eyes as she said: "*Yerpeck chemornas* (Never forget)! If ever you need anything or anyone to help you or just to talk, please know I'm here. I'll be here for you – always."

I put my arms around Serpouhi and held on tightly. I'd found a devoted, steadfast friend – someone who understood my pain, someone who cared what happened to me, someone who had extended her hand and heart in deep, abiding friendship that would span a lifetime.

TWENTY

Serpouhi

I valued my close friendship with Serpouhi. She had a rejuvenating effect which helped so much in conquering my despondency. Consequently, I took greater pride in my work, and I enjoyed chatting with the other nurses during our off-duty hours. Nearly seven years older than I, she was a warm and gregarious person who, despite the painful loss of her own loved ones, evinced a vivacious disposition.

Like all Armenians deported from their homes, Serpouhi had experienced all of the exile's barbarities – famine, thirst, disease, death of family members. During the many hours we'd spend talking, Serpouhi told me about her life before we met.

She was the lone remaining child of four children born to *Maryam* and *Haratoon Kalayjian* in Fenese which was the twin village of Everek, my favorite town. Her two brothers had died during childhood and her older sister had died during the exile's second year. Serpouhi's mother was her only genocide-surviving relative; and she believed her father, a sales agent for several exporters of Turkish goods, was still in Buenos Aires, Argentina, where he'd gone on business a year before the deportation orders were announced.

"I'm glad he didn't try to get back; he'd have been killed. Every day, I think of him and pray he's safe somewhere in South America. If fate is kind, I'll see him someday," Serpouhi said hopefully.

Unlike her sister, *Makrouhi*, who never attended school and married at a very early age, Serpouhi completed seven years of schooling at the Girls' School of Fenese.

"I loved school! I just wish I'd continued," she said in discernible regret. "I was stupid not to insist on going to school until I graduated. But I wanted to go to Everek and live for a while with my *moreyeghpyr*, my mother's brother. He had a large, bustling household. My darling grandmother lived there and so did lots of my other relatives. Besides, I loved being with my uncle's daughters who were close to me in age."

Serpouhi paused and asked: "Did you ever hear of my *moreyeghpyr, Krikor Ohanian?*"

Before I could shake my head, she continued. "He was one of Evereg's most prominent men and he had a very successful import-export business. My uncle was a close friend of Evereg's *Kaimakham,* the town's mayor. In fact, they were just like brothers."

"What happened to your uncle?"

"He convinced the authorities that he and his family had accepted Islam, and he stayed behind in Evereg with most of his family."

Pensively silent for a few minutes, Serpouhi spoke softly, "I wonder what's happened to *Boghos.*"

"Who's Boghos?" I was curious.

"My betrothed. We became engaged before he left for the United States in '09, and we always wrote letters to each other until this deportation mess started."

I'd already told Serpouhi about my negotiated betrothal to Armenag when I was not quite eight years old, and we wondered if our fiancés lived near one another. We didn't know the distance between Wisconsin where Armenag lived, and the strange-sounding Con-nec-ti-cut where Boghos had settled.

Serpouhi told me she'd first seen Boghos at the home of a close friend who, at the time, was engaged to Boghos' best friend.

"I'll never forget that Sunday. A lot of young people gathered to celebrate Boghos' return from Smyrna where he'd just been released after many months of political imprisonment. Oh! There was so much joy in that house on that day. Everyone was so carefree!"

Serpouhi laughed impishly in remembering the events at her friend's home. "Boghos has a wonderful personality and he was the center of attention that entire day! You should hear him sing! He has a glorious voice and he sang a lot of our favorite songs that day. And, Vergeen, you should have seen him dance the *zehbeck* – you know, the Greek dance where the men slap the back of their heels while twirling!"

"Oh, yes!" I remembered seeing Papa dance the *zehbeck* once.

"Well, Boghos grew up in Smyrna. You know how modern people from that city are. That's why I think he's so bold because he wasn't the least bit bashful about asking me to dance with him."

"*Aman!* What did you do?" I gasped.

"I said 'yes', of course! I wasn't going to pass up the chance to dance with him. After all, I was just thirteen years old and, I've got to tell you – I was a real rebel. But our dancing together became the scandalous talk of the day because – as you know – it's forbidden for unmarrieds to dance together, even when there's no touching."

Serpouhi quickly rose from her chair and simulated her dance with Boghos. "He snapped his fingers to the music as we circled around each other while I tried to sway my hands and arms like this."

"Oh, that's wonderful!" I applauded as I watched Serpouhi glide gracefully around the room with her arms stretching out to the ceiling.

"Did you see him often?"

"Only a few more times when our friends got together for picnics. I knew he liked me by the way he always smiled and asked, '*eench bess ess*' (how are you)?"

"What happened? How did you end up getting engaged?"

Serpouhi's effervescence and exuberant story-telling fascinated me and I wanted to hear more about her fiance.

She told me Boghos was born to the large *Mikjian* clan in Evereg, but he'd spent most of his youth in the family's nail manufacturing business in Smyrna on Turkey's west coast. After the death of their father, Boghos joined his older brother, *Garabed*, in the business and they built it into a highly successful enterprise.

A great concern of the brothers, however, was the deteriorating political atmosphere for Armenian subjects in Turkey. During the years preceding the genocide, both Boghos and Garabed, like their

Mikjian clansmen, secretly supported the *Dashnaks*, an Armenian nationalistic party. But they all paid dearly for this affiliation when one of the Mikjians fatally ambushed the son of a Turkish general. Every member of the Mikjian clan, including Boghos and Garabed, was arrested and imprisoned for a year or more. Yet, the cousin who provoked all the turmoil managed to escape to Switzerland.

There were growing rumors that many *Dashnak* supporters might be arrested again, so Garabed urged his young brother to go to the United States for a while until Turkey's political climate stabilized. Thus, right after his release from prison, Boghos went to his family home in Everek so that he could secure the necessary papers to leave Turkey.

Totally exasperated one day because he could not cut through the obstacles impeding his access to the necessary documents, Boghos dashed into the headquarters of Everek's *Kaimakham* and complained angrily. He noticed the delighted astonishment of a white-bearded, blue-eyed man who was seated next to the all-important *Kaimakham*; and Boghos was enormously encouraged when he heard the distinguished-looking gentleman say: "I really like your audacious spirit, young man. Whose son are you?"

The elderly, influential gentleman was Serpouhi's *moreyeghpyr* (mother's brother), Krikor Ohanian, and he helped Boghos get his papers that day.

"Before Boghos returned to Smyrna, he came to the house to thank my uncle for his help and to say goodbye." Serpouhi recalled sentimentally. "I saw him very briefly that morning. We just exchanged smiles."

"But what happened next? How did the betrothal come about?"

"Well," Serpouhi began slowly and her face creased into a sly grin. "Six months later, two of Boghos' relatives came to my uncle and asked for my hand. And, without even consulting with my parents, my uncle immediately said: 'Yes! I really like that young man! I think he'd be a great husband for my niece.'"

Still grinning, Serpouhi said: "Can you imagine how my parents felt! They were very angry at my *moreyeghpyr!* But as the family's venerable patriarch, he kept reassuring my parents about Boghos and finally convinced them that this was a great match for me."

Serpouhi shook her head remembering her own reaction. "I cried for a week after the *ghoskgob*, claiming I didn't want to get married even though, secretly, I really liked Boghos a lot. But I didn't understand what he saw in me. I was only thirteen, too young for marriage, I thought; and he was a twenty-one year-old, worldly young man from a big city. Besides, I wasn't even physically matured yet either. I was much too tall for my age, I was very skinny and really a little homely."

I couldn't believe the picture Serpouhi drew of herself. Now, at twenty-two, she was enviably curvaceous, engagingly attractive and elegant in her bearing.

"Vergeen, I wish you could have been there when Boghos' family brought me a large gold coin on a chain – you remember, the customary engagement gift. Boghos was not with them; he was in Smyrna. My cousins and I went into the parlor to greet them and, as we bent to kiss their hands, I heard a woman whisper: 'Which one is Boghos' fiance?' And someone answered: 'I think it's that tall, skinny girl.'"

Serpouhi burst into cackling laughter. "Then I heard someone else say, '*Khetch deghan, eeraghan varav!* (Poor boy! He really got burned!') But I guess Boghos didn't mind that I was so thin and awkward. Later on, his sisters told me that he was very insistent with his mother. He told her he wanted me for his wife and no one else."

"*Aman!* You mean – he went against his mother!"

"That's right! She was the one who'd insisted he get engaged to someone before leaving for America because she figured it might make Boghos return home in a few years. But I wasn't so sure. Actually, I was angry at my uncle for promising me to someone who was going to be thousands of miles away and who may never come back."

"Did you see Boghos before he left?"

"No! It's been more than nine years since he left for America, and I really don't believe he'll ever return to this part of the world. Sometimes I wonder if I'll ever see him again," Serpouhi reminisced sadly.

"But I must tell you, Vergeen, I nearly had a chance to be with him. Just before the war started, Boghos wrote to his brother, Garabed, who was not yet married then. Boghos warned him about the troubles spreading through Europe which might even effect Turkey. He urged Garabed to leave as soon as possible and to take me with him to France where Boghos planned to meet us and escort us to America. He even sent the passage money! But, unfortunately, Boghos mailed the money in care of his mother. I think she was so afraid Garabed would also end up in America that she gave away all the money. It was a lot of money. She gave it all to a cousin for some crazy business venture."

"*Aman*, Serpouhi, how awful!"

"I know. It just breaks my heart when I think about it, and it's not just because I missed a chance to escape the horrors of the massacre. It's mostly about Garabed. He was a kind, wonderful man! A tall, gentle giant – really a prince! He stayed behind to take care of the family's business when he saved his brother's life by insisting that Boghos leave for America. Of course, at the time, his poor mother didn't know it but by stopping Garabed from going to America, she condemned him to death."

When the plan to go to America crumbled, Garabed, now in his mid-thirties, had married a spinster from Evereg. For safety reasons, he'd thought it best to return to the business in Smyrna while his pregnant wife remained in the care of her family. Near the time of the baby's birth, he'd sneaked into Evereg from Smyrna to see his wife and newborn son. But, within days, he was spotted and arrested.

Enormous tears flowed from Serpouhi's eyes as she remembered Boghos' heroic brother. "I saw him a month before we were deported. *Asvatz!* (God!) It was terrible! He was shackled to a dozen men, and they were being led slowly by the Turkish guards right in front of our house. I could see that he'd been tortured badly by the guards who may have tried to force some information from him about the underground activities of the Armenians. The tops of Garabed's bare feet were cut and grotesquely swollen from the acid poured into his wounds. His fingernails were torn from his hands. Blood was spurting from his head and face. Yet, when he saw me, he managed a smile and shouted: 'Serpouhi, please tell my family I'm being taken to Kayseri where we're told we'll be released.' But, Vergeen, we both knew he was headed for the gallows."

Serpouhi told me her uncle heard of the perils facing all Armenians in Turkey long before anyone else did in Everek. Through his close friendship with the town's *Kaimakham,* Krikor learned about the deportation plans of the Turkish leaders. Yet, to avoid alarming his family, he told no one about the Turks' plot to exterminate all Armenians. Acting swiftly to save the lives of all his loved ones, Krikor insisted that Serpouhi's mother and sister move from Fenese into his home since both their husbands were still in South America. Then, for the protection of everyone in his household, Krikor duped officials into believing his family had converted to Islam. Furthermore, he continually bribed officials to stop them from arresting the young men in his family – his only son, *Sarkis,* and his son-in-law, *Haji Sahag.* Thus, both escaped the fate of the town's other able-bodied young men who eventually were killed.

In her haunting reminiscences, it was obvious that Serpouhi worshipped her uncle. "The rest of us knew something was terribly wrong during the early summer of '15 because my dear *moreyeghpyr* suddenly became very depressed, and he'd sweep away our concerns with a wave of his large hand. Still, we all sensed disaster, especially when many of the town's Turks boldly started to explore marriage possibilities with young Armenian girls. In fact, my uncle saved me from one persistent Turk by claiming I was already married to a man in America.

"By mid-August, when word came that we had to vacate our

homes within the week, *moreyeghpyr* tried desperately to dissuade all of us from leaving. Every day, he'd beg everyone to stay. Over and over again, he told us we'd be safe from harm only if we remained in his home; otherwise, we'd surely die on our journey to nowhere. *Myreek* (mother) and I were certain he was right! We wanted to stay. But the two Christian fanatics in our family – my sister, *Makrouhi*, and my cousin, *Gulu* – fiercely refused to listen. *Moreyeghpyr* pleaded with his daughter and my sister to pretend they'd accept Islam, they didn't have to practice it. They refused to listen. Those two were so stubborn. Instead, with supreme confidence, both Makrouhi and Gulu claimed Jesus would protect them from all harm.

"Finally Myreek decided she had no choice. I agreed. We could not let my sister leave without us. And my unrelenting cousin, Gulu, was repeatedly warned by her husband, *Haji Sahag*, about the hazards the exile held for her especially since she was in her second or third month of pregnancy. But he, too, failed to convince his obstinate wife of the folly of leaving."

Serpouhi paused to blow her nose and wipe her eyes. "Myreek as well as the rest of us honestly believed that, after spending a few wretched days on the dusty road, Makrouhi and Gulu could be persuaded to return home. So, ten of us left my uncle's home that hot August morning. In addition to Myreek, Makrouhi and me, there was Gulu, her husband, Haji Sahag, and their adorable four-year-old daughter, *Rosie*. Then there were four members of Haji Sahag's family, including his aunt and her small son, his sister and her little girl who was a beautiful three-year-old.

Beset with emotion, Serpouhi sat down before continuing. "As we headed out of Evereg on our donkeys alongside our deported friends, we heard our Turkish neighbors jeering: 'Farewell, Christians! Your vineyards are ours now!'

"Within a few hours, our caravan met up with two hundred other *Everegtzee* families And, for several days afterwards, we tried so hard to convince Makrouhi and Gulu that we should go back home. After a while, we just gave up and continued on our miserable march toward Syria."

Bitterly, Serpouhi recalled the subsequent months of abject savagery and degradation: the long, forced marches through muddy terrain with swollen feet sinking into the bellies of the dead; the constant pillaging by hordes of civilian Turks; the merciless abduction of young girls who were raped or sold to harem masters; the frequent self-burials by frightened girls in bundles of bedding in order to foil discovery as the suspicious guards plunged their sabers through the bundles in search of hidden girls.

Serpouhi was reminded of her good friend, *Markarite*. "Months before we left Evereg, this poor girl refused to marry a neighboring Turk who hounded her day and night with his pledge of love. When she and her mother started on the exile with our caravan, that young man followed us on horseback for two days until he was able to drag Markarite out of her tent and toss her on top of his horse. An elderly neighbor of ours screamed and grabbed the horse's tail, trying to stop the abduction. But the guards clubbed that sweet, old man to death. Four nights later, the Turk who'd claimed so much love for Markarite returned her, completely naked, and dumped her in front of her mother's tent. That poor mother! That poor girl! She couldn't eat or sleep or even speak. She got morbidly despondent. A few weeks later when our caravan camped near a river, Markarite slipped away unnoticed and killed herself by drowning."

Remembering how she was able to thwart sexual assaults, Serpouhi said: "I was lucky. My cousin's husband, Haji Sahag, did everything he could to protect me. He made sure I darkened my face with soot or mud every day, that I concealed myself under beddings in our tent. And he was also aware that the guards were only interested in young virgins, so he spread the word throughout the camp that I was married. That's how I was safe for a while until we reached the outskirts of Aleppo. Otherwise, I may have suffered the same fate as *khetch* Markarite."

In our inevitable exchange of holocaust experiences, Serpouhi and I discovered we'd both traveled for months, mostly by foot, over the same mountains and through the same towns and villages before reaching the huge refugee camp outside Aleppo in the late fall of 1915.

"My pregnant cousin must have been in her seventh or eighth month when she suddenly became seriously ill," Serpouhi recalled sadly. "Immediately, Haji Sahag bribed some officials so that he could take his wife to Aleppo for medical attention; and he took his daughter, his sick sister and his little niece with him while the rest of us stayed behind in the refugee camp."

Serpouhi's gaze fixed on her clenched hands. "Well, Haji Sahag returned alone a week later with the sad news that Gulu had been unable to withstand the trip and both she and her baby died en route. He'd come to take us back to stay with him in the room he'd secretly rented in Aleppo from a sympathetic Syrian family. This kind Christian family had agreed to look after his daughter and the others until he returned.

"We were crushed by Gulu's death. She was the first one we lost in our group and, honestly, our situation was so hopeless that some of us wished for death, too. You know how that is, Vergeen, don't you? But we had to go on for the sake of the three children in our care.

"All of us stayed in that one, crowded room for weeks. Not only were we afraid for ourselves, we were apprehensive about the safety of the Syrian family who'd helped us because a new government order warned Syrian citizens that anyone caught harboring Armenian refugees would be severely punished.

"In the midst of our constant fear of being discovered, we lost two more members of our group – Makrouhi and Haji's sister, *Eskoohi*. First, my beloved sister bled to death after losing her diseased uterus while urinating into a pan. Then, later that same night, we lost Eskoohi. She just couldn't go on any longer. In her last words, she begged my mother to take care of her little girl, saying she trusted no one else, not even her brother.

"We had two sheets left from all of our bedding and we used them to wrap my dead sister and cousin. While it was still dark, I helped Haji load their bodies on the horse-drawn wagon which passed by the house each day before dawn to collect corpses."

Serpouhi paused to draw a deep breath. "I'll never be able to get that sight out of my mind. I'll never forget my anguish as my grieving Myreek and I watched the bouncing bodies of our loved ones until the wagon disappeared."

Serpouhi stopped abruptly. "*Neroghutyun!* (Forgive me), Vergeen. I can't talk any more right now," she apologized, dabbing her eyes. "I'll finish the rest of my story during our off-time tomorrow. Let's have some tea."

The next day, resuming her story, Serpouhi told me how Haji Sahag, now a widower with a small child on his hands, stunned her with a marriage proposal.

"I loved little Rosie like she was my own child and I assumed the responsibility for her care after Gulu died. But I just could NOT agree to marry her father. NO! Not my dead cousin's husband! I just couldn't! Even for Rosie's sake, I couldn't. Myreek was just as much against such a union as I was. But Haji did not take too kindly to my rejection and I think Myreek and I paid for it later on. Oh, we really paid for it!"

Serpouhi described how her mother and Haji Sahag bickered bitterly about his sister's little girl. He insisted on taking his niece to the orphanage in Aleppo while Serpouhi's mother argued passionately to keep her solemn promise to the child's dying mother.

"Myreek was so distraught," Serpouhi described her mother's despair. "She kept telling Haji that she'd made a sacred pledge to his sister and that she swore on the cross to take care of her child. But he insisted he knew what was best for the child, claiming she was HIS blood kin, not Myreek's. So, he stormed off, carting his little niece to the orphanage.

"Haji returned two weeks later just to inform us that a wealthy Swiss couple wanted to adopt his niece, and he indicated that he planned to stay with the couple."

"The next day, we learned the Swiss couple had also offered to help Haji's relatives get the necessary permit to remain in Aleppo, but Haji told the couple he had no one else except his daughter."

"That's terrible!" I was appalled. "That was an awful revenge because you refused to marry him!"

I felt an angry contempt toward a man I didn't even know. How could he have forsaken his relatives with whom he'd shared so much misery, so much deprivation, so much grief all those months of exile? Suddenly, I was reminded of my own abandonment by Joseph! The reasons differed, but the painful impact was absolutely the same.

Serpouhi continued. "The wonderful Syrian family hid the remaining four of us for a while – Haji's aunt, her son, Myreek and me. When we heard the soldiers were going from house to house searching for refugees, we managed one night to slip back into the refugee camp on the city's outskirts."

Serpouhi covered her moist eyes with her long, slender fingers. "*Aman, Asvatz*! That was the worst part of all those months of misery! There were rows and rows of tents where thousands of deported Armenians existed in indescribable squalor, waiting and waiting and waiting for fate's next blow. The suffering was unbearable for all of us, especially for Haji's aunt and little boy. Both died within a week after we left Aleppo."

Although spent emotionally, Serpouhi continued to describe the intolerable conditions: the long months of famine, the gruesome epidemics, the growing number of dead.

Serpouhi ran her fingers through her thick, black hair. "And there were the miserable lice – *aman*, millions of them! Myreek and I had to shave our heads several times in trying to get rid of them."

Standing up to pace around the room, Serpouhi stopped and looked up at the ceiling and, in a quivering voice, avowed: "To the day I die, I'll NEVER, NEVER forget those babies!"

Still pacing, Serpouhi kept threading her fingers through her hair. "In the tent next to ours, there must have been forty to fifty tiny orphans – not one could have been more than a year old. They were starving, mostly sick infants left alone to die. Their pitiful cries were unbearable! Myreek and I as well as other refugees tried so hard to go into that tent, but we were always pushed back and beaten by the guards."

Serpouhi looked toward the ceiling, fighting back the stream of tears. "*Asvatz* (God), where were you? They were BABIES! Precious, innocent babies! You didn't even allow them the loving touch of an adult during their last hours."

Exhausted, Serpouhi decided to continue her story another time. A week went by before we sat down again to talk about our holocaust experiences.

Serpouhi described the fearful night she and her mother succeeded in escaping the destined extermination of the encamped Armenians by slipping unobserved back into Aleppo, to the home of the same Syrian family who'd helped them before.

"They were kind, caring people," recalled Serpouhi. "They really saved Myreek and me. They kept us hidden in a closet-like room for over a year. They fed us and protected us until it became safer for Armenians to emerge from their hiding places."

The improved conditions in Aleppo made it fairly safe for refugees to look for work. Thus, soon after leaving the Syrian family, Serpouhi found a job at the military hospital as well as a place to live for her mother and herself.

"I'd like to meet your mother one day," I told my friend.

"I'll make sure you do. Myreek is a sweet, loving person. I know you'll like her and she'll embrace you like you're her own child."

Talking about Serpouhi's mother, I longed for Mama. My heart ached as I remembered the last time I saw her – how she kissed me on the cheek, how gently she tucked the coverlet around my shoulders, and how calmly she told me to go back to sleep. Glorious, but poignant memories of my darling Mama filled my dreams every night that week.

While living at the hospital, I continued to spend many more hours with Serpouhi, talking mostly about what we'd do after the war. One afternoon, almost six months after we first met, Serpouhi dashed into the nurses' room to share her great news.

"I've just been told I'm getting a new assignment," she said straining to catch her breath.

"What will you be doing? Her excitement was contagious.

"I'm the new head nurse in the *Pansement* section!

"Eench eskancheli lur! (What wonderful news!)"

I was happy for my dear friend. I knew she'd be one of the best head nurses the hospital ever had.

TWENTY-ONE

The War Nears End

"I hear the British are getting closer," Nartouhy told us one day in mid-November of 1917. The news made us all uneasy because we were unsure of what the British takeover would mean for the Armenian refugees working in the Ramanazania Army Hospital.

The perpetual signs of the battle lines moving toward Aleppo appeared daily in the increasing numbers of wounded soldiers filling the hospital's wards, especially the seriously injured men who required extensive medical care. As the number of wounded grew, the need for surgeons and additional equipment became imperative.

Dr. Sertabid, the hospital's administrator, sent word to government authorities that the hospital needed more medical personnel and equipment – urgently! And he ordered the total conversion of the nurses' quarters into a surgical unit.

At first, all of the nurses – including Serpouhi and me – silently bemoaned the loss of our peaceful leisure room with its large window and balcony overlooking the splendid fig orchard; but our resentment vanished with our precise focus on expanding assignments and our need to adjust, as quickly as possible, to all the new hospital equipment.

One morning, in my rush to keep up with my new schedule, I bumped into Dr. Sertabid in the second-floor corridor. He grinned and gently grabbed my arm.

"Slow down, girl. We have enough patients. We don't need to have one of our nurses become a patient, too." Then, examining my face closely, he said, "You don't have to tell me how you got those tattoos. I know what happened to you. Tell me, would you like to have them removed?"

"YES! Oh, yes," I exclaimed, unable to conceal my joy at the thought of having the ugly markings on my face erased. Dear God,

I thought, please make it possible.

"When we finish fixing the operating room, I'll see what can be done. I'm sure you've heard that Dr. Jamal will be coming to the hospital in a few days. He's an exceptionally fine surgeon; he's highly experienced. Let me check with him."

The happy thought of freeing my face of the hideous brands etched by my captors was almost more than my emotions could handle. I wanted the surgery RIGHT AWAY! I could not wait to be rid of those ghastly, blue reminders of my servile life with the Bedouins! You must be patient, I kept telling myself. Just BE PATIENT! They'll all be gone soon.

A few days later, Dr. Jamal joined the hospital staff. He appeared to be a gentle, mild-mannered man in his middle years. I wanted to rush up to him and ask when he could schedule surgery for me; but I wavered, mindful of the protocol which demanded that, as an employee of the hospital, I wait at least a couple of weeks before approaching him about any possibility of surgery on my face.

One morning during his second week, Dr. Jamal stepped into the nurses' room during one of our brief rest periods. "I know it's your off-time," he said, "but will someone please help me in the morgue?"

"Why does he need our help there?" I murmured to the older nurse next to me.

"I really don't know why," she answered, shaking her head. "I think that's where they bathe the corpses. I believe it's a requirement of the Muslim religion. The dead can't be buried until the *Hoja*, the cleric, bathes them first."

I visualized the strange ritual in my mind. Curious to see it and, more importantly, anxious to use the opportunity to discuss my own problem with the noted surgeon, I raised my hand before anyone else had a chance.

"Do you know where we're going?" Dr. Jamal realized I was the youngest member of the nursing staff and he wanted to make sure I was prepared for what was in store for me.

I nodded as we entered a large, dimly-lit room. In one corner, there were two big, black sinks where the Hoja was praying as he washed one of the corpses stretched on a narrow table.

Wanting to impart some levity into this gruesome scene, Dr. Jamal looked at me and whispered: "The Hoja is praying for each corpse one at a time, but not one of the dead soldiers is listening to him."

I smiled only to let the doctor know I acknowledged his little humor.

"Doctor, I believe this is the one you want." The Hoja pointed to another corpse on a table and dragged the table close to the window.

Dr. Jamal turned to me. "This solder died last night," he started to explain. "The poor man had a rapidly growing tumor in his brain. I think it's a rare form of tumor."

Hesitating a moment, Dr. Jamal asked: "Have you ever seen anything like this before?"

"No, but I'm very interested," I replied sincerely; but I had little self confidence in my ability to witness what I realized was going to be an unpleasant carving of a corpse's head.

"Well, I'm about to make an incision right here." Dr. Jamal bent over the corpse and then suddenly looked up at me. "If you can't take it, you'd better tell me now."

"I'm sure I'll be fine, doctor."

"All right. Stand by and hand me the instruments I ask for, beginning with that small knife."

Starting from the dead man's forehead, Dr. Jamal slit a wide opening up to the top of the head, and he proceeded to dig deep into the brain. I felt queasy, hoping the procedure would not last long. Working rapidly, the doctor requested certain instruments by pointing to each one on the table and he specified his findings in medical terms. Even though I did not understand a single word, I was totally riveted by his probing procedure.

"This is one way we doctors can learn about rare diseases," he said looking up at me. "You seem to be fascinated by what I'm doing."

"Yes, doctor. I've learned so much today."

Later that afternoon, I told my colleagues in the resting room: "You should have been there! I actually saw what a brain looks like."

"That must have been very interesting. Did it bother you to see Dr. Jamal open the brain?"

"Not one bit!" I lied. I didn't dare let my friends know that I felt a little nauseous and quite uneasy during the doctor's entire procedure.

The increasing number of casualties coming from the battlefront strained the hospital's entire staff, especially the surgical unit. Dr. Jamal was forever dashing back and forth to keep up with his rigorous surgery schedule. One day, I saw him resting in the hallway outside the surgical room and, seizing my opportunity, I approached him.

"Excuse me, Dr. Jamal. Did Dr. Sertabid speak to you about me?"

"Yes, he did," he said, conveying a genuine wish to help me. "But I must tell you that I'm not that kind of a surgeon. I've never removed tattoos from anyone's face before. I've seen only one special surgeon do such an operation. It involved cutting each tattoo and patching over it with skin peeled from other parts of the body."

Noting my disappointment, Dr. Jamal tried to explain the difficulty of the surgical procedure and the possible harmful consequences. "I'd like to tell you that I'd be willing to try removing those marks. But, unfortunately, serious infections sometimes follow this kind of surgery, and this hospital is not equipped to treat such infections."

I was thoroughly disheartened when I heard him conclude: "Really, Vergeen, it's best to leave those tattoos alone. Risking your life is not worth it, believe me. Forget about any surgery."

I was crushed. Crushed deeply! Why did I think removal of the tattoos would be simple? Why had I been so optimistic that any surgeon could blot out the ugly marks on my face? Get used to it, I told myself bitterly. You'll have to live with them to the end of your days. I shuddered at the thought of continuing to look at those marks in the mirror every day.

I brooded haplessly for a few days until our nursing supervisor announced the start of a special class on the fundamentals of nursing, and, fortunately, I was among several staff members selected to attend. For an hour each day, we were required to take copious notes as Dr. Sertabid lectured us in Turkish. This was awkward for some in our class whose knowledge of the Turkish language was meager, and several of them dropped out of class because they could not understand the lectures.

I was lucky; I was fluent in Turkish. Besides, I loved the challenge of learning. Usually, I spent my rest period each afternoon to study in the second floor bandage-dressing room; and sometimes I'd hear Dr. Sertabid and the chief nurse making their daily rounds. A little apprehensive about using the room for study, I hoped they would not disapprove.

One afternoon, from the corner of my eye, I saw a long, white coat float by; and, for one fearful moment, I thought it was Yousuf looking for me. Yes, it's Yousuf, I said to myself. I'd better hide.

"Don't be frightened. I came here to see what you're doing."

Relieved, I recognized Dr. Sertabid's distinguishable voice before he came through the door.

"I'm working during my rest period," I said, edgy that I might be breaking a hospital rule. "I hope it's permissible for me to study here."

Nodding slowly, Dr. Sertabid smiled and left.

Three weeks later, a message from our supervisor indicated that three of the nurses were summoned to Dr. Sertabid's office – I was among the three. As we entered the empty office, a boy was delivering three small boxes; he put them on the desk and quickly left.

"Do you know why we're here?" We murmured to each other,

fearing a reprimand of some kind as Dr. Sertabid walked in. His bearded face wrinkled into a wide smile, and I relaxed.

"Three weeks ago, I wanted to check on the working habits of the nurses," he said, still smiling. "And I noted that you three – yes, the three of you were still working on your breaks. I thought such hard work deserved to be rewarded."

He reached for the boxes which had just been delivered by the messenger and he presented one to each of us. Stunned, we stood for a moment before thanking the good doctor and we walked out of his office, eager to find out what was inside the box. Each contained a pound of cubed sugar – a veritable treasure during wartime.

※ ※ ※

The battlefront was getting closer to Aleppo, and our hospital bulged with the seriously wounded. Frequently, space was unavailable for those with minor injuries, so they were bathed, bandaged and sent to Turkey.

Repeatedly, Dr. Jamal urged the authorities to supply the hospital with critically needed x-ray equipment; but the helpless government was unable to fill the need. Finally, Dr. Jamal's persistent search resulted in the acquisition of an x-ray machine from the Germans who sent an engineer along to install the equipment.

After two days of work on the difficult installation, the German engineer offered to train a technician to operate the machine.

"Does anyone here speak German?" Our chief nurse asked us the day after the installation. No one answered.

"The engineer knows a little French. Does anyone speak French?"

"I do! I can even read and write French," I boasted brazenly.

"All right, Vergeen, you'll work in the x-ray room from now on."

I was thrilled with my new assignment. I loved having a new challenge! Neither the engineer nor I was proficient in the French language, yet we managed to communicate well, mostly through gestures and our reliance on the pictures in the instruction manual. Regularly, Dr. Jamal would join us to learn more about operating the machine; and, when the engineer left, I was assigned by the doctor to be his all-around assistant in the x-ray room. I relished the work and I was elated that Dr. Jamal had so much confidence in me. Those were uplifting times for my self-esteem.

※ ※ ※

The advancing battlefront caused chaos in our hospital: disagreements erupted daily between the administration and other hospital personnel on how to handle the enormous increase in patients; inexperienced young doctors and medical students were summoned to help treat patients; and dozens of untrained aides were hired to assist the overworked nurses. Still, the whizzing turmoil continued unabated.

"We're expecting still more patients from all over the occupied territory," our chief nurse, Nartouhy, cautioned us one morning at a special meeting. "The hospital is depending on those of you who are more experienced to do whatever you can to make sure every patient receives the proper care. You must also supervise the aides; make certain they do their jobs well."

Although always efficient and generally soft-spoken, Nartouhy was beginning to show the effects of the hospital's frenetic activities. It was especially noticeable that day when she adjourned the meeting before completing her report.

"Wait! Come back. I have another announcement," Nartouhy shouted. "Nurses are needed immediately to volunteer for duty on the battlefront. Of course, you're not forced to accept such an assignment, but you may want to consider it because it pays a lot more."

Nartouhy scratched her head with a pencil and added, "And there's always the chance you might win a medal for bravery."

There was no response to Nartouhy's call for volunteers until I raised my hand and everyone in the room gasped, surprised and shocked at my ready willingness to risk my life.

"*Khent es, eench es?* (Are you crazy?)" Serpouhi confronted me angrily after the meeting. "What's possessed you? If you go to the front, you're bound to be killed – maybe on the very first day! Vergeen, *khentrem*! Please give up this ridiculous notion."

I was obstinate. "But, Serpouhi, I'm not going to be right at the front. I'll be behind the battlelines providing first aid for the wounded."

"You're being very foolish, stupidly naive!" Serpouhi's impatience turned into consternation when I refused to be persuaded.

Nartouhy was equally concerned. "Why do you want to go to the front, Vergeen? Tell me. What's so noble about going to the front and risking your life? Are you looking for medals?"

"It's not for any glory," I told her in an earnest attempt to explain my bold decision. "I figure if I get to the front, I might be able to escape into the British territory. And that way I'll be free, free of Turkish persecution in the years ahead. I don't care what you and Serpouhi say; I'm going. The British are Christians; I know they'll help me."

"My dear girl, don't you understand!" Nartouhy was exasperated by my intractable behavior.

"In a few months, the British and the French will be all over this country, and we'll all be under their control."

"How do you know that?"

"Just ask anyone. The British will soon be knocking on our doors here at the hospital."

Within a few days, the wounded transported from the front included soldiers of the Allies as well as Turks and Germans. It was yet another confirmation of the advancing British, and I was finally convinced that duty on the front lines could be a horrible mistake.

Were it not for the wisdom and efforts of my two best friends – Serpouhi and Nartouhy, I probably would have gone to the battle front and died along with the doomed soldiers.

TWENTY-TWO

Peace Comes to Aleppo

The daily stream of incoming wounded continued around the clock. The hospital crews – everyone of us – became accustomed, even hardened to the frenzy of long hours, rare rest breaks, and the unending stretches of cots cradling the injured warriors in the crowded, noisy corridors.

I had a hard time keeping up with the demands of Dr. Jamal for the development of the x-ray films in preparation for various surgery on patients. One morning, carrying an important set of films for the doctor, I tiptoed carefully into the surgical room and was stopped immediately by a medical student.

"That's Vergeen! She's got the x-rays for me." Dr. Jamal sounded harassed. "Give her a coat and mask so that she can help."

A husky man lay on the operating table flanked by Dr. Jamal and his helper, Dr. Ahmat, along with two surgical nurses, and the male anesthetist – a young Armenian named Dr. Vahan.

Quickly, an orderly helped me put on a white coat and mask, and then he pushed me to the corner sink for the mandatory, antiseptic scrub of the hands and arms.

"Stand at the foot of the table, Vergeen, and grab that swollen leg by its ankle as soon as the patient goes to sleep." instructed one of the nurses.

Dr. Jamal waited until Dr. Vahan administered the chloroform before charting the amputation area just below the knee, and he motioned me to hold the patient's ankle.

I had a hard time watching the procedure, and turned my head away a few times. But I still noted how carefully and efficiently Dr. Jamal worked with his surgical team, first cutting deep around the area to be amputated, then pinching and tying each blood vessel before using a saw to complete the amputation.

For a moment, I stood petrified; my unblinking eyes fixed on the man's severed leg hanging from my hand. Instantly, an orderly grabbed the decayed limb and threw it casually into a large trash bin in the next room.

"You did just fine," Dr. Jamal patted me on the head. "Maybe I'll ask for your help again when we need it," he said as he walked out of the room.

Being a helper in the operating room was intriguing, I told myself at bedtime. But, for a while, I preferred not to witness another amputation.

The young Armenian we called Dr. Vahan was actually a medical student assigned to our hospital for his practical training. We worked together in the x-ray room occasionally and we'd exchange views about what the war's end was going to mean for all the Armenians in Aleppo. I discovered he was a hard-working, ambitious young man – qualities I greatly admired in a person.

He was curious about my goals and one day asked me: "What's your ambition in life, Vergeen? What would you like to do?"

"To be a midwife," I said, quite innocently.

"I'll bring you some books on the subject."

Vahan returned the next day with two books. "Read these in your spare time. I'll help you anytime with any questions you may have."

The books contained material far too advanced for my comprehension, and I decided I had no time to pore over them. Besides, I found Vahan was becoming much too attentive, much too obvious about his romantic feelings toward me; and I wanted to discourage him as quickly as I could in case he misinterpreted my friendship as a prelude to a romantic relationship.

I avoided him as much as I could until he stopped me in the corridor one afternoon. "I haven't seen much of you lately; are you evading me?"

"No. I just think you really should concentrate on your studies," I replied.

Fortunately, he was a bright young man; he understood I didn't share his feelings.

※ ※ ※

Within two months, the hectic atmosphere in the hospital began to dissipate, yet we could hear the far-off sounds of the war. Soon after, the number of incoming wounded soldiers declined and suddenly many of the staff were absent. One day, Dr. Jamal disappeared and, the next morning, all the other Turkish doctors were gone. Inside of a week, most of the medical staff was replaced by new physicians, two of whom were Armenian. One was a native of Aleppo, and the other came from my home city of Kayseri. He knew my father well and occasionally he'd stop me in the corridor to chat.

Still remaining was the hospital's administrator, Dr. Sertabid. He sent a message that he wanted to see me. I headed to his office immediately and saw him angrily engaged in a heated discussion on the hospital's lone telephone outside his room.

He turned to me and muttered: "Wait for me in my office." Visibly upset, he continued on the telephone for several more minutes before ending his important call. The harried doctor dropped into his chair and spoke rapidly. "Vergeen, the enemy is advancing fast."

Thank God, I said to myself; but I made certain I showed no joy.

"I want you to get ready to leave with me. We'll pay for your transportation, and you'll still get the same wages or probably even more."

"Are the other nurses going, too?" My question was really a stall so that I'd have time to think of a way to avoid leaving.

"No. Just you!"

"But, doctor, if the other nurses are staying, I want to stay here with them." I started to worry. Could he make me go with him?

"Listen to me!" His commanding tone startled me. "This is an army hospital and you're considered a soldier here. When the army orders you, you GO where we say you go!"

Dr. Sertabid stood up and pointed his forefinger at nurses passing by his door. "We don't need those nurses. We need you! You have to operate the x-ray machine; so wherever the x-ray equipment goes, you go with it."

I needed an alibi quickly. "I'm sorry, Dr. Sertabid; but I can't leave my aunt and uncle."

"Don't try to fool me! You have no aunt, no uncle, no other relatives here. I know you live in the hospital."

I was trapped. What could I do now? I needed a way out of this situation before I was forced to go back to Turkey with the Turkish doctors.

"Get ready to leave tomorrow." Dr. Sertabid's admonishing voice ended any more thoughts of faking excuses.

Throughout that sleepless night, I tried to consider my options. I almost panicked when I realized I had none unless I just left the hospital. But where could I go? I had no place outside the hospital.

The following morning, with my courage waning, I went to my regular work station in the x-ray room. All the equipment was GONE! Peering outside the dark room, I saw large crates and figured the equipment was being readied for shipment.

My heart thumping, I walked nervously to Dr. Sertabid's office and peeked through the corner of the glass window to see if he was there. Someone else was sitting in his chair, giving instructions to a group of unfamiliar men in white coats, plainly a new team of Syrian physicians.

Not daring to interrupt the new medical personnel, I returned to the x-ray room, wondering what I should do. For nearly two hours, I shuffled papers on the shelves, but mostly I watched and listened as the new medical staff assumed their duties.

Fear leaped inside me again when the man who'd been sitting at Dr. Sertabid's desk entered, and asked: "Are you wondering what happened to the x-ray equipment? As you can see from those crates outside, the equipment will soon be on its way to Adana in Turkey. So, there's nothing for you to do here."

A tall, pleasant-looking man, much younger than Dr. Sertabid, the new Syrian administrator surveyed the room and looked at me again. "Where did you work before you started here in the x-ray room?"

"In the bandage-and-dressing room, doctor."

"Then go back to that room and resume your duties there."

Thank, God! I did not have to go to Adana! My joy escalated as I almost skipped down the hall to the bandaging room.

❈ ❈ ❈

Wild rumors buzzed through every corridor of the hospital, alleging atrocities by the Black soldiers serving in the victorious British Army. Although false, reports about the pillaging of homes and the raping of women in villages near Aleppo terrorized all the nurses. And since Ramanazaria Hospital was located on the city's outskirts, many of the nurses dreaded the travel to and from their homes for fear of being assaulted; and some never returned to their jobs.

There were, however, grave concerns emanating from reports of the British bombing areas outside Aleppo and that the hospital may be too close to most of the targets.

One late afternoon that week, Serpouhi came into my room.

"There are too many rumors flying around about this hospital being bombed and what the British soldiers are doing to the villagers," she said. "I don't know if all the rumors are true or not; but I'm going to listen to my worried mother, and I'm quitting my job today. Honestly, I don't think it's safe to stay here."

"Oh, NO!" My heart sank; I was going to lose my dear friend.

"You can't risk staying here either," Serpouhi said firmly.

"I know. But, I have no where else to go."

"Vergeen, listen. I've already discussed the matter with my mother and I want you to come home with me. I've told my mother all about you and I'm sure she's going to let you stay with us. So, hurry and pack some things. Let's leave before it gets dark."

I was so grateful to my friend. I just hoped her mother would accept me. In case she didn't, I just bundled a few clothes to take with me. We walked at least five kilometers before reaching Serpouhi's residence within the city limits of Aleppo. The building reminded me of the houses in Kayseri with a similar entrance from the street into a large courtyard. The building had several doors which led to different living quarters housing mainly refugee families.

Serpouhi ushered me down a few stairs on the far left side of the building and we entered a small room. Immediately, my eyes focused on three steps leading to a tiny indoor balcony; yet it was large enough to accommodate a fair-sized bed. An elderly woman, rocking in a wooden chair, kept staring sullenly at Serpouhi and me.

"Vergeen, this is my mother," Serpouhi said; and I turned to be greeted by a smiling, lovely woman with delicate features and nearly snow-white hair.

"*Hrammetsek, zhakess,*" she said warmly. "Welcome, my child. Consider this your home."

"Thank you. You are so kind to me," I said in profound gratitude. Although older, she reminded me of my own mother and I wanted to wrap my arms around her.

"My mother's name is *Maryam*," Serpouhi explained. "And that woman in the balcony shares the rent with us for this room. Her name is *Annah Doodoo*."

I remembered that *Doodoo* was a Turkish word, usually tagged on to an older woman's name and considered a term of respect for a mother with adult children. Even though everyone called Serpouhi's venerable mother by the name *Maryam Doodoo*, I decided that I preferred to call her by the endearing Armenian word for mother, *Myreek*.

Serpouhi and her mother began preparations for the evening meal. On the roof, a very small flat area, about two-by-four feet, was used for cooking. Myreek cooked over a fire she lit in a large tin can while Serpouhi spread a clean cloth on the floor and on it she placed three forks, three pieces of bread and a small jug of water. I don't remember exactly what we ate that evening; perhaps it was because I was more engrossed in the wonderful, warm conversation I enjoyed with my friend and her mother.

Annah Doodoo had finished her supper before we did; and she remained seated, still sullen, watching us from her balcony.

"We call that place the throne," Serpouhi whispered to me, suppressing a great urge to giggle.

We'd not yet finished our meal when Serpouhi began to speak in a loud voice: "Yes, Myreek, the purpose of Vergeen's visit tonight is to consider whether she can live here with us."

I realized Serpouhi's comments were meant for the ears of the unfriendly balcony dweller, Annah Doodoo.

"Vergeen wants to leave the hospital for the same reasons I do," Serpouhi continued. "As you know, Myreek, we think it's rather risky for refugees to keep working there. So, I'd like Vergeen to stay with us as long as it is acceptable to you and Annah Doodoo –"

Myreek interrupted right away. "My child, of course. You're welcome to live here with us. I'd like to think that you're replacing my oldest daughter who died not long ago during this wretched *oxor*."

The generosity of this gracious woman touched me deeply. "I'm truly grateful that you wish to look upon me as your daughter," I said. And I wanted her to know how much I hoped she would accept me in a similar way. "I think Serpouhi must have told you that I lost my mother more than two years ago. I wish you'll allow me to consider you as my Myreek."

Tears filled both our eyes as our conversation revived memories of our loved ones, and we were silent in our recollections for several minutes.

Lowering my voice to avoid being overheard, I said: "Myreek, would you please ask Annah Doodoo if she would mind if I shared your quarters with you and Serpouhi."

When asked the question, Annah Doodoo paused and answered, "I really don't care if she lives here as long as she stays in your part of the room. But, I want the rent divided into three shares instead of two."

"Oh, I'll be happy to take care of my part of the rent." I was glad the woman in the balcony raised no objection. I think she rather liked the idea since it meant she'd be spending less for her rent.

"Myreek, I also want to split other living expenses with you and Serpouhi."

I was delighted that the arrangement satisfied everyone, even the balcony dweller. The only thing left to complete my move was to return to the hospital in the morning to resign from my job, and to collect the rest of my belongings.

"I don't know if I can carry everything by myself," I told Myreek.

"Don't concern yourself," she said. "I'll be at the front gate tomorrow afternoon to help you bring your bundles back here."

That was settled, too; except I could not fall asleep the first night. I was too excited about my new home and my wonderful, new family. I kept thinking of my incredible good fortune. Here I was, sharing their only bed. Serpouhi and I lay at the head of the bed while Myreek was in between, on the opposite side. As I tossed during that sleepless night, I was very careful not to hit dear Myreek with my active feet.

Returning to the hospital next morning, I bundled all my things before reporting to work; and I went to see the administrator to tell him I was quitting my job. When he asked why I wanted to leave, I told him I was frightened by all the rumors about the bombings and the British takeover of Syria.

"Nonsense, actually this is the safest place you can be during these crucial days." The Syrian administrator was surprised by my reasons for leaving the hospital.

"As you've probably heard," he said, "all the Turks are gone.

They've gone into the interior or they returned to Turkey. This is no longer the Ramanazaria Army Hospital; it's a Red Cross facility now and it's been renamed the Elalhamad Hospital. In fact, there's a huge white sheet bearing the Red Cross insignia on the roof to alert all the British war planes that THIS is a Red Cross building. So, we're very safe here."

The administrator waited for me to say something before he went on.

"It's true we don't have many patients anymore, but I plan to keep the nurses who are willing to stay and I'm going to increase their wages. Of course, I can't compel you to work here; but, if you change your mind, you're always welcome to come back."

I was determined to leave at the end of my shift at five o'clock. Before departing, I said my farewells to my colleagues, some of whom had also planned to quit that week. And I promised Nartouhy I would try to visit her as often as I could. She had agreed to remain as the chief nurse under the hospital's new administration

As she'd promised, Myreek was waiting for me at the gate, watching patiently while my exit was approved by the guards. She grabbed one of my heavy bundles and we walked slowly and silently toward my new home.

Once again, my young life was changing. Although only sixteen, I felt I'd lived a long time, through many enforced adjustments. What was going to happen next? I kept reminding myself: at least you've found a lovely family.

"I'm really happy that you'll be living with us," Myreek broke the silence. "I honestly feel you're like a daughter to me. You know, Serpouhi was very upset when her sister died. I'm so glad she has you now; and I hope you'll always be like sisters to one another."

"I promise we will, Myreek," I replied. "I've admired Serpouhi from the first day we met and, ever since then, she's been my best friend. I know we'll remain close until the end of our lives."

Serpouhi was waiting for us when we reached home. That night, we had cheese and bread for supper; it was a feast for me with my new family.

The following morning, Serpouhi and I lounged in bed while Myreek prepared breakfast. How pleasant it was not to report for work; we talked, giggled and ate leisurely, enjoying every second of our relaxation. Nevertheless, we understood our leisure would be for a short time only and we'd have to find other work.

The British occupation of Syria was imminent, and all the Turks in wartime governmental positions had already fled with their families. The Syrians, especially those who were Christian, looked forward to the takeover by the British and some even boldly announced plans to welcome the conquerors.

Two weeks after I left the hospital, Myreek came home with the news that the British would be entering Aleppo that Sunday. Excitedly, she described the festivities planned for the British soldiers' scheduled victory march. "You should see the decorations on the shops, up and down Aleppo's main street, the Babul-Tarash. A friend of mine is going to let us watch from her building's rooftop. What an opportunity to see history!" Myreek's excitement seemed to mount with her every word.

Serpouhi loved the idea of watching the parade of the victors; but I was skeptical, secretly afraid of the Black soldiers in the British Army. For some inexplicable reason, I compared them to the sun-darkened men I knew in the desert – like Yousuf.

"Come on! This is a historical occasion. Let's go and watch." Serpouhi was insistent and convinced me I had nothing to fear.

I was glad I joined the revelers who greeted the occupying forces on Babul-Tarash street that Sunday morning. All the shops were closed; large crowds lined the festive streets for miles; and even more people, mostly women and children, were jam-packed on flat rooftops. Busy gendarmes on horseback tried to keep the streets cleared and held back the jubilant crowds behind wooden barricades.

By ten o'clock that morning, we heard music and the parade started with the passing of artillery trucks followed by other trucks full of cheering soldiers. Then Black soldiers shouldering rifles marched stalwartly ahead of a large band of uniformed musicians and endless rows of other soldiers. It was a joyous sight, especially for Armenian refugees whose bursting hope for unbounded liberation centered on the conquering Allies.

"Thank you, thank you," I told Serpouhi, intoxicated by the sights and sounds around me.

"I'm so glad you insisted that I come with you and Myreek to witness the occupation. I'll never forget it."

Although we realized we'd eventually have to find new jobs, Serpouhi and I enjoyed our leisure for the next few weeks and we indulged ourselves with sight-seeing and shopping in occupied Aleppo. Since we shared all expenses, we'd been able to save some money to buy dress fabrics and new kinds of food items which had not been available in the shops before.

Three weeks after the occupation, one of the doctors Serpouhi had known at Ramanazaria Hospital sent a message asking to see her. A Syrian-Armenian who specialized in venereal diseases, Dr Emil was starting his own practice and he wanted Serpouhi to work for him. He'd also been authorized by the government in Aleppo as the city's official physician responsible for providing the compulsory monthly, medical examinations of the licensed prostitutes.

"It's a good job, and the salary is going to be very generous. So, I agreed to work for Dr. Emil," Serpouhi told Myreek and me. "I just have to wait until he finds the right office space."

A few days later, Serpouhi received a note from Dr. Emil saying he'd located an office and he wanted her to see it before he rented it.

"It's a nice, four-room house with a big kitchen in the back on the second floor." Serpouhi could barely contain her enthusiasm. "Dr. Emil is going to use the large front room as his office and, instead of moving his own family into the house, he said he wanted to give Myreek and me the rest of the rooms to live in rent-free. Can you imagine! We don't have to worry about paying rent!"

Before I could ask about my situation, Serpouhi hurried to tell us the rest of the good news.

"I told him I was delighted to accept, but a young girl – just like my sister – is living with us; and I asked if she can stay in our part of the house with Myreek and me?"

"What did he say?" I was concerned, yet buoyed by Serpouhi's euphoria.

"That wonderful man said: 'Of course!' Just think, we can get out of this place and live together in a real house with a real kitchen."

We settled into our relatively spacious quarters the following week. Perhaps the happiest one was Myreek who finally had her own small bed while Serpouhi and I slept in the larger bed in the room.

On many of Serpouhi's off days, we'd visit our friend, Nartouhy. She'd decided to remain at Elalhamad, the Red Cross hospital which had continued to operate under the auspices of the Syrian government.

"I really miss you girls," Nartouhy would often say. "Let's have a photograph taken of the three of us so that we'll never forget one another. I'm afraid that once you locate your family members, you're not going to remain in Aleppo. You're bound to go your separate ways – maybe you'll even go to America."

I disagreed emphatically. "I don't know about Serpouhi, but that will never happen to me. I have no relatives left; except maybe my step-uncle. I think he's still in Egypt."

Luckily, the three of us had our picture taken together by a professional photographer. It's the only memento I have of Nartouhy, and I've treasured it.

Even though I was comfortably situated with Serpouhi and Myreek in our rent-free living arrangement, I tired of doing nothing and, besides, my money supply was dwindling. I wanted to work, but I was in a quandary about the kind of job I could get.

※ ※ ※

When the war ended, thousands of Armenians poured into Aleppo from Damuscus and the Arabian Desert – in fact, from all over Syria. The vast influx of refugees strained the capacity of Aleppo's small Armenian Church and the ability of its clergy to help the genocide survivors relocate. At the same time, the governments of the Allied forces ordered the Turks and Arabs to return their captives, both girls and boys who'd been sold to harems and to the nomads, so that they could be reunited with their relatives. And the Allies obtained the cooperation of the Syrian authorities to provide temporary housing for the refugees.

The unoccupied army barracks were converted into shelters for the refugees. The armory became a dispensary and it was equipped with beds, medicine and supplies. Nartouhy as well as several other members of Elalhamad Hospital's staff began to work there, administering to the needs of the sick every day.

Regularly, Sunday after Sunday, Serpouhi and I would accompany still devout Myreek to the Armenian Church. However, for Serpouhi and me, the purpose was not to pray nor to attend mass, but to see if we could find our lost loved ones among the new refugees being cared for by the clergy. (My faith in religion destroyed, I hadn't prayed or gone to church since fleeing from my Arab captors; and my aversion to prayer has continued since then.)

I hoped I'd find some family members of my Uncle Melkon or my Aunt Veronica or that I'd see Armenag's parents, Elimon and Sarkis agha. But enviously, I'd watch others reunite with their families, and I'd leave church with my spirits sagging at not seeing a single familiar face.

※ ※ ※

Early in the war, the Near East Relief had been established with the dedicated input of Henry Morgenthau who, as the United States ambassador to Turkey from 1913 to 1916, was one of the first foreign diplomats to recognize the Ottoman government's intent to exterminate the entire Armenian population in Turkey. While ambassador, Morgenthau had repeatedly, yet unsuccessfully appealed to Talaat Pasha and Enver Pasha, the absolute despots of Turkey, to stop the slaughter of Armenians. Thus, in continuing his benevolent interest in the welfare of the Armenian refugees, Morgenthau devoted his highly-respected leadership efforts to the work of the Near East Relief.

One of the first missions undertaken by Morgenthau and the other leaders of this relief organization was to establish several child-care institutions as quickly as possible for the tens of thousands of orphaned children whose families had perished. Enlisting the help of established Armenian orphanages, the relief group asked *Reverend Cheradjian*, a Protestant minister and already the administrator of a child-care institution in Aleppo, to open another facility for 2,500 new orphans.

One day Nartouhy sent a message through her nephew that she wanted to see me at her home. It must be important, I thought; Nartouhy must have some good news for me.

"Vergeen, I have a great idea for you!" My dear mentor displayed more excitement than she'd ever shown before. "I heard that Reverend Cheradjian is opening a day school in the new orphanage, and he's looking for teachers. You should apply for a teaching job there."

"How can I? I'm not qualified," I objected. "I don't have the necessary education to teach school."

"Now, don't be scared. There aren't many Armenians who survived the holocaust who know more than you do. Go ahead and apply for one of the jobs! I'm quite sure that you'll be hired."

I was still dubious about my ability to handle a teaching position without any training or experience.

Look," Nartouhy was persistent. "I know a girl who's teaching in one of the orphanages set up by the Near East Relief and, if you're hired, I'll ask her to instruct you on the basics of teaching. Come on! Go down there tomorrow and apply!"

Encouraged by my friend's prodding, I went to Reverend Cheradjian's orphanage the next day and, although not as hopeful as Nartouhy about being hired, I sought a teaching position. I was not alone, ten other young women had the same idea; they looked older and more qualified than I. Some even claimed previous teaching experience; but none had attended a French school. I almost left before my name was called when two or three of the women before me emerged from their interviews smiling, and I assumed all the positions were filled.

The interviewer was Reverend Cheradjian's daughter who asked many questions: "Where are you from? How old are you? What schools did you attend? Have you worked before? Do you have any parents or relatives?"

"My parents are dead, and I'm not sure the few relatives I had even survived the deportation," I explained.

"You know, you're eligible to live here since you're only sixteen. We take care of orphans up to your age."

"Thank you, that's very kind. But I stay with a family." I stressed that what I needed was a job and a chance to earn my own living again.

"I understand," the young interviewer smiled warmly. "Although I've hired all the instructors we need right now to teach Armenian and English, I'm sure we're going to hire more teachers, especially ones who know French. Many, many new orphans are coming to us every day."

I was heartened to hear that I might have a chance for employment at the orphanage because of my knowledge of French.

"Since you went to a French Jesuit School, we can use you. We'll start you out as a teacher's aide next week and, when we're able to secure more space, we'll begin our French classes and we'll assign you to one of them."

I was delighted about finding a good job, but I had anxieties about my need to develop some teaching skills. Fortunately, Nartouhy's young friend, a teacher at another orphanage, agreed to coach me on the basics of teaching; and, finally, I gained enough gumption to start teaching an elementary class.

※ ※ ※

I asked Myreek if she'd help me make new bedding for myself. "Since I'm about to start my new job, I feel I can afford to have my own bed so that both Serpouhi and I can be more comfortable at night. I'd like to have a mattress, a quilt and a pillow."

"I'll be glad to help you." Darling Myreek was always eager to make things easier for Serpouhi and me. "I only know one place where wool is sold and that's at the street bazaar run by the Arabs. It's only open on fridays."

The following friday, Myreek and I walked to the bazaar and ran into large crowds sauntering from stall to stall. Unaware that it was taboo for young girls to be seen there, I was startled by the obscenities being shouted at me by some of the shoppers who also jostled me, pushing me away from a pile of wool displayed in front of a stall.

"Let's go home, Myreek," I grumbled, afraid for both of us; and we began to walk toward the road when a young man, dressed in an Arabic garb, scolded the crowd.

"Haven't you seen a young girl before," he yelled. "Go about your business and leave her alone."

He reached for my arm and said, "I noticed you were looking for wool. Come with me; I have all kinds of wool. I'm sure you'll find just what you're looking for at my shop."

I walked alongside him, dragging uneasy Myreek with me. Aghast at my daring, she whispered, "Vergeen, where are we going with this strange man?"

I assured her that the man seemed honest, and he just wanted to sell me some wool.

The man's shop was filled with numerous grades of wool, and we found exactly what we needed to make good bedding.

"How much is all this?" I was preparing to try out my skills at bargaining, a generally-observed custom when purchasing merchandise.

"Usually, I'd want four mejidia; but for you, it's just three mejidia," was the man's surprising answer. Myreek stared at me wide-eyed, flabbergasted at how little he was asking for all we'd selected.

"I'd like to give you a special price because I know you." He smiled and waited for my response.

"Come, Myreek," I said as I turned toward the door, fearing he was one of Yousuf's henchmen who must have been looking for me. "Myreek, come, please! Let's get out of here!"

"Wait! Don't you recognize me?" The young man followed me. "Let me show you my arm." He pushed up the sleeve of his white robe to show me a long, deep scar marking his entire forearm.

"Remember? I was hit by shrapnel at the front lines and I was brought to Ramanazaria Hospital a few months ago. You were the kind nurse who dressed my wound every day."

Suddenly, I recognized him as the badly wounded soldier whose mangled arm was almost amputated. "Oh, of course, now I remember you! I'm glad to see you've recovered so well."

I thanked the young man for the special rate on my purchases; and Myreek and I headed home, toting the heavy bundles of wool.

As soon as we got to the house, Myreek began working first on the shaping of the mattress; and then she concentrated on sewing the quilt and pillow. I helped her whenever I could, saying little to Myreek except to thank her for her efforts. I didn't dare let her know how impatient I was, waiting for her to finish what ultimately turned into very comfortable bedding.

TWENTY-THREE

Mending Torn Lives

The beginning of the orphanage's school, named *Sabon Kan*, was hectic for everyone, the teachers and children alike. Located on the second floor of a huge building, the school entrance opened into an enormous hallway facing newly converted classrooms, situated side by side along the long, dusty corridor. On this opening day, the hallway was filled with noisy boys and girls as well as the frantic teachers, all waiting for their room assignments.

"You'll be working with *Deegeen Mandouhy* for a while," the principal informed me. I was pleased that I would start as an assistant before facing a classroom of children by myself; and working with an experienced teacher, Mrs. Mandouhy, proved to be a satisfactory arrangement for me.

Although the school was operating fairly well, the unprecedented increase in the number of incoming children soon posed major accommodation problems for Reverend Cheradjian and his staff. There were not enough beds and blankets, not enough clothing and food; and all the newly arrived orphans, most of them famished and contagiously ill, slept on cold floors and drank water, all using a single, eventually contaminated dipper from a pail. The overwhelmed staff, at both the dormitory and school, tried conscientiously to contain the communicable diseases. But, leprosy spread through the orphanage; and several staff members, including me, contracted the loathsome disease from the children. And, unknowingly, I exposed Myreek and Serpouhi to it.

Fortunately, both Myreek and Dr. Emil found ways to help us overcome the dreaded pestilence. Myreek used an effective salve while Dr. Emil medicated us with large doses of a special drug.

While working with Dr. Emil, Serpouhi spent a great deal of time assisting him in the required, monthly examinations of all the prostitutes licensed to work in the city's Red Light district. Since prostitution was legal in Aleppo, the busy brothels were popular haunts for many of the discharged soldiers. Whenever a Red Light girl became infected with a venereal disease, she was denied renewal of her license and prevented from working until she was treated by Dr. Emil and finally authorized to continue her activities.

Serpouhi spoke frequently with compassionate sadness about the young women who had resorted to prostitution to keep from starving.

"Nearly all of these girls are so young, maybe no more than thirteen or fourteen years old," she told Myreek and me. "And many of them are Armenian refugees who were rescued from harems."

Sometimes, Myreek and I saw the young prostitutes enter the doctor's office for their routine check-ups, and we'd wonder if any had relatives who could help them get away from their imperiled environment.

"I really feel so badly for these girls," Serpouhi told us one evening. "There's a particular young girl who calls herself *Rosette* who never smiles; she always looks sad when she comes for her monthly examination. She's really just a child who can't be more than fourteen. You should see her. She's petite and very pretty with long, curly hair and beautiful green eyes."

Serpouhi shook her head, showing her frustration. "It breaks my heart every time I see her. I wish I could do something to get this child out of that awful place."

A few weeks later, while Myreek and I were preparing the evening meal, Serpouhi walked slowly into the kitchen and sank into the room's only chair. We could see she'd been crying.

"What's wrong?" Both Myreek and I knew it was something terrible because Serpouhi seldom allowed herself the luxury of tears.

"It's that sweet girl I was talking about a few weeks ago."

"What happened to her?" Myreek was curious, yet tentative about finding out why her daughter was so upset. "Is she all right?"

"*Voch*, Myreek. No! She's not all right; she's dead."

"*Aman, Asvatz!*" Myreek, always tender-hearted, usually appealed to God whenever she heard bad news.

"Let's go to the other room so that we can hear all about it," I said, escorting Myreek to the bedroom and seating her in our only upholstered chair.

I'd never seen Serpouhi so distraught. Her straight, narrow nose looked like a small, crushed rosebud as she kept wiping it and her tears continued to flow.

"Now, tell us what happened." Both Myreek and I couldn't wait to hear what was upsetting Serpouhi so much.

"Well, Rosette was supposed to come in for her examination yesterday and, when she didn't show up, I checked around to find out why she'd missed her appointment. This morning, I heard from one of the prostitutes who came in for her examination that Rosette was killed two nights ago."

"*Aman, Asvatz!*" Myreek uttered her familiar words once again. "What happened?"

"I just found out," Serpouhi said, trying to compose herself. "You know, don't you, that most of the men patronizing those brothels are soldiers who have just been mustered out of the army. Well, two nights ago, a young soldier went to the place where Rosette worked. He chose her from a line-up of all the young prostitutes and they went up to her room. After having sex, the young man sat down to talk awhile with Rosette; and he found out that she was Armenian who'd been kidnapped and sold to a harem. Since her recent rescue from the harem, she told him, she'd ended up working as a prostitute because she couldn't find a job anywhere else."

Serpouhi stopped to blow her abused nose once again before continuing.

"Apparently, he became very interested in Rosette and they talked a lot more, discovering that they both came from the town of Talas. An Armenian himself, he'd been working here in Aleppo for a long time when he was inducted into the Syrian army. I guess that was around the same time that our *oxor* (exile) started in Turkey."

Serpouhi sat down next to Myreek, still dabbing her eyes, before going on with her story.

"According to what I heard, the young man had talked a lot about his parents, and he'd said he was trying to find out what happened to them. The last time he'd seen his family was several years ago when his little sister was only six or seven years old."

As Serpouhi paused once more to wipe her continually leaking nose, she looked at Myreek and me and caught our horrified expressions.

"Yes!" She exclaimed, "Oh, YES! The more they talked, the young man suddenly realized this girl was his SISTER."

"*Aman, Asvatz!*" Myreek clasped her hands over her mouth.

"I guess he just couldn't deal with the knowledge that he'd just had sex with his sister – and that she was a prostitute. He must have lost his senses. I was told he quickly pulled out his revolver and shot Rosette in the head, and then he turned the gun on himself."

Myreek shook her head and mumbled, "Oh, God! Those poor children."

"*Khetch* Rosette died right away," Serpouhi continued. "But the brother was seriously wounded and rushed to the hospital where he passed away this morning. Before he died, he told the doctors he was very remorseful; he'd lost his head over his shocking discovery."

"How awful! How awful!" Momentarily, I could find no other words to describe my horror.

"I know. God, I feel so terrible that I couldn't do anything about getting that child out of that hell. Maybe if I'd been able to help her get away, she'd still be alive."

"Listen to me." I wanted to help Serpouhi overcome her feelings. "You couldn't have done anything to save her. It's almost impossible to get any girl out of the Red Light district. You know that."

"I know! You're right, but it's so hard not to feel some guilt."

Trying to divert Serpouhi from blaming herself, I asked, "How did you find out what happened?"

"Through Dr. Emil," she explained. "He told me everyone was talking about it at the hospital this morning, and he got all the details from the doctor who'd been with the young man during his last hours."

This incident was a particularly tragic one; but, day after day, we heard about other incredibly sad stories, especially about very young, lone survivors of families who'd perished during the Turkish death marches. Even though the war had ended and the reparations demanded from Turkey by the Allies helped to ease the existence of many of us in Aleppo, it was still extremely hard for the refugees to repair their lives after so much suffering.

After the Armistice, more and more Armenian refugees found their way into Aleppo; and they, along with the rest of us who survived the genocide, expended every energy trying to locate loved ones all over the world – children, husbands, parents, sisters, brothers, aunts, uncles, cousins, even in-laws. And, painstakingly, people shared with each other whatever information they found about the whereabouts of relatives.

One Sunday afternoon, we checked with the Armenian priest for new information and he told Serpouhi that the church had just received a letter from someone in America named Boghos who was looking for his betrothed.

"In his letter, he mentioned that his fiance's name is Serpouhi Kalayjian and that she's from Everek," the priest explained. "So, it must be you this man is looking for. If so, I'm sure you'll want to write to him immediately. Here's the letter with his address."

"Thank you, *Der Hayr*," Serpouhi said, a bit shy about revealing her excitement.

In his letter, Boghos indicated that he'd been searching for her for a long time which pleased Serpouhi greatly; and she wrote to him that same day. Despite the distance for the mail to travel between America and Syria, Boghos' response came surprisingly fast, saying he was so happy she was a survivor. For the next several months, they continued to correspond with increasing frequency.

"We've heard from my father, too!" Serpouhi told me one afternoon. "Myreek and I are so relieved!"

Serpouhi was comforted by the news that he was still safe in Buenos Aires. Since Myreek was unschooled, Serpouhi used a lot of her spare time writing to her father on behalf of both of them; and it seemed she wrote just as many letters to Boghos in America.

I recalled that Armenag lived with his older brothers in a place called Wisconsin; and I wondered if he ever thought about our betrothal years ago. Continually, I checked with the church's clergy who'd become the main source of communication for refugees trying to locate their people; but I found no one who could give me any information about Armenag.

One day, while on my way home from school, I recognized a former neighbor from Kayseri walking on the opposite side of the road. Excited by my good luck, I shouted his name; the elderly man turned, but he was unable to identify me until he came closer.

"Oh, my GOD! Vergeen, *aghcheekes* (my girl), is that you?"

I nodded and we hugged tightly. For a brief period, we answered each other's queries about our lost family members, and then I asked if he'd heard anything about Armenag's parents.

"No, I'm sorry, I haven't heard anything," my neighbor said solemnly. "Weren't you engaged to marry their youngest son, Armenag?"

"Yes, but, unfortunately, I don't know how to reach him in America."

"I think I can help you find him. I'm sure my brother-in-law, who lives in America, knows where Armenag and his brothers live. Give me your address and I'll mail it to my brother-in-law so that he can let you know how you can reach them."

I'd found a way to contact Armenag! I was so happy! I couldn't wait to hear from the brother-in-law in America; and when I finally got his letter, I was disappointed to discover he'd sent me the address of Armenag's brother, Krikor. Immediately, I wrote him a short letter, telling him a little about my situation and expressing regrets that I could not find information about his parents despite my efforts to check on their whereabouts.

In less than a month, I received an answer from Krikor who wrote: "Armenag's not here. He's in the United States Army waiting to be discharged. But, I'm writing to him today to let him know you're alive; I know he's going to be very glad to get the news. Meantime, I'm mailing some money for you in care of the Bank of Aleppo; watch for it, the money should get there shortly."

I was elated! And I was ecstatic when a letter arrived from Armenag just ten days later with another check. I wasted not a minute in sending him a long letter, thanking him for the money and giving some details about my circumstances since being exiled from Kayseri.

Careful to make it strictly a friendly letter, I didn't want Armenag to think I expected consummation of our betrothal. "That was almost ten years ago," I wrote, "and so much has happened to both of us since then. You may have other goals and other interests."

Also, in my letter, I told him I was working as a teacher in an orphanage and I was making enough to support myself.

Once again, I received a prompt reply, and this time it was heart-warmingly affectionate and signed "Armen," an abbreviated version of his name.

"I've saved quite a bit from my army allotment," he wrote. "I'm going to send you money regularly so that you don't have to work."

He mentioned that he'd started law school before enlisting in the American Army and he planned to complete his law studies after his discharge.

"One more thing you should know," Armen said in his next letter, "I'm changing my last name legally from *Balian* to *Meghrouni*. I hate the thought of having a Turkish surname like *Bal* with an *i-a-n* attached to it. I prefer the pure Armenian version, *Meghr*, with the ancient ending of *ouni* that was used on all Armenian surnames in the olden days."

The idea of the name change is amazing, I told myself. I was tremendously impressed by Armen's ingenuity. By translating the Turkish word meaning "honey" into Armenian, he was severing his emotional connection with the country responsible for the massacre of his people. What an extraordinary young man! I was quite taken by Armen's brilliance and charm. Somehow Mama's predictive words kept reverberating in my mind: "He's very good, very smart; he'll be somebody one day." And to think that I was able to find him after all those miserable years; luck had singled me out at last.

I was thrilled beyond words and accepted eagerly when Armen reiterated his proposal of marriage; and he began working on the long process of obtaining the necessary documents for me to join him in Wisconsin. Meanwhile, our touching letters, filled with loving messages to each other, crossed the ocean nearly every day.

My weekly search for relatives finally produced information about my step-uncle, Parsegh, who lived in Egypt with his wife and four sons. He had listed his name and address with Aleppo's Armenian Church in the hopes of finding me. I was so pleased to know that my step-uncle's efforts helped me locate him. At least, I had one relative who was still alive. I wrote to him promptly, explaining my situation and that I was waiting to go to America where I planned to marry Armen. In his immediate reply, my step-uncle discouraged my plan to live in the United States. Instead, he invited me to stay with him and his family, and he enclosed transportation money to join them in Cairo.

"You don't have to follow a stupid, old country custom," he wrote.

"There's no need for you to honor a betrothal that was arranged when you were just a small child. Come here. There are a number of fine young men here; and we'll arrange a good marriage for you."

That was not what I wanted; I was definitely going to the United States. I had made up my mind to marry Armen. He was the kind of man I hoped for in a husband – someone who was true to his word, someone who was genuinely devoted to my well-being, and someone who wanted to share his life with me without any reservations.

In my next letter to my step-uncle, I thanked him for his kind offer to live with him and his family; but I stated that my decision to marry Armen was irrevocable.

※ ※ ※

Every day, on my way to and from my job at the orphanage's school, I had to use the street where the Bank of Aleppo was located and where I knew Joseph had once worked. I always made a point of walking on the opposite side of the road as if any proximity to the building would conjure up aching memories of a betrayed love. Not to risk arousing such feelings, I'd look straight ahead without glancing at the bank building or to see who was loitering in front of it. One gray morning, while walking to work, I heard someone shout, "Vergeen! Vergeen! Wait!"

I turned around and saw three well-dressed men in front of the bank; and one of them was JOSEPH! I stopped as he ran across the street toward me.

"Vergeen! I'm so glad to see you! How are you?"

"I'm fine," I answered with an uneasy smile as he came alongside me. Running into Joseph after such a long time rattled me. I felt a wave of the deep hurt which had nagged me for so long. I wasn't sure how I should conduct myself.

"I just returned from Baghdad a few days ago," Joseph quickly explained.

"I have an appointment at the bank right now about getting my old job back, and I don't think it'll take long. Would you wait for me here?"

"I'm sorry, but I can't because I'm on my way to work. I'm teaching at the orphanage school."

"Then, will you please give me your home address so that I can come by to see you. I'd like to talk to you." Joseph appeared anxious; and I really wanted to know why he had not contacted me during the past eighteen months. I wanted to know why he had abandoned me after so many pledges of his commitment to me. I wanted to know! Absolutely, for my peace of mind, I HAD to KNOW!

"Here's where I live," I said, pulling a pencil and a piece of paper out of my bag, and I wrote down the address of the house I occupied with Serpouhi and Myreek. "Yes, I'd like to talk to you, too," I declared formally as I handed him the slip of paper.

"Goodbye, for now," Joseph smiled and shook my hand. "It's so good to see you, Vergeen! Honestly! I'm so glad to see you! I'll be by on Sunday."

I walked away slowly, my head spinning. I'd never expected to see Joseph again. I kept wondering what he was going to tell me. That evening, I told Serpouhi about my accidental encounter with Joseph, and that he might be coming to the house in a few days.

Concerned about my reaction, Serpouhi asked, "How do you feel about seeing him again."

"I really don't know how I feel," I answered truthfully. "After all, he did save my life and he was very good to me. And there was a time my love for him smothered me completely. Also, I have to believe that he cared for me once. I must find out what happened."

The following Sunday morning, Serpouhi accompanied Myreek to church; I knew it was her way of making certain I was alone when Joseph came to see me.

At precisely eleven o'clock, there was a strong knock on the door; it was Joseph. He looked exceptionally dapper. He was dressed in a dark, neatly pressed suit; and he wore a red flower in his lapel.

"Here, this is for you," he smiled, handing me the flower before he sat down in a chair.

"No, thank you." My refusal sounded curt; but I was anxious to hear why he wanted to see me, why he'd cut off communication during all those months.

Instead, he first asked, "What do you teach at the orphanage?"

"Mostly, I teach elementary French," I replied.

"Do you remember the time when I was your French instructor?"

Joseph's brows arched upward and his face broadened into an affable grin. "I remember you were a good pupil. I hope those sessions have helped you in your teaching."

"Yes, thank you; they've helped a lot."

I knew my short, stiff responses made Joseph a little tense, but I was getting impatient with his proclivity for small talk. First, I wanted him to disclose the reasons for his silence before I was forced to broach the matter. Perhaps, I thought, it would help to defrost the somewhat chilly atmosphere I'd created if I offered him something to drink.

"Would you like a cup of tea?"

"Yes, that would be fine."

I rose from my chair to go up to the kitchen, and he followed me.

"Vergeen, I realize it's been a long time since we last saw each other; but, thank God, our destiny meant for us to be together again."

I said nothing as I prepared the tea, with my back to him. Suddenly, I felt his warm lips on the nape of my neck and his long arms encircled my waist.

I pulled away quickly. There may have been a time when I'd have encouraged Joseph's caresses; now I just wanted answers to my questions.

"I'm sorry, Joseph; it's too late for that. I'm going to America to marry someone I've known since my childhood."

Joseph was quiet for a few seconds and finally retorted, "I don't believe it. I think you're just saying that out of anger because I didn't write."

"No, Joseph. I'm really getting married and I'm going to America as soon as the necessary papers are arranged."

"Vergeen, please listen!" Joseph seemed sincere. "Things are different from what they were during the war. I'm back here in Aleppo and I've been able to get my old job at the bank. In a few months, I'll be making enough money for us to go through our marriage plans."

I couldn't believe what I was hearing. He wanted to resume our relationship as if nothing had happened to shatter it; and, yet, he was not forthcoming on any explanation for his many months of silence.

"I know my sisters did not treat you well," he continued. "But, things have changed now. I don't have to be beholden to my sisters any more. You know why I was in a dilemma; they were working their fingers off to take care of my family while I was away during the war. But now, I can help support my mother and young brother. They can remain in their home, and we can have our own place."

"I'm very sorry, Joseph; it's really too late for us. I've made up my mind to go to America to be married."

Joseph glared at me for several seconds, clearly at a loss for any more persuasive words. "I guess I'd better leave," he spoke softly. "Forgive me, but I don't think I can stay to have tea with you. Perhaps some other time, but not today."

"Just a minute, Joseph!" My indignant annoyance showed in my voice. I was incredulous. Not once did he offer an explanation, not even an excuse, for virtually deserting me during a vulnerable period in my life. I was angry; I had to get some answers.

"Before you go, I want to know why you never wrote to me. At first, you never let me know where you were or how you were. Why didn't you? You knew I'd be concerned! Most unforgivable of all, you knew I had no one; I had nothing! Didn't you ever wonder what had happened to me during all those months? If you had any feelings for me, why didn't you have enough interest to try and find out how I was getting along?"

He turned his face away, unable to look at me.

"I want you to know, Joseph, that you hurt me deeply, very deeply." I hesitated somewhat to control the tremor creeping into my voice. "You knew that you were all I had."

Surprisingly, Joseph said nothing. He just let me go on.

"Can you understand why I felt rejected, totally abandoned

when I didn't hear from you? And now, after eighteen months, you see me on the street and you want to renew everything as if we just saw each other last week. It's too late; much too late!"

Joseph shook his head. "You knew how much I cared for you."

"Please think about it; how could I trust your feelings when I had no word from you. All I wanted was a letter, not money, just ONE letter to let me know how we could stay in touch. That's all I wanted."

"Do you need any money now?" He reached into his pocket and started to hand me a lira.

"I don't need your money," I said sadly, woefully disappointed in his inability to comprehend the emotional pain he'd caused me.

In a display of what I perceived to be blind resentment, Joseph tossed the lira into the chair and walked toward the door. "I can see you're angry right now, and you're not going to listen to me today," he said casually. "I'll come back another time, perhaps next week; and we can talk then."

After that day, Joseph came to see me twice; Myreek and Serpouhi were at home and their reassuring presence, at least for me, prevented any further discussion about renewal of a relationship. I thought it was best to end the visiting, for both our sakes; and I told Joseph that I didn't think it was a good idea for him to come by anymore. "The front of this house is a doctor's office," I stressed. "It really doesn't look good for us to receive visitors here."

Only on my way to work, when I passed by the bank, did I see Joseph again. A few times, we stopped to exchange greetings and finally I told him, "It's best this way, Joseph. Your family never would have accepted me."

Joseph nodded, admitting his understanding. He took my hand, kissed it, and held it for a few seconds; then he walked away.

I never saw him again.

TWENTY-FOUR

Beginning Anew

Armen was discharged from the army in the Spring of 1919 and he sent a long letter informing me that he'd invested money in a tire shop with a friend in Chicago.

"My friend will run the shop while I go to law school in Chicago," he wrote, sounding fairly confident that this was a good business deal.

A short time later, another letter from Armen stated that the tire shop had failed. He was returning to Milwaukee to be with his brothers and that I'd hear from him soon. But, for the next several months, I received nothing. There were no replies to my letters, and I started to fret about the state of our relationship. Maybe Armen changed his mind about marriage, I'd tell myself; but then, at other times, I'd be consoled by the notion that there must be a very good reason for the break in our communication. I hoped it was temporary and that I'd hear from him shortly.

༺ ༺ ༺

In early 1920, we learned that the United States was relaxing its immigration requirements. It was great news for the hundreds of Armenian refugees who had already connected with relatives in the United States; and they were getting ready to leave Aleppo to become reunited with their loved ones.

Nearly every day, travel money arrived at the Armenian Church from many countries for refugees who'd been located by family members. Yet, most of this money came from men in America for the transportation of their wives, children, parents, siblings, their fiancés. One of the generous checks came for Serpouhi from Boghos; he suggested she should buy whatever she needed and to use the rest for her trip to America. Simultaneously, Myreek received money from her husband to join him in Buenos Aires.

Unfortunately, arguments about Serpouhi's determination to go to the United States sparked hurt feelings between mother and daughter. Myreek kept insisting Serpouhi should go with her to Buenos Aires.

"I know Myreek is upset about my decision," Serpouhi lamented. "But I think I can have a better life with Boghos in America. Once I'm married and settled, I'm going to send for both of my parents to live with us. Boghos is a very generous man; I believe he'll agree to it."

A few days later, Serpouhi told me she was taking Myreek to Mersin, a Turkish port city not far from Aleppo where most of the refugees made arrangements to sail to their individual destinations. Some Allied forces still remained in Mersin to insure the safe departure of Armenian refugees.

"Come with us, Vergeen," Serpouhi said insistently. "I don't want to leave you here when you've not yet heard from Armen."

I shook my head emphatically. "No, Serpouhi! I never want to step foot in Turkey again."

I looked at my dear friend who was saddened by the thought of our separation, and her eyes became moist. "Don't worry about me," I said, trying to comfort her while choking back my own tears. "I've decided to go and stay with my step-uncle in Cairo for a while. He can help me find out about Armen."

Both Serpouhi and I resigned from our jobs; and, the following week, she and Myreek left for the Turkish port city of Mersin. Our parting was extremely painful. Serpouhi and I pledged that we'd find each other no matter where we ultimately settled in America. But, saying goodbye to Myreek was agonizing; I hugged her tightly, not wanting to let her go because I knew I would never see her again. And I never did.

Even though Serpouhi and Myreek were gone, Dr. Emil let me stay in the back section of the house because he knew I, too, would be leaving soon.

Several times, before leaving for Cairo, I saw Deegen Timourian, the resourceful woman who helped Mama and me get out of Katma on an ox-drawn cart. She, too, was planning to go to America and she wanted me to accompany her for a special reason.

"I'm looking for two nice girls to take with me for my nephews," she told me. "And you'd be perfect for either one."

Although this kind of matrimonial match for the young men in America was arranged customarily, I did not like the idea and I kept reminding Deegen Timourian that I was engaged to someone else in America. Even so, she tried to pressure me with her frequent visits and she always brought photos of her nephews.

"Let me take you to America with me," she persisted. "If you don't like my nephews, you can look for your fiance."

I convinced Deegen Timourian that I was not interested.

Surprisingly, I received a similar offer from my dear mentor, Nartouhy, who wanted to arrange a marriage with one of her sister's boys in America. In fact, she'd sent them a copy of the photo she'd taken with Serpouhi and me.

Even though Nartouhy tried to talk me into a marriage agreement, I could not be persuaded and claimed I could not wed anyone I didn't know.

I wrote Armen a final letter from Aleppo, informing him that I was leaving for Cairo to stay with my step-uncle's family. Enclosing Uncle Parsegh's address in my letter, I requested a reply from Armen about his commitment to me. "I'd understand," I contended, "if you want to back out."

Since the Armenian Church still served as the clearing house for all mail addressed to refugees in Aleppo, I asked a friend at the church to forward all my letters to my new residence in Egypt.

I boarded the train to Cairo with a female acquaintance and her daughter; and, fortunately, we were able to stay together all the way, even on our four-day stopover in Damascus.

Reaching Cairo, my reunion with Uncle Parsegh was very emotional. We clung together for several minutes, unable to speak. It was wonderful to be greeted so warmly by his entire family – his wife, his four sons and daughter-in-law. I was saturated by their outpouring of affection.

On the day of my arrival, my step-uncle told me I had two letters forwarded from Aleppo. I was delighted to see that they were from Armen. In the lengthy first one, he explained the reasons for his belated reply. He'd been totally immersed in starting a new grocery store and he'd also returned to law school in Milwaukee. Both activities, he stated apologetically, had occupied him almost day and night.

Armen's second letter, dated just ten days later, included a check in a huge amount. "Dear Vergeen, this is your travel money for your trip here," he wrote in his note. "I've also enclosed the papers required by American authorities, but you'll have to arrange for your visa there. Perhaps your uncle or cousins can help you."

It was such a relief to know that Armen had not changed his mind about me. I was really going to America! All I needed now was securing my visa. I solicited my step-uncle's help in depositing the check in the bank until I could get my visa.

The parents of four sons, my step-uncle and his wife continually expressed their delight in finally having a girl in the family, and they treated me like royalty. My male cousins were even more attentive. They introduced me to Cairo's marvelous streetcars, the first I'd ever seen; and every Sunday, we'd board a streetcar and my enthusiastic cousins would chaperon me on sightseeing trips around the city.

While the youngest son was still in school, the other three had followed their father in the shoe business. The eldest, *Hagop*, owned a wholesale shoe shop just a few blocks away from his father's wholesale place while the second son had a retail shoe store specializing in leather bootery.

Hagop was married and the father of an adorable, eight-month-old boy. His young wife, *Myranny*, was especially kind and loving; we got along very well. Together, we spent many enjoyable mornings when the men went off to work and my step-aunt always went to the market. Shopping for the day's family meals was an early morning chore for every homemaker in Cairo because of the city's unbearable afternoon heat and the unavailability of refrigeration.

During my stay in Cairo, I met another Armenian family originally from Kayseri. The couple had an unmarried son who was a few years older than I. One evening, my suspicions about the purpose of their frequent visits were confirmed when my step-uncle sought my opinion of the son.

"He's really a fine, young man, don't you think?"

"I can't say, Uncle Parsegh; I really don't know him."

"Well, I think I'd better tell you that his father came to see me today to discuss the possibility of a 'match' between you and his son."

"Didn't you tell him I was already promised to someone else?"

"No, I didn't tell him that; I did say I had no objection, but I told him the decision was yours."

"I'm sorry, Uncle Parsegh. You can tell him tomorrow that I'm not interested."

"Vergeen, think carefully." My uncle felt he needed to press on. "I've known this family for a long time; they're wonderful people and, if you marry into their family, you could be living here, close to us. But if you go to America, you'll have no family there to look out for you; and, frankly, I don't like the fact that I don't know anything about Armen."

I appreciated my step-uncle's paternalistic, protective feelings for me; nonetheless, I repeated my wish to go to America.

"If anything goes wrong for you, remember, you'll be way across the ocean; and there's no way we can help you," he said, overtly annoyed; and his voice quivered with emotion – a hurt I knew I'd inflicted, and I regretted it deeply. However, I was aghast a few days later when my step-uncle conceded he'd returned my transportation money to Armen.

"I was certain I could persuade you to stay here with us, so I returned the check," he explained. "But, when you would not listen to me, I wrote to Armen again and asked him to come here so that we could meet him; and then you could get married in my home. We'll have a nice wedding for you."

"But, uncle," I objected. "Armen can't take the time away from his law studies. Besides, it would cost him double. No! I think it's better for me to leave for America as soon as I can."

I wrote to Armen to disregard my step-uncle's request. "Please remain in school. I'll get there as soon as I can get my papers in order."

In another letter to my step-uncle, Armen specified why he could not come to Cairo, citing his business and studies as main reasons. He also enclosed another check for my travel expenses.

Finally, acquiescing to my firm resolve, Uncle Parsegh and my cousin helped me obtain my visa; and they escorted me by train to Port Said where, on November 26, 1920, I boarded an English cargo ship, named the City of Marseilles, destined for New York.

All second-class accommodations were already taken, so I settled happily for a very spacious, first-class cabin. Both Uncle Parsegh and my cousin came aboard to make sure I was comfortably situated and, when the ship's bells warned departure time for guests, they hurriedly wished me luck, kissed me goodbye, and left.

Suddenly, a flutter of panic seized me at the thought of being alone on my way to a strange country; and I rushed to the ship's deck to look for my dear relatives on the dock, but they were gone.

The ship was scheduled to sail early the following morning, so I used the time to quiet my nerves by looking for Armenians. Finding none in the first-class section, I went down to the crowded second-class level where I met only three Armenians; two of them were from my hometown of Kayseri. One was a young member of Kayseri's *Dabanian* family and he was headed for Detroit. Another young man, also from Kayseri, was joining relatives in Boston.

I returned to my cabin, selected the largest of the three beds in my cabin and luxuriated into a restful sleep until I was awakened in the morning by the ship's captain.

"Good morning." The captain grinned and, speaking in French, he introduced me to a robust woman who looked like she was in her thirties. "This Armenian lady will share your cabin. Since you speak the same language, I'm sure you'll enjoy each other."

I was glad to have the company; I really didn't like the idea of being alone in the cabin. But, having someone to talk to didn't matter because I, like so many passengers, was seasick during the entire fifteen days of the ship's crossing. Yet, every day, my roommate blithely enjoyed her three meals and promenaded on the breezy deck. I couldn't lift my head off the pillow.

Whenever our ship docked at a port to unload cargo, I had a little respite from my vile illness; and I'd wonder how I would find Armen, how he'd look, if we'd be happy in our marriage. My thoughts would go back to the time our parents arranged our betrothal. My God, I'd say to myself, I was only seven years old. Now, at eighteen, I was no longer a child and I'd experienced so much. In my mind, I kept figuring that Armen must be a mature man of twenty-nine by now. My anxieties about how we'd recognize each other disturbed me occasionally. No wonder, it had been nearly ten years since the last time we saw one another in Mama's kitchen in Kayseri before the war.

We reached New York's harbor on December 10 at 4 o'clock in the afternoon. It was a cold, partially sunny day; and the glorious Statue of Liberty seemed to soar out of the ocean. At last, I was in America! America and freedom! In all my excitement, I did something very strange. I stood on the busy deck and looked around to see if I could spot the golden streets; I'd heard the streets in America were paved in gold.

Trembling with emotion, I watched the disembarking passengers rush into the waiting arms of their loved ones. It was an unforgettable sight; tears flowed from all eyes and the noisy chatter was unrestrained as the newly reunited relatives clung to each other.

I searched the happy faces below me to see if I could recognize

Armen; but I saw no one who might resemble him. Where was he? Almost everyone had left the ship, except two blonde women and me. No one had come for either one of us.

Don't panic, I told myself when I saw a woman in uniform approaching and motioning us to follow her. She helped us climb into a boat and she got in herself along with a crewman who did the rowing. Not one of us understood what the uniformed woman and the man were saying; nor, could we understand each other. We remained quiet, altogether confused about where we were headed. Within minutes, we arrived at an island, got off the boat, and entered a large building.

Crowds of people, in different attire and speaking different languages, were walking back and forth, in and out of offices. The uniformed woman, who'd accompanied us, ushered me into a room where empty double-deck, bunk beds lined the walls. She pointed to one of the lower beds and, through motions, she indicated I was supposed to spend the night in the room.

My head started to throb with intolerable pain and, pointing to my forehead, I let the woman know I had a bad headache. She left and returned immediately; she gave me two pills and a glass of water. With my headache finally subdued, I fell asleep for a few hours on one of the bunk's lower deck. Around seven o'clock in the evening, I was awakened by several women sand children entering the room; and lo, to my delight, I recognized one of my pupils from the orphanage in Aleppo. I walked over to talk to the little girl, hoping that the adult with her could speak Armenian.

"Hello, *Kater*," I said, glad that I'd found someone I knew in this strange place.

"This is my mother," Kater smiled and shyly fingered her dress.

"We're waiting for my husband to take us to Detroit," the mother said apprehensively. "We haven't heard from him for five days."

She asked, "Why are you here at Ellis Island?" That was the first time I learned where I was. Ellis Island? I'd never heard of it before.

"Did you come second-class?"

"No, I couldn't get second-class because it was full," I replied. "I had to take a first-class cabin."

"Then, you should be on the second floor, not here. All first-class ship passengers are upstairs."

Even though I believed Kater's mother, I was too tired to pursue better quarters upstairs; and I returned to the bunk bed to sleep that night.

The next morning, after showing my first-class ticket stub to one of the room attendants, I was transferred to the second floor to a pleasant room with five single beds and an adjoining lavatory. I sat on the edge of the only unoccupied bed until my name was called at noon by another uniformed woman. She escorted me to a mess hall where I had lunch of red beans and ground meat, and the woman returned a half hour later to take me to the interrogation room.

While waiting, almost to three o'clock that afternoon, I wondered what had happened to Armen. Why didn't he meet me at the dock? Maybe we just didn't recognize each other.

"Vergeen Kalendarian, *hos yehgur.*" A female, speaking in Armenian, asked me to enter an enclosed office where a uniformed man was seated behind a desk. The female interpreter slowly translated the man's questions.

"*Oor deghen yehgar?* (Where did you come from?)"

"*Yehkeepdos en yehgah.* (I came from Egypt.)"

"*Amerigayeen vor kaghak beedy yertas?* (To which American city are you going?)"

"*Kaghak een anun eh Milwaukee eh.* (The name of the city is Milwaukee.)"

"*Hon azkagan unees?* (Do you have a relative there?)"

"*Voch. Eem neshanadzes hon geh pnagee.* (No. My fiance lives there.)"

"*Anuneh eench eh?* (What's his name?)"

"*Armen Meghrouni.*" From my large bag, I dragged out the papers and letters he'd sent me and showed them to the interrogator.

Hedet vor chop trom oo nees? Hesoon dolar? (How much money do you have with you? Fifty dollars?)"

I showed them the sixty-five dollars I had in my bag.

"*Lav! Hima, amusnutyun affidaveet oo nees?* (Good! Now, do you have your affidavit to marry?)"

"*Voch.* (No.)"

The interpreter then told me that they would send a letter to Armen right away requesting the affidavit; and it would probably take three or four days to get his response.

Catching the worried expression on my face, the interpreter said in Armenian, "Don't be afraid, Vergeen. We'll see that you get together with your fiance. But, you'd better write to him, too. If we don't receive the affidavit, he must come to Ellis Island and you can be married here before going on to Milwaukee."

As soon as I returned to my room, I wrote to Armen that the authorities wanted some kind of a paper called an "affidavit" that would insure our forthcoming marriage; or he'd have to make a trip to Ellis Island.

"I was very disappointed not to see you when my ship docked," I said. "I hope everything can be arranged soon. It's not easy to stay here."

I waited patiently for five days for a reply; nothing came. On the sixth day, I wrote to Armen again, describing how difficult it was to be detained at Ellis Island; and it was especially hard not knowing what was going to happen to me if the authorities got no response from him.

The next day, I sent a letter to his brother, Krikor, as well as another letter to Armen. Still no response!

On the eighth day, I wrote a letter to Armen's other brother, Movsess. In the hopes of reaching at least one of the men, I wrote to each one alternately for the next three days. Still no word. Nothing!

On the eleventh day, I was summoned to the interrogation office again. Through the same interpreter, I was asked the same questions. Where did you come from? To which city will you be going in America? Are you sure you didn't misplace the affidavit your fiance must have sent to you? I answered all their queries the same way I'd responded before; except, this time, I trembled with undisguised apprehension.

Detecting my trepidation, the Armenian interpreter intervened. "Vergeen, don't be frightened. But, do you have any idea why we haven't heard from your fiance?"

"No!"

"The authorities are saying they will wait for the affidavit until the Christmas holiday is over; but if they receive nothing, they'll send you back to Egypt." The interpreter tried to be kind. "I'm sorry, Vergeen."

Why was this happening to me? Going back to Egypt? To my uncle? He'd warned me over and over again about the difficulties of having no family in America. He was against my coming here to marry Armen. How could I go back and face him?

I returned to my room, exhaustively distressed. I did not feel well and thought I'd better lie down; I fell asleep. I was awakened by a stabbing pain in my right ear, and I felt feverish. The pain in my ear continued unabated the entire night. I didn't dare tell anyone about my earache or fever for fear of being hospitalized and missing any news about the affidavit from Armen.

When I stopped going to the mess hall for my meals, the room attendants realized I was ill and they offered to bring my meals to the room. They'd use sign language to find out what I'd like to eat, and I could only make them understand "eggs". That's all I ate for the next two days.

I felt a little better by the morning of Christmas Eve; and, tired of my egg fare, I went to the mess hall early to have breakfast. Happy workmen were completing the construction of a platform, and placing flags around it. Other workers were on top of tall ladders, near the huge ceiling, busily adding red and green balls to wires already bearing ornaments of every kind.

Admiring all the decorations, I was reminded of a cousin back in

Kayseri who had attended an American Missionary School; and I remembered his elaborate description of how Christmas was celebrated in America. The decorations were just like he depicted. For a while, my problems paled in my mind, and I yielded to the genial spirit of the holiday.

Returning eagerly to the balcony of the mess hall for the holiday supper that evening, I thoroughly relished my first taste of ham and mashed potatoes, especially after all the eggs I'd eaten the previous two days.

When supper finished, a large number of people filed into the hall below and sat down, crowding each other on benches or standing in rows against the walls. I knew many more new immigrants were arriving from Europe and Asia every day; but I was unaware of the large number being detained at Ellis Island because of legal problems. The knowledge that others, like I, were experiencing the same immigration complications helped me feel a little better. I didn't feel so isolated and I turned my attention to the festivities starting in the hall.

When the band started to play, a fat, white-bearded man, wearing strange-looking red clothes, dashed into the room, waving his arms and uttering weird sounds. He climbed on the platform and lifted the large, heavy sack off his shoulder and dropped it on the floor.

"That's just like my cousin described," I murmured to the Armenian woman at my table.

The band started to play Christmas music and those familiar with the carols sang in piercing, off-key voices. It was wonderful! The whole holiday atmosphere was so joyous, filled with merriment and laughter. The evening was topped off with the distribution of gifts for everyone. The uniformed staff made sure everyone got at least two or more packages; they included toys for the children and mostly toiletries for the adults. The staff even dashed upstairs to present gifts to those of us seated in comfortable chairs on the balcony. They smiled and shouted, "Merry Christmas! Merry Christmas!."

This was my first celebration of Christmas in America, and it was immensely enjoyable.

My respite from problems was brief, however. A few days after Christmas, I had excruciating pain in my ear and higher fever than before. This time, I was sure I needed medical attention. I called the night attendant and somehow, through gestures, I let her know I needed to go to the hospital.

"Tomorrow morning," she repeated until I understood what she was saying. She gave me two pills – aspirin, I think – and I did get a little relief.

At nine in the morning, a doctor came to examine me and ordered my admission to the hospital. A few minutes later, a young women came in and asked, by gesturing, for all my money and what little jewelry I had; and she handed me a receipt.

"Don't lose the receipt," she cautioned me. "After you came back from the hospital, we'll return them to you." She, too, had to repeat her words and gestures several times before I understood her.

She returned a half hour later to report there was no room for me in the hospital. "There will be a bed available tomorrow," she said, gesturing. "Here are some pain relievers that the doctor said you should take every four hours."

I remained in bed all day, taking the prescribed pills, and fell into a long, deep sleep. I felt better the following morning and wondered whether I really needed to be hospitalized. The young woman who'd taken my money and jewelry entered the room and returned them. "How do you feel?"

I understood her and nodded, indicating I felt better.

"Well, then, get ready," she ordered. "You're not going to the hospital. I've got good news for you! We received the affidavit from Mr. Meghrouni and you'll be leaving for Milwaukee this evening."

Just the words "affidavit" and "Milwaukee" and "this evening" were all I needed to understand! I forgot my earache and, although I still felt weak and tired, I managed to scurry for my important trip.

Within the hour, another female staffer came and took me to the train depot along with three other immigrants who were scheduled to depart for different cities. The worker gave each of us a box lunch and pinned a destination card on each of our coats, and she waited until we all boarded the train at six o'clock in the evening. After grabbing the first available seat, I put my lunch box and baggage near my feet and, overcome by total exhaustion, I fell asleep.

Awakened by the train's shrill whistle, I opened my eyes and peeked out the window to catch a glimpse of the morning sun partially emerging from behind a gray cloud. Snow covered the desolate landscape; and the train wheels clicked, clicked, clicked monotonously.

The train passed a railroad station and, instantly, I was reminded of the awful rail depot of Ras-al-Ayn in the Arabian Desert. To clear my thoughts, I quickly erased those dark memories and concentrated, instead, on the scenery outside my window – and on Armen. What will he say? How would he look now? We'd never even exchanged photographs during our correspondence. Not only had our separation been caused by war and geography, but the years had stretched to nearly a decade since we'd last seen each other. Would I be disappointed?

Wait a minute, I told myself. What if HE'S disappointed in me? What if he's turned off by the ugly tattoos on my face? What if he's troubled by the disgusting experiences of my nomadic life in the desert? What if he rejects me when he finds out I was sexually molested?

Oh, God! I hoped I hadn't made a mistake coming to the United States. Was my step-uncle right in opposing my decision to marry Armen?

Another concern crossed my mind. Would Armen be able to adjust to married life after all those years as a bachelor, without having had responsibilities for someone else?

My head kept buzzing with all these reproachful thoughts throughout the three nights and two days it took to reach Wisconsin.

Along our route, before each stop at a train station, the conductor would check the destination cards pinned to the coats of the immigrants, and he would alert each person on when or where to get off the train. Several of the immigrants, embarking from New York, reached their destinations before I did.

Suddenly, I heard the conductor call: "South Milwaukee! Next stop, South Milwaukee!"

Quickly, I grabbed my baggage and got up from my seat to head for the door. The conductor looked carefully at my card, shook his head, and shouted: "NO! You don't get off here!"

"Milwaukee! Milwaukee!" That was all I could say waving my destination card at the conductor; I could not understand why this man would not let me get off the train.

"Young lady, this is SOUTH Milwaukee. You're not supposed to get off here!" The conductor smiled and spoke very slowly hoping I'd understand him, but I did not.

I returned to my seat near the back of the car; my agitated mind pictured Armen waiting at that station, wondering where I could be.

A short time went by and the train stopped again. No one got off, but two men came aboard. One of the men took a seat; the second one looked around at everyone and began to talk to the conductor.

Could that be Armen, I asked myself at first; but then, I did not think we'd reached the city of Milwaukee yet. Maybe that is Armen. The young man sort of resembled the teenaged Armen I remembered from Kayseri nearly ten years before. But, did this man really look like him?

Utterly confused, I stared at the standing passenger while he kept talking to the conductor who, after a few minutes, pointed to the back door leading to the next car.

The young man looked around again and walked up to a couple seated in the front. He started to talk to the woman who had blondish hair, and I noticed both she and her companion shook their heads rather vigorously. My mind raced. That could be

Armen; maybe he remembered me the way I was as a little girl. My hair was dark blonde then.

Oh, it had to be Armen!

The young man looked toward the back, and headed for the next car behind me. As he swept by, his coat brushed my leg. I tried to speak; but all I could get out of my mouth was a whimper: "*Toon Armen nes?* (Are you Armen?)" Obviously, he did not hear me or he really was not Armen because he walked on, into the next car. He returned a short time later and, when the train stopped, he was the first to get off.

"This is Milwaukee," the conductor called and motioned to me that it was my stop.

As soon as I stepped down from the train car with my baggage in hand, a woman from the Travelers Aid Society greeted me and directed me to a group of immigrants who were huddled together.

I looked around for my large suitcase. "Where's my baggage?" I asked, alarmed by its disappearance. I tried asking the Travelers aide in Armenian and in French what happened to my bag. Somehow, the helpful woman understood what I was trying to ask and she let me know, mostly through gestures, that my suitcase was being sent on another train and I'd get it shortly. I did not believe her.

"The people at Ellis Island told me that my suitcase would be in the baggage compartment on the same train," I muttered in my aggravated state. "I know my suitcase is lost."

While waiting with the group of immigrants, I noticed the same young man from the train in front of the newsstand. He bought a newspaper and, leaning against a post, he started to read it.

"Sit down here on the benches," instructed the Travelers aide. "Don't get up. Don't go anywhere, not even to the lavatory." The woman spoke very slowly and, to my astonishment, I was beginning to understand some of her directives. As she began to call out the names of the immigrants on a list, some raised their hands; and I thought I heard my name. I got up to glance at the list, and I saw the name "Virginia" next to "Kalendarian". I knew the French version of Vergeen was spelled V-i-r-g-i-n-i-e, and I let the aide know that I was that person.

"Stay right there," she said pointing to a spot. While standing still, I watched the young man fold the newspaper and tuck it under his arm; then he climbed the stairs and stepped in front of a telephone.

"Your fiance is not here yet," the aide said to me. "Stay here while I go upstairs and try to call him."

I nodded, guessing what she said as I watched her go to the telephone next to the one the young man was using. When she asked for Armen Meghrouni on the phone, the young man heard her and turned around; he smiled at the aide and pointed to himself. They talked just a second or two, then they both looked down and waved at me.

IT WAS ARMEN! He rushed down the stairs toward me, smiling broadly. I hurried to meet him half way up the steps.

"Vergeen! You're here," he exclaimed and quickly extended his hand, gripping mine tightly. "When I didn't find you on the train, I was concerned. I hoped you'd be on the next one."

"But, I was on the train." I laughed. "You walked right by my seat."

"I did? Oh, I'm sorry." Armen examined my face quickly, chuckled and squeezed my hand in a show of affection. "Well, how could I recognize you? You've changed a lot since I last saw you." Standing back to take another direct look, he said, "You look good, very good; and I'm so glad you got here safe and sound."

Unconsciously, I covered my tattooed chin; and Armen gently pushed my hand away from my face. "You don't have to hide those marks from me," he said quietly. "Please, Vergeen, remember this: I will always regard those marks as symbols of your valor and honor."

I smiled in profound gratitude and buried my face inside my coat collar to conceal my happy tears from onlookers at the station. My fears of rejection melted in that moment.

Once again, Armen clasped my hand tightly and guided me outdoors where we got into a taxi. We chatted, laughed and just enjoyed ourselves. As I sat close to him, I could see that Armen had not really changed much in the last ten years. Perhaps, his hair was a little thinner, and he was a little heavier; but his marvelous, almond-shaped eyes were as I remembered them: large, dark and dramatically expressive.

Actually, I was surprised at how much I was at ease; I don't remember an awkward moment during that entire taxi ride. We were so engrossed in each other that I felt it was an inappropriate time to ask about the delays causing my detainment at Ellis Island. Instead, I inquired about mundane things, such as the whereabouts of my suitcase. Armen assured me it was being forwarded, and apparently it was; I received it two weeks later.

"This is Krikor's shop," Armen said as we pulled in front of a shoe store; and he told the driver to stop and wait. "Come and meet my brother."

Krikor greeted me warmly. Although I'd never met him before, I recognized him from the photo I'd seen in Aunt Elimon's house back in Kayseri; and I remembered how much she and her husband, Sarkis Agha, treasured the picture of their three boys.

Krikor was bustling with incoming customers, so we didn't stay long; we returned to the waiting taxi and headed home. I learned that the brothers shared an apartment. "It's only temporary," Armen explained. "Krikor will be moving out after we're married."

It was early afternoon when we arrived at the apartment; like so many of the family dwellings of those days, it was located over a store.

"You go up and I'll be along in a minute," Armen said, ushering me up a long flight of stairs.

First, I entered a dimly-lit room where a hard coal stove, the first I'd ever seen, occupied one corner. Next was the parlor; it was an empty, but bright room with three large windows flooded by the warm rays of the sun. My continuing exploration of the apartment led to two bedrooms, each had a dresser and a bed; and, beyond these rooms, I found a lavatory and a kitchen with a small table and two chairs.

"Vergeen, I hope you're not cold," Armen called out to me. "I've got a pail full of coal, and this place should be warm in no time."

After he attended to the stove, Armen showed me how to pull the unusual chain to flush the toilet; its peculiar water tank was up high, nearly touching the ceiling. He showed me how to turn the gaslights on and off; the apartment was not yet wired for electricity. Most extraordinary, at least for me, was the gas stove for cooking.

"All you have to do is turn a knob and light a match to the burner – and *voila!* You'll be ready to cook." Armen chuckled, watching me inspect the knobs intently.

What a great way to light a stove, I thought. Nothing like the battle I used to go through in the squalid Arabian desert, with thorny twigs and the repulsive camel dung, just to start a flame.

Leading me into the sun-soaked parlor, Armen said, "This will be your bedroom for the time being. Later today, we'll be getting new furniture for this room. I hope you like it."

Before the delivery of the furniture – a bed, mattress and two chairs, we sat down in the kitchen for a snack of feta cheese, black olives, halva and Armenian bread.

Armen told me he attended classes until 11:30 every morning and he worked in the grocery store below the apartment until seven each evening.

"You must be very tired," he said. "Why don't you get some sleep while I go downstairs to the store. Unfortunately, I have to work this afternoon; but, I'll be back up in time for supper."

I was very tired; in fact, I was exhausted, and I welcomed Armen's suggestion to get some rest. He gave me a pillow, clean sheets and a heavy comforter before dashing downstairs. As soon as my head touched the soft pillow, I sank into a deep, dreamless sleep.

I awoke to darkness, and I didn't know where I was for a moment. Then remembering that Armen might be back from work by now, I hurried out of bed and went to the kitchen. All the gaslights were turned on; and he was standing at the stove preparing supper, with an apron around his middle.

"Did you get enough rest?"

"Oh, yes!" I replied, sniffing the spicy aroma floating from the pots.

"What are you cooking? It smells so good!"

"Meat stew with vegetables and bulghur pilaf!" He announced the menu for our first meal with a whimsical self-appreciation, waving a large wooden spoon over his head.

Armen had every right to be pleased with himself; the food was delicious. We talked, lingered over tea, and cleaned the table together.

"Is this a custom in America?" I could not get over Armen being the dishwasher and I was merely his helper.

"Of course! In this country, husbands try to help with the housework." He laughed and added: "So, get used to it!"

"I will! I will!" I loved the idea. "What a wonderful country!"

After dinner, we talked and talked, heedless of the passing hours. First, Armen speculated that the reason for my detention at Ellis Island was caused by a combination of mix-ups: immigration officials were being inundated by the paperwork involved in the great influx of foreigners, and his recent change of address impeded the flow of mail to and from me and the New York authorities. All the reasons for the misconnections didn't matter much at that moment, I was happy to be with Armen.

"Do you like living here in America?" I asked, wanting to learn more about the country where I'd be spending the rest of my life.

"Absolutely!" Armen's response was so reassuring. "This is a free country where anyone can go as high as they're able. Look at me. I found the opportunity I wanted here for higher education. I worked and with the help of my brothers, I went to night school and I made enough money to go to Lawrence College – that's in Appleton."

I had no idea where Appleton was. I thought it was a strange name for a town.

"You know, don't you, that I served in the American Army during the war."

"Yes, of course."

Well, when I got out of the army, I went back to my classes and now I'm in law school right here in Milwaukee. I have almost two years yet to graduate."

What an ambitious young man, I thought. I was so proud.

Armen had so many long-pending questions about my experiences and those of others we both knew in Kayseri. I tried to answer every query except, unfortunately, I could not give him any news about his father and stepmother. I described how I ran into them briefly in Katma, but never saw them again. And I thought it best to withhold the information about their poverty-stricken state. I knew it would be too upsetting for him.

We discussed the possible date of our wedding and, since it would be small and simple, we decided it could take place within two weeks.

"I think that should be enough time to shop for your wedding dress and other clothes you might need," Armen noted. "We also have to invite a few friends."

His desire to hasten the wedding date pleased me.

As we sat and talked endlessly, I felt I was living a dream. Here I was in the happy home of my childhood love who would soon be my husband. The time Armen and I spent together that evening was indescribably precious. It was remarkable how much he'd turned my life around in just one day. He nurtured my long-held feelings of emptiness; he seemed to replace every loss I'd had – my father, my mother, my sister, my brother, my uncles, my aunts, my cousins, and all the other loved ones who were the ill-fated victims of Turkey's attempted annihilation of the whole Armenian nation.

Suddenly, I heard the crackling sound of gunshots! Startled and frightened, I bolted out of my chair and ran to the window. There was an amazing sight on the street below! Children and adults were pouring out of their homes, blowing strange-sounding horns, and dancing in circles.

"My God! What is that?"

"Oh, don't be afraid," Armen said, laughing. "It's New Year's Eve, and that's the way the start of another year is celebrated in this country. Some people think it's fun to make a lot of noise by shooting their guns in the air. Everyone has a good time!"

Gently, Armen turned me away from the window to face him. "Vergeen, I want you to listen to me. Please listen carefully. All the horrors of the past are over! Remember, they're over! And whatever bad happened to you in the desert makes no difference to me; it doesn't matter. I'm only sorry you had to go through so much – so much hell. Also, I want you to know I'm going to try everything I can to keep you safe and to fill your life with all the important things that's been denied you for so long."

Then Armen held my face in both hands and pledged: "I want to be the husband you deserve."

Kissing me tenderly, he whispered, "Happy New Year, dearest. This is the beginning of your new life."

Epilogue

On the afternoon of January 9, 1921, nine days after her arrival in Milwaukee, Vergeen married Armen in a brief ceremony conducted by Reverend Charles A. Garriel of the Bethany Presbyterian Church. The wedding took place in the home of a Meghrouni cousin with a small group of relatives and friends in attendance.

A son, Victor, was born on Armistice Day, November 11, 1921; and, five years later, on September 10, 1926, Vergeen gave birth to another son, Vahe.

The young couple remained in Milwaukee after Armen graduated from the Marquette University Law School and passed the Wisconsin Bar in 1922. But, after contacting Serpouhi and her new husband, Paul Boghos Mikjian, in Detroit, Vergeen and Armen decided to move to the rapidly growing motor city in 1925 where many more Armenian immigrants had settled and where opportunities to develop a thriving law practice were deemed more favorable.

Starting in the early thirties, Armen's successful law practice was strained by both the economic burdens of the Depression years as well as the service he provided, usually without remuneration, to needy members of the Armenian community. Consequently, he discontinued the practice of law in 1944; and the Meghrouni family then moved to southern California where Armen bought a grocery store and operated it together with Vergeen.

Despite their separation, the families of Vergeen and Serpouhi maintained their lifelong, close friendship and continue to do so.

Vergeen continually demonstrated her indomitable pride and profound regard for learning. Before moving out west, she earned a high school diploma in 1943. After eight years of hard study and with the help of her supportive family, she graduated from Detroit's Northern High School and was honored by the school as a commencement speaker. Her remarkable achievement also generated public recognition by the city's metropolitan newspapers.

After Armen's death in 1962, sixty-year-old Vergeen learned to drive a car and maintained the grocery store for seven more years.

In the spring of 1964, Vergeen decided to tour Europe, visiting some relatives and traveling extensively in Greece, Spain, France, Italy, Switzerland and Egypt. When she visited the Soviet Republic of Armenia, her holocaust memories forbade any thought of stepping foot inside her birthplace, the adjacent country of Turkey.

For thirty-six years, after coming to the United States, Vergeen was obsessed by the tattoos on her face; they caused deep embarrassment and depression. The marks attracted people's stares in shops and on the streets; and, anguished by the ugly reminders of her servitude during her year in the desert, Vergeen wanted to get rid of them as soon as possible.

Trying to find someone knowledgeable about the removal of his wife's facial marks, Armen consulted several physicians; yet, none could provide a satisfactory correction. Finally, in 1952, when Vahe was in medical school, he took his mother to see his professor of surgery. Even though the doctor expressed doubt about erasing the mark on Vergeen's lower lip, he became keenly interested in attempting the removal of the other tattoos on her forehead and chin. It took one full year to eradicate the tattoos surgically and, amazingly, the tattoo on Vergeen's lip turned out to be the easiest to remove.

"I owe it all to my two wonderful boys," Vergeen often said. "Vahe was determined to find a surgeon who could do the job; and Victor continually took me back and forth to the doctor's office without once uttering a complaint."

Her first-born, Victor, an accountant, is now a retired businessman who has two grown sons, Vincent and Marc; and he currently lives with his second wife, Theda, in Anaheim. Vahe, a retired radiologist, is married to Armine, also a physician; and they split their time between homes in Anaheim and Carmel. They have four grown daughters: Alexis, Andrea, Michelle and Sara.

Epilogue

❈ ❈ ❈

Although both Vergeen and my mother, Serpouhi, have passed on, the bond between their children, even their grandchildren, remains very strong despite the great distance between California and Michigan where all of my mother's descendants live today. And, remarkably, the grandchildren of both women draw enduring inspiration from their grandmothers' triumphant survival.

M.M.D.

Historical Notes

Armenia is one of the most ancient of nations. Many centuries ago, it occupied a large portion of western Asia between the Caspian and Black seas, south of the mountain range of the Caucasus and east of the Mediterranean. Within its boundaries were the sources of the Tigris and Euphrates rivers and Mt. Ararat, the resting place of Noah's Ark after the flood.

Historical accounts, dating back more than 2,000 years, contend Armenia served as an advanced post of civilization, rivaling the great empires of the East. These documentations of Armenia's indisputable leadership in cultural achievements depict the force and splendor of the early nation which, in 301 A.D., was the first to adopt Christianity and which, in 405 A.D., developed its unique, still-in-use alphabet. From the very beginning, Armenia fiercely defended its national and spiritual independence against ruthless, neighboring nations – the Assyrians, the Medes, the Persians, the Arabs, the Byzantines, the Tartars.

Starting in the 11th century, Armenia lost her independence to a succession of conquerors and, by the late 15th century, the Turks became the final victors. Yet, to this day, Armenians, although scattered the world over, have held on tenaciously to their Christian faith and to their national character.

In the early 1900s, more than two million Armenians lived in Ottoman Turkey, concentrated in the country's eastern provinces. Since Islam was the rule of law, the Christian Armenians had no legal rights; they were a persecuted minority periodically subjected to senselessly ruthless pogroms to dominate them. In 1908, Armenians joyfully welcomed the revolt of the Young Turks against the oppressive rule of Sultan Abdul Hamid II. Persecuted for centuries, Armenians saw it as the beginning of much-needed reform in Turkey. However, they soon learned any talk of reform was maliciously misleading; the new government proved to be just as despotic as the one it replaced.

By 1914, dictatorship was formed by a power-hungry triumvirate: Enver Pasha, the Minister of War; Djemal Pasha, the Minister of Marine; and Talaat Pasha, the Minister of Interior. The Young Turk government was determined to purify the country's race of people and to expand Turkey's territory, and thus began the goal to take care of the "Armenian problem" once and for all. Entering World War I on the side of Germany, the Ottoman dictators relied on their ally to help achieve their plan of genocide: first weaken the Armenians by assassinating all their leaders, intellectuals and able-bodied men; then disperse the remaining Armenian subjects into remote areas; and finally exterminate all remaining Armenians systematically.

Implementation of the diabolical scheme started in January of 1915 when the Turkish government disarmed and forced its loyal Armenian soldiers into labor crews assigned to hard road work. Driven for months by whips and bayonets, all ultimately were slaughtered.

Three months later, on April 23 and 24, Turkish authorities arrested more than 600 prominent Armenians in Istanbul and took them to secluded regions where they were murdered. The shocking news reverberated through every Armenian community, signaling the imminent peril endangering all Armenians in Turkey. (Since then, on April 24 every year, Armenians worldwide memorialize and honor all victims of the genocide.)

On May 30, 1915, the Turkish government issued its general decree of deportation. Despite the government's attempts to censor information about banishing Armenians, the text of its decree was discovered eight months later by an American journalist, Eleanor Franklin Egan, who smuggled it out of Turkey. Her provocative, eye-opening account of the Turkish plan of deportation was published by the *Saturday Evening Post* [1] along with the entire proclamation ordering the deportation of all Armenians within five days.

Even though, for decades, Turkish governments habitually committed wholesale massacres of Armenian communities to

---

[1] *Behind the Smoke of Battle*, Saturday Evening Post, by E.F. Egan, February 5, 1916

quell offenses by individuals or by small groups of rebels, only a handful of Armenians and a few organized groups sporadically resorted to independent aggression when no longer able to withstand Turkish oppression. Thus, weary of Turkish brutality, several Armenians living near the Turkish-Russian border joined the Russian army to fight the Turks at the beginning of the war. Moreover, some Armenians in Turkey's eastern city of Van organized armed opposition against Turkish forces in a courageous, but futile defensive action which cost more than 55,000 Armenian lives. Several thousand more Armenian lives were lost in the early months of 1915 when valiant self-defense attempts were made in other locales, including the heroic forty days' siege on top of the Musa Dagh mountain in Syria.[2]

By the autumn of 1915, nearly the entire remaining Armenian population of Turkey was expatriated, forced into a death march. Yet, other Armenians in Istanbul and in Smyrna, Turkey's second major seaport, escaped deportation since, according to subsequent observations by diplomats, foreigners living in these large cities would have been eyewitnesses to the atrocities.

The persistence of Turkish officials to suppress the news about their atrocities against Armenians almost succeeded because reports were being transmitted slowly from Turkey's interior areas, and diplomats failed at first to comprehend the real intent of the deportation. In fact, many doubted the extent of bloodshed; but, after a while, journalists' first-hand reports of the unprecedented barbarity against Armenians began to trickle through the underground into the foreign news bureaus located in Istanbul.

At first, Germany told the world it refused to interfere. Eventually, however, it was forced, in some instances by its own people, to acknowledge Turkey's diabolic butchery of the Armenians. Protests to Germany's foreign office came from many German missionaries in Turkey and Syria. One letter, in

---

[2] *Forty Days at Musa Dagh,* Franz Werfel, The Viking Press, November, 1934

particular, was forwarded from the entire faculty of the German high school in Aleppo. It read, in part:
"In face of the horrible scenes which take place daily near our school buildings before our very eyes, our school work has sunk to a new level which is an insult to all human sentiments... death is reaping a harvest... girls, boys, women, all practically naked, lie on the ground breathing their last sighs amid the dying." [3]

Another letter, directed by four German missionaries to their government and published fully in the Swiss newspapers in 1915 and only partially in the German documents, detailed the "unspeakable horror" of the treatment against exiled Armenian women and children. German censors suppressed such stories.

In the Fall of 1915, the German ambassador to the United States labeled the reported massacres as "pure inventions." (After World War I, official German documents, collected by Dr. Johannes Lepsius, the dedicated German pastor in charge of the German relief work, fully substantiated Germany's complicity in the genocide.) [4]

Attempting exculpation, an official Turkish statement, published by *The New York Times* in October of 1915, blamed the deportation and alleged atrocities on the Armenians' support of Russia, a bitter foe; and the Turkish counsel general in New york claimed: "The Armenians have themselves to blame." [5]

However, in a contradiction of Turkey's claim, *The New York Times* published a 600-page report, containing 150 authentic documents obtained through the Summer of 1916 from American and other neutral workers in Turkey, which detailed the wholesale massacres and deportations committed by Turkish troops against Armenians and other Christians. Author of the report, Viscount James Bryce, formerly a British Ambassador to the United States, claimed the evidence revealed the deliberate purpose of the Turkish

---

[3] *Protest of German Teachers Against Massacres of Armenians,* New York Times Monthly Magazine, November, 1916
[4] *Germany and the Armenian Massacres,* The New York Times Current History Magazine, November, 1919
[5] *Turkish Official Denies Atrocities,* The New York Times, October 15, 1915

authorities was to exterminate the Armenian nation, calling it "the most colossal crime in the history of the world." [6]

Henry Morgenthau, America's Ambassador to Turkey, was another resolute diplomat dedicated to revealing the truth about the carnage. As early as July, 1915, he began to send regular cables to the U.S. Department of State, reporting the persecution of Armenians had assumed unprecedented proportions.

Repeatedly, the U.S. State Department expressed its outrage and vainly tried to halt the deportations; but, since Turkey was an enemy of the Allies, America's hands were tied and nothing could be done to pressure the Turks into stopping the massacres.

A few years later, as national vice-chairman of Near East Relief, Morgenthau wrote: [7]

"More than 2,000,000 persons were deported. The system was about the same everywhere. The Armenians – men, women and children – would be assembled in the marketplace. Then the able-bodied men would be marched off and killed by being shot or clubbed in cold blood at some spot which did not necessitate the trouble of burial.

"Next the women would be sorted out. Agents of the Turk officers picked the youngest and fairest for their masters' harems. Next the civil officials had their pick, and then the remainder either were sold for one medjidi – a silver coin valued at about eighty cents –or were driven forth to be seized by the lower class Turks and Kurds.

"As a last step, those who remained – mothers, grandmothers, children – were driven forth on their death pilgrimages across Syria's (Mesopotamian) desert with no food, no water, no shelter, to be robbed and beaten at every halt, to see children slain in scores before their eyes, and babies dashed to death against rocks or spitted on the bayonets of the soldier guards."

Nearly one-and-a-half million people perished during what historians have since described as the 20th century's first genocide. The fortunate half-million survivors fled to other parts of the world

---

[6] *Lord Bryce's Report on Turkish Atrocities in Armenia,* The New York Times Current History Magazine, November, 1916
[7] *The Independent,* Henry Morgenthau, February 28, 1920

— western Europe, South America, Canada, and the United States.

In news accounts by the American press from 1915 to 1922, collected in his informative book, *The Armenian Genocide*, Richard D. Kloian points out, "the same combination of dictatorship, racial elitism, and nationalistic expansion recurred in Germany in the 1930s and again led to a major World War and to a government-planned extermination of the Jews."[8]

Still today, the Turkish government insists that the genocide never happened. Even some uninformed or lobbied members of the United States Congress have accepted Turkey's false version of what took place.

Critical of Turkey's attempt to alter history, Kloian prefaced his book of news articles, writing:

"That an event of such proportions should be so relegated and so easily dismissed from the body of world opinion, and today even fall victim to increasing attempts to alter the facts to show that these events did not even occur must be abhorrent to all who truly understand the facts. It should be no less abhorrent to those who profess their active support for human rights today."[9]

One need only to look at the individual memoirs of victims like Vergeen for demonstrated validation of the holocaust perpetrated against the Armenian subjects of Turkey during World War I.

---

[8] *The Armenian Genocide*, Richard D. Kloian, Anto Printing, Berkeley, California, 1980
[9] Ibid, Kloian

List of People
Vergeen's Family, Relatives and Friends

Anoush – *Nvart's daughter and Vergeen's cousin*
Lousaper Balian – *Vergeen's mother*
Filor Balian – *Haji Hagop's wife*
Haji Hagop Balian – *Lousaper's uncle*
Dr. William Dodd – *an American physician and missionary*
Elimon – *Soultan Kala's daughter*
Haji Marie and Seranoush – *Vergeen's classmates*
Dr. Vahan Hershdakian – *an Armenian physician stationed in Ras-al-Ayn*
Baron Heymak – *Principal, Armenian Girls' School in Kayseri*
Maryam Indjejian – *Hagop Tachdjian's second wife*
Parsegh Indjejian – *Maryam's son*
Soultan Kala – *Lousaper's great-aunt*
Baghdasar (Tachdjian) Kalendarian – *Vergeen's father*
Melkon (Tachdjian) Kalendarian – *Baghdasar's young brother*
Veronica (Tachdjian) Kalendarian – *Baghdasar's sister*
Khenarig Kalendarian – *Vergeen's sister*
Manoog Kalendarian – *Vergeen's brother*
Arshalous Keshishian – *Lousaper's mother and Haji Hagop's sister*
Boghos Keshishian – *Lousaper's father*
Haiganoush Keshishian – *Lousaper's sister*
Mardiros Keshishian – *Lousaper's brother*
Melanie – *Vergeen's playmate in Kayseri*
Nvart – *Lousaper's cousin*
Stepphan – *Veronica's husband*
Hagop Tachdjian – *Baghdasar's father*
Lisabett Timourian – *a Kayseri neighbor who helped Vergeen and her mother*

Armenag's Family

Armenag (Balian) Meghrouni – *Vergeen's fiance*
Krikor Balian – *Armenag's brother*
Movsess Balian – *Armenag's eldest brother*
Sarkis Balian – *Armenag's father*
Yeghsahpett Balian – *Armenag's mother*

The Bedouins and Their Captives

Yousuf – *Vergeen's abductor*
Aisha – *Yousuf's niece*
Aneche – *Yousuf's wife*
Ani – *an Armenian girl adopted by Bedouins*
Fatima – *Aneche's helper*
Hamad – *the nomad who bought Senat and married her*
Hilmi – *he Arab assigned to kill Vergeen's mother*
Mounla Abdulah – *Yousuf's brother and Zegariard's husband*
Mounla Salman – *Yousuf's brother and tribal sheik*
Noura – *Arabic name given to Vergeen*
Saliha – *Mounla Salman's wife*
Senat – *the Armenian woman searching for her kidnapped children*
Vartouhi (Zenab) – *the Armenian girl abducted with Vergeen*
Vahan (Hassan) – *the Armenian boy abducted by Yousuf*
Yalal – *an Arab offering marriage to Vergeen*
Zahra – *Fatima's daughter-in-law*
Zegariad – *Aneche's sister*

German-Turkish Railroad Company Personnel

Souren Gondjian – *an assistant engineer*
Jacob – *railway station manager and Joseph's friend*
Georg Kazan, Ghon and Salim – *secretaries*
Hans Kislenge – *he chief engineer from Germany*
Joseph Nacouz – *the accountant*
Nazig – *an Armenian refugee working as a cook*

Joseph's Family

Habib – *Joseph's brother*
Lizbeth – *Joseph's mother*
Miriam, Antoinette, Suzanne and Louise – *Joseph's sisters*

The Hospital's Personnel

Annah – *a head nurse*
Nartouhy – *a head nurse and Vergeen's mentor*
Dr. Emil – *specialist in venereal diseases*
Dr. Jamal – *the hospital's surgeon*
Serpouhi Kalayjian – *a nurse and Vergeen's close friend*
Dr. Sertabid – *the hospital's administrator*
Dr. Vahan – *a medical student*

Serpouhi's Family

Eskoohi – *Haji Sahag's sister*
Gulu – *Serpouhi's first cousin*
Haji Sahag – *Gulu's husband*
Haratoon Kalayjian – *Serpouhi's father*
Makrouhi – *Serpouhi's sister*
Maryam – *Serpouhi's mother*
Boghos Mikjian – *Serpouhi's fiance*
Garabed Mikjian – *Boghos' older brother*
Krikor Ohanian – *Serpouhi's uncle*
Rosie – *Gulu and Haji Sahag's 4-year-old daughter*

Glossary

A=Armenian   T=Turkish   a=Arabic

Aad chojoogh nereh eech ehghan (A) – What happened to those children?
achdachi (a) – man's robe
Aghcheekes (A) – my girl
Ahdee shad tzhvareh (A)– that's so hard
Ahss onkom ohkneh mezhee (A) – help us this time
Alhamdullah (a) – thank God
agha (T) – sir; a title of respect for a gentleman
allakum salami (a) – response to greeting
Aman (A)– oh!
amhiet (a) – Bedouin soup
Asvatz (A) – God
ayyoh (A)– yes
booyourahnez (T) – welcome
chojoogh nereh (A) – the children
dallyseen (T) – are you crazy?
Deegen (A) – Mrs.
dehgha (A) – boy
Der Hayr (A) – priest
disini (a) – Arabic symbols tattooed on a woman's face
djellabas (a) – a white caftan worn by men
eerahghan (A) – real
eench eskancheli lur – what great news!
effendi (T) – sir
endahneek choonees (A) – have you no family?
Ermini millet (T) – Armenian people
Everegzhee (A) – a native of the village of Everek
ghoskgob (A) – arrangement sealing bethothal of a couple
giaour (T) – dog, infidel
Hegheeyes (A) – are you pregnant?
hoja (T) – cleric
horahkooyr (A) – father's sister

hos yehgur (A) – you come here
Kaimakham (T) – civil head of a town, city or district
katah (A) – special Armenian bread
kefyah (a) – a crown anchoring a head scarf
kehshare paree (A) – goodnight
khentrem (A) – please; I beg of you
ketch (A) – pitiful, poor
kohlez (A)– butter-flour filling in katah
lira (T) – Turkish money
Meenag yes (A) – Are you alone?
me vaghnare (A) – don't be afraid
meghah (A) – my goodness!
mejidia (T) – Turkish coin, worth less than a dollar
moreyeghpyr (A) – mother's brother
morahkooyr (A) — mother's sister
myreek (A) – affectionate word for mother
Mousoudaman (a) – I'm a Muslim
neroghutyun (A) – forgive me
nargileh (T) – water pipe
Naserany (a) – a Christian
Nehdeerorsun (T) – What do you say?
Nerdehseen (T) – Where are you?
neroghutyun (A) – forgive me
oghloom (T) – my son
okneh inzhee (A) – help me
oxor (A) – exile
salami-el-allakum (a) – polite greeting
Sourp Garabed (A) – St. Charles
varav (A) – burned
voch (A) – no
Vor kahghaken es (A) – From what city are you?
yerpek chemornas (A) – never forget.
yorghan (T) – bedding
zehbek (T) – a dance performed by males
Zhairkez (T) – Turkish cossack

About the Author

A native Detroiter, Mae M. Derdarian attended public schools in Detroit and Wayne State University before entering the communications field, primarily in advertising and public relations. She spent most of her professional years directing the public relations operation of a metropolitan United Way organization, garnering several awards along the way for professional and community leadership.

Since her retirement in 1985, Ms. Derdarian has been devoting a great deal of her time to community service, especially programs for the elderly.

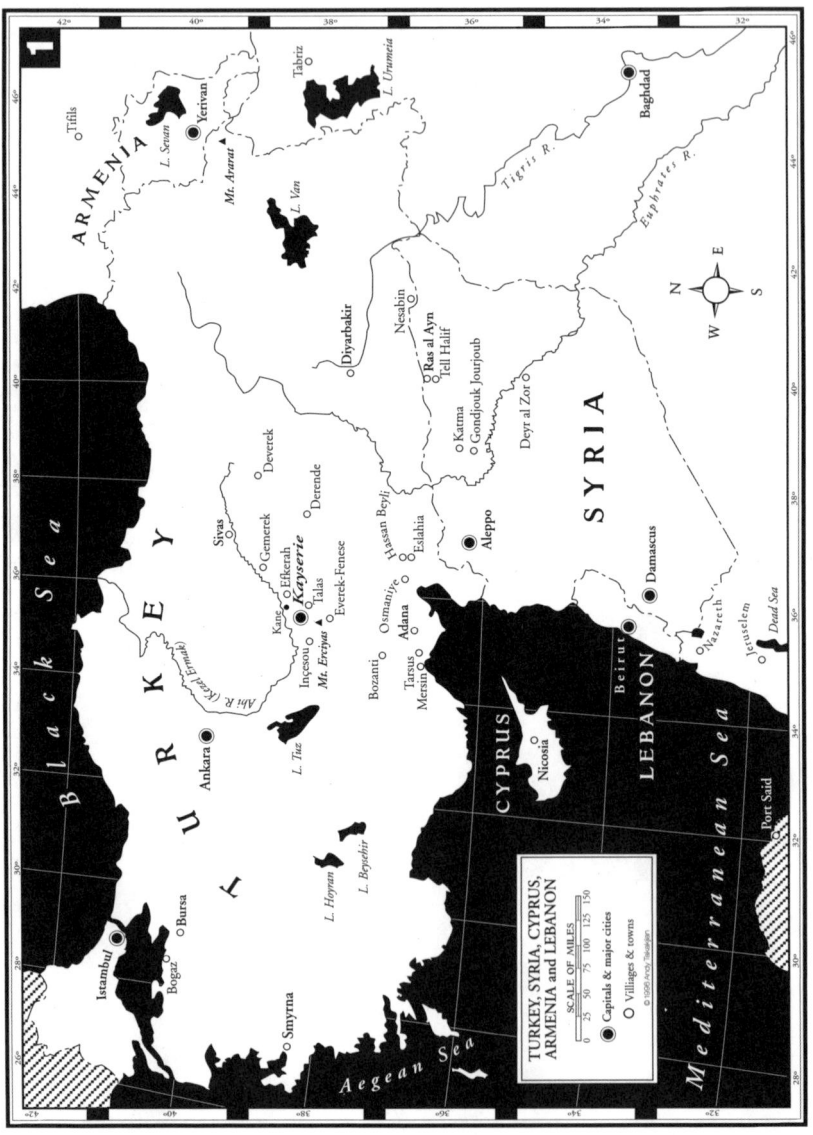